Netsuke

100 miniature masterpieces from Japan

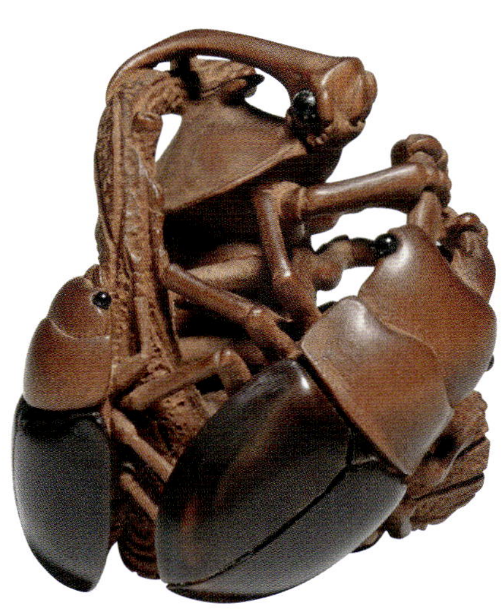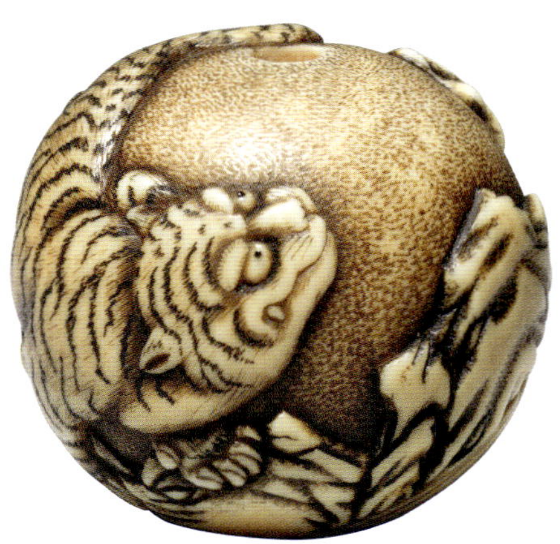

The **BRITISH**
Museum

Netsuke

100 miniature masterpieces from Japan

Noriko Tsuchiya

With assistance from Max Rutherston

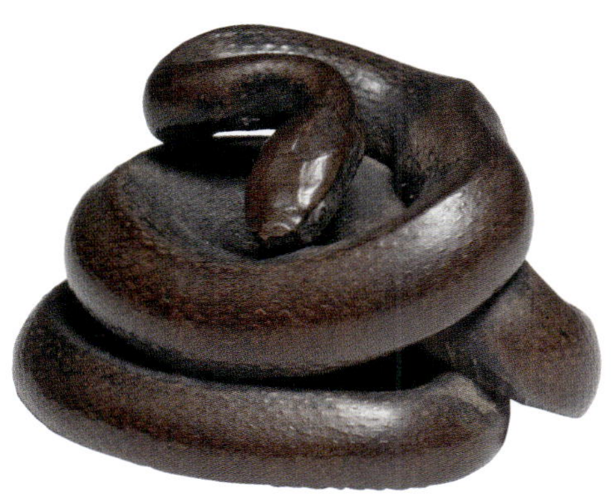

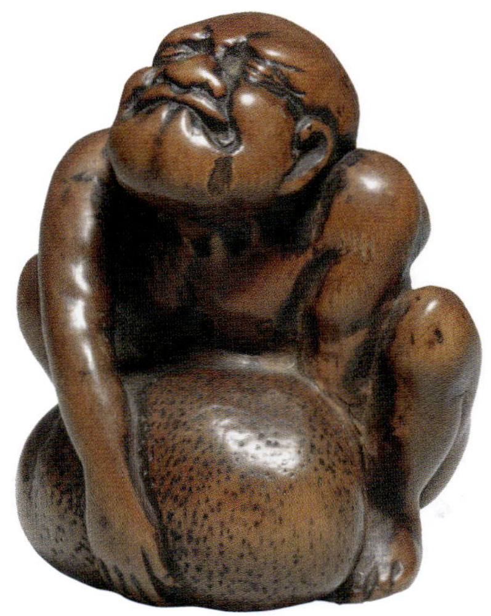

This publication has been generously supported by Peter and Faith Coolidge.

First published in 2014 by The British Museum Press
A division of the British Museum Company Ltd

The British Museum

Great Russell Street, London WC1B 3DG

britishmuseum.org/publishing

ISBN 9780714124810

Reprinted 2024

A catalogue record for this book is available from the British Library

Designed by Grade Design
Printed and bound in Poland by Drukarnia Dimograf

Front cover see pp. 40–41
Back cover see pp. 176–177
Title page see pp. 34–35, 114–115, 166–167. Third netsuke from left: Coiled snake
by Kōmin. Wood, Edo (present-day Tokyo), c.1860–80. w. 3.6 cm. British Museum F.282.
Given by Sir Augustus Wollaston Franks.

The papers used in this book are recyclable products and the manufacturing processes
are expected to conform to the environmental regulations of the country of origin.

The objects illustrated in this book are from the collection of
the British Museum. The British Museum registration numbers for these objects are
provided in the accompanying captions. You can find out more about objects in all
areas of the British Museum's collection on the Museum's website at britishmuseum.
org/research/search_the_collection_database.aspx

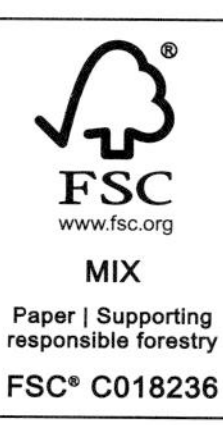

Contents

Director's foreword

Accessories for the global businessman that complement his dark suit are necktie, watch, cufflinks, designer eye-glasses and wallet, with the occasional foray into eye-catching socks and braces. The latest smart phone is now another means to impress. The situation for a male of the townsman class in Edo period (1615–1868) Japan – a merchant or artisan whose dress code was constrained by the laws laid down by his samurai rulers – was not, in practice, so very different. His basic robe had, by edict, to be subdued, but this could be offset with spectacular accessories, providing these were worn discreetly: a flashy lining to an otherwise plain jacket and lavishly crafted personal accessories hidden in the folds of his robes. These ranged from a tobacco pouch, pipe and pipe-case to the single sword permitted to some merchants, and also beautifully lacquered medicine- and seal-cases. With no pockets in a traditional kimono, smaller accessories were hung from the sash using silk cords. This is where the need evolved for a special toggle to secure the cord at the top of the sash – a netsuke. These were the pride and joy of their owner, ordered from named specialist carvers working in a variety of materials, principally ivory, bone and wood.

With great inventiveness and unmatched skill, netsuke makers drew on centuries of Japanese visual culture to produce miniature masterpieces of sculpture on an extraordinary range of themes. In the late nineteenth century, foreign collectors of Japanese art became fascinated, obsessed even, to amass large holdings of the full range of subjects, techniques and makers. Over the last century and a half, the British Museum has been the beneficiary of much generosity from these passionate collectors. Already in the 1860s, very soon after Japan reopened to world trade, Sir Augustus Wollaston Franks, pre-eminent British Museum curator and benefactor, was acquiring netsuke and other Japanese decorative arts. In 1978–1984 the Museum received a spectacular gift of netsuke and related medicine-cases (*inrō*) from Professor John and Mrs Anne Hull Grundy. Along with these two great gifts have been many more acts of generosity.

In featuring here one hundred netsuke from the British Museum's collection of more than 2,300, the guiding criteria have been quality and interest. We have been much assisted by the keen connoisseurial eye of Max Rutherston, to whom we give thanks. The Museum is grateful also to the Duke of Omnium Fund, which has supported the netsuke project overall.

Netsuke are designed to be scrutinized at close quarters and the book features close-up views of the objects, which we hope you will enjoy. We invite you also to visit the Museum's Mitsubishi Corporation Japanese Galleries where a selection of the originals is always on display.

Neil MacGregor
Director, British Museum

Introduction

The Japanese netsuke is a unique form of miniature art which has attracted attention and many enthusiasts from all over the world. For over two centuries, the shogunate (military government) had enforced a policy of maritime restrictions which prevented Japan trading with the rest of the world. When this period of relative isolation finally ended in the 1850s, a wide variety of Japanese decorative arts began to be exported. Netsuke in particular caught the eye of Western visitors to Japan, who were attracted both by their exquisite craftsmanship and their small size – making them eminently transportable and collectable. Europeans purchased and brought back large numbers of netsuke, and these miniature masterpieces have gone on to form the basis of many of the important public collections in Europe and the USA. The British Museum has some 2,300 netsuke in its collection, which were acquired by donation and purchase from the 1860s onwards. One hundred netsuke have been selected for this book primarily for their quality and interest, but also to illustrate other aspects of this fascinating art form – its history, subject matter, and its associated meaning, the materials employed and the various schools of carvers.

What is a netsuke and how was it worn?

Netsuke – literally meaning 'root' (*ne*) 'to attach' (*tsuke*) – were practical fashion accessories worn by Japanese men of the Edo period (1615–1868). During that time, both men and women wore the traditional wrap-over robe called a *kosode kimono* (that is, a robe with a small sleeve opening, hereafter simply 'kimono'), with a sash, *obi*, that was tied around the waist. Kimono had no pockets, and only the woman's garment had places in the sleeves to keep small objects. In contrast, men would carry their personal accessories by hanging them from the sash. Such *sagemono* ('suspended items') comprised money pouches, smoking accessories (see opposite), small sets of writing equipment, and compartmented boxes (*inrō*) to store personal seals or herbal medicine (see pp. 188–189). Each item would be attached with a woven silk cord to a netsuke, always working as a unit or ensemble. These *sagemono* were usually kept closed by drawing the cords tight using a sliding piece, a kind of spherical bead with a hole through it called an *ojime*.

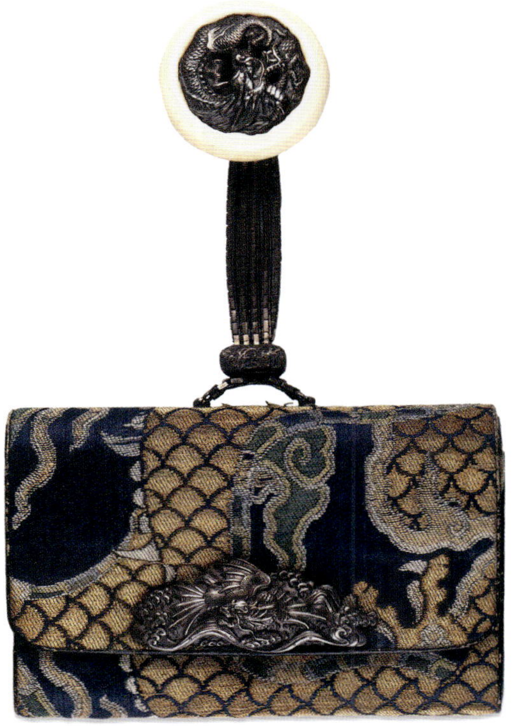

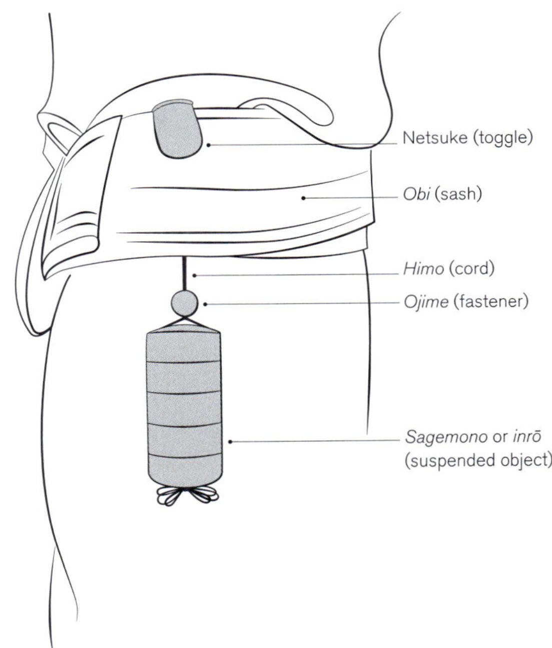

Above left Tobacco pouch. Brocaded textile and leather with dragon-shaped metal clasp. At the top is a *kagamibuta* netsuke, a metal disk carved with a dragon in an ivory bowl. 1800s. w. 9 cm; L. 13 cm; D. 5 cm. British Museum HG.158.a&b. Given by Professor John and Mrs Anne Hull Grundy.

Above right Drawing showing how to wear netsuke and *inrō*. Illustration created by Anna Wilkinson.

When the ensemble is worn, the cord is tucked behind the sash and the netsuke then functions as a toggle or stopper, displayed over the top edge of the sash, preventing the item from falling to the ground (see above).

Netsuke and *sagemono* were used by all classes of society. Throughout the Edo period, the Tokugawa shogunate imposed a strict social hierarchy of four classes: in descending order, samurai warriors, farmers, craftsmen and tradesmen (*shi-nō-kō-shō*). Because craftsmen and tradesmen were regarded as less productive according to Confucian ideology, they were ranked at the lower end of the hierarchy. Craftsmen and tradesmen together were generally referred to as townspeople, or *chōnin*. However, it was the townspeople who increasingly had large disposable incomes and consequently purchasing power. The richest and most powerful merchants were patrons of various arts, such as tea gatherings, painting, calligraphy, classical music and poetry. Naturally these wealthy merchants aspired to emulate their social betters by expressing themselves through luxurious material goods. In reaction, sumptuary laws were periodically issued by the samurai authorities to limit private expenditure and regulate what clothing and material goods could be worn and owned, depending on social rank. Accordingly, townspeople were banned from wearing richly embroidered fabrics and certain other materials, and could wear only clothing of dark silk, or cotton with simple patterns. Instead they spent their money on fashion accessories, particularly *inrō* and netsuke. These accessories, which could be discreetly worn in the folds of the kimono or under a jacket, allowed them to flout the sumptuary laws and express their personal taste. Thus netsuke were both miniature masterpieces of sculpture and a source of sartorial pride. In a woodblock print by Kitao Masanobu (1761–1816), a merchant is depicted dangling a smoking pouch and pipe case attached to a netsuke from his right hand (see right). It is notable that the well-known ukiyo-e ('floating world') artist Masanobu, also famous as a popular author using the name Santō Kyōden, was not only a celebrated man of culture but also opened up his own shop selling tobacco accessories in Edo (present-day Tokyo), creating new ranges that set many of the latest trends.

As outlined above, netsuke were functional objects, toggles intended for everyday use by Edo-period men. We can imagine that these men chose their netsuke with care to coordinate with the different suspended items, to suit the weather, season, occasion – and also their mood. This could be compared to the watch fobs or cufflinks worn by Europeans in the eighteenth and nineteenth centuries, and to some extent to male accessories used today. There were various practical considerations: the shape of the netsuke needed to be comfortable to wear but also aesthetically pleasing; it should be comparatively small and not too heavy to carry around; it needed to have a smooth contour, with no sharp corners

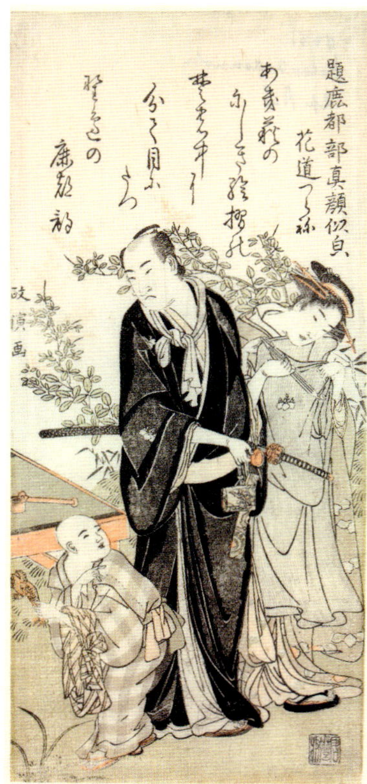

Portrait of Shikatsube no Magao. Kitao Masanobu, colour woodblock print, mid 1780s. 32.2 x 14.5 cm. British Museum 1932,0223,0.3. Given by R. N. Shaw.

that might damage the fabric of the kimono; it should be made of strong and durable materials, such as wood and ivory; finally, it needed to have two holes or *himotōshi* through which the silk cord was passed and tied. Within these limitations, netsuke carvers were free to demonstrate their skill and creativity. By skilful planning, they could exploit a natural opening in the raw material as an alternative to cord holes within the design; or the form of the sculpture could be shaped to create a suitable hole – for example, the arm of a figure bent against the body (see pp. 24–25). With regard to compactness, dragons and snakes were good subjects: both have long bodies which were usually carved in a coiling pose to make an effective toggle (pp. 122–123 and 124–125).

Types of netsuke

There are a number of types of netsuke. The majority are carvings in the round, called *katabori* (literally, 'carved form' or 'sculpture netsuke'), and most of the netsuke in this book are of this type. The subjects of *katabori* netsuke range from human figures and animals to plants and still-life objects. The size can range from a life-sized copy of a nut to a huge elephant represented in a piece less than 3 cm in size (pp. 152–153). *Sashi* ('inserted') netsuke are a longer and slender type, and were worn by simply tucking into the sash. Most *sashi* netsuke have some kind of hook at one end to prevent them from slipping through the sash: in the case of the netsuke shown on pp. 170–171, the hook is the bended head of a sea horse-like creature. The second most numerous type is *manjū*, featured in the last section in this book (pp. 179–187), named after a round, flattish rice-cake filled with bean paste. They are often made of ivory; sometimes also wood, horn or lacquer, with engraved, inlaid or carved details in semi-relief. The cords were attached to a ring inside, passing out through a central hole, or, in the case of a solid piece, were tied to a metal ring or ivory plug with a hole attached to one side of the *manjū*. The *kagamibuta* ('mirror-lid') netsuke consists of a metal plate set into a round wood or ivory bowl (pp. 190–191). The disc is the focal point of the decoration, and the incising and embossing of this metal disc was often done by specialist metalworkers, generally makers of sword fittings.

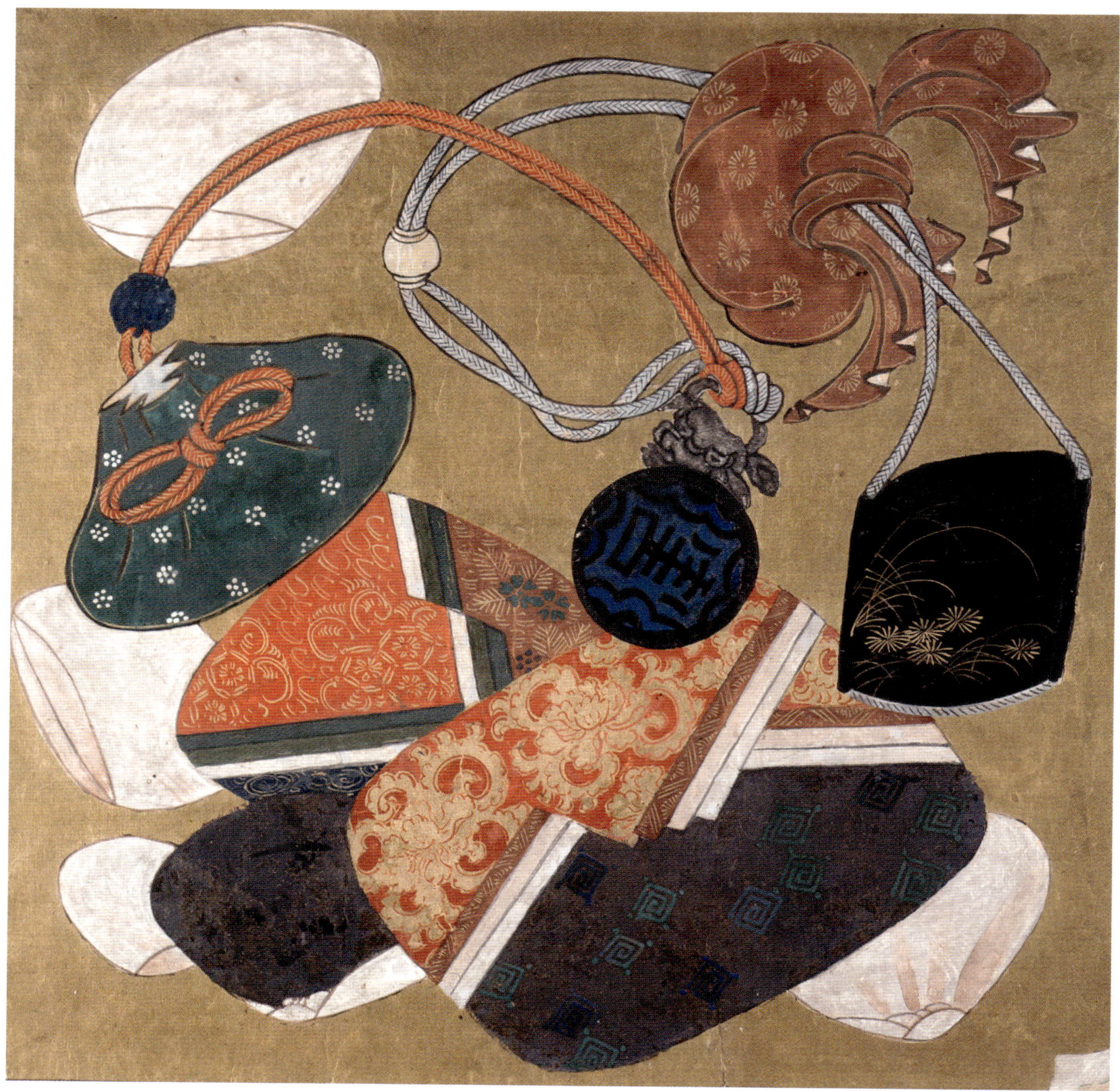

History of netsuke

The simplest functional netsuke could be a piece of stone, a twig, a dried gourd, nuts or shells, and the origin of netsuke is likely to be found in these naturally occuring objects. The custom of suspending objects from a belt can be seen in many cultures of the world and traced back to ancient times. However, few netsuke dating from before the Edo period have survived, and documentary records regarding the earliest purpose-made netsuke are extremely scant. Pictorial evidence from the seventeenth century shows that in their earliest stages of development, netsuke were for the most part functional toggles, such as ring-type netsuke to which a closed loop could easily be attached. Seals were also among the first sculpted objects to function as netsuke. For example, the image opposite shows many types of personal accoutrements and accessories in decorative arrangements, dated to around the Kan'ei era (1624–1644). Here a brocade pouch and a lacquered *inrō* are attached to a gilt seal with a sculpture of Chinese lion (*shishi*) on top. During the late Ming period (1368–1644), a large quantity of Chinese seals was imported. These seals were made of various materials such as wood, ivory, bronze or semi-precious stones, and were themselves sometimes adapted as netsuke, as seen here. In addition, the sculptural carvings often attached to the top may have served as a source for designs by netsuke carvers, especially for *katabori* netsuke.

The development of hanging items like *inrō* and smoking accessories had a great influence on netsuke. The practice of smoking tobacco, first introduced to Japan by Portuguese merchants in the late sixteenth century, had become widely adopted by the early seventeenth. It was not until the first half of the eighteenth century, however, that personal and portable smoking sets came into widespread use. Wealthy merchants now required fine tobacco pouches and pipe cases, along with their complementary netsuke. From that time netsuke became more decorative and ornamental in the manner that we know today. The earliest printed account of netsuke carvers is included in the seven-volume *Sōken kishō* (*Strange and Wonderful Sword Fittings*), first published in 1781. The writer, Inaba Tsūryū Shin'emon (1740–1786), was a sword-fitting dealer in Osaka, and in the

Sagemono and dress accessories, from a set of ten paintings in album leaf (originally made as ceiling panels). Artist unknown, ink and colour on gold-leafed paper, about 1624–1644. 34 x 33 cm. British Museum 1978,0724,0.5. Acquired with funding from the Brooke Sewell Bequest.

final volume of the book, he lists fifty-four netsuke carvers together with short biographies and illustrations of their works. The carvers are mostly from Osaka, but also Kyoto, Edo and regional towns, indicating that a fully professional netsuke industry had already developed in these centres.

Netsuke production could be a side-product of other types of carving, particularly in the early Edo period. Buddhist sculptors were certainly among the first makers of netsuke in wood. Other craftsmen who likely turned to netsuke included seal-makers and makers of plectrums for stringed instruments, as they were skilled in the working of ivory. A pictorial encyclopaedia *Jinrin kinmō zui* (*Illustrated Instructions for Proper Behaviour*), published in 1690, illustrates an ivory worker (see opposite). Among the products on the floor, which the artisan has just made, can been seen combs, plectrums, as well as conveniently sized pieces of ivory for netsuke. Netsuke in other materials, such as lacquer, stoneware, porcelain and metalwork, were usually made alongside these long-established crafts, as a side-product.

However, there were many changes in Japan towards the middle of the nineteenth century and these changes had a considerable effect on the production and use of netsuke. In 1853, U.S. Commodore Matthew Perry (1794–1858) arrived with his squadron of Black Ships to request the establishment of trade relations with Japan and the Treaty of Kanagawa was duly signed in 1854. This officially brought to an end the government's policy of isolation which had lasted for more than two centuries. Treaty ports were presently opened and Western culture flooded into Japan. The country embarked on a course of rapid modernization leading in 1868 to the collapse of the Tokugawa shogunate and the Meiji Restoration, the chain of events that restored imperial rule to Japan under the Meiji Emperor. Subsequently, many Japanese people started to wear Western dress rather than kimono. The netsuke and hanging pouch gave way to the pocket and wallet, and the traditional pipe and tobacco set were replaced by cigars and matches. Netsuke and *sagemono* were no longer needed, and were sold in large numbers to Western visitors. Many netsuke carved after this time were purely decorative, and no longer made for practical use; although fine pieces continued to be made and worn in the Meiji era (1868–1912). Today netsuke are produced by

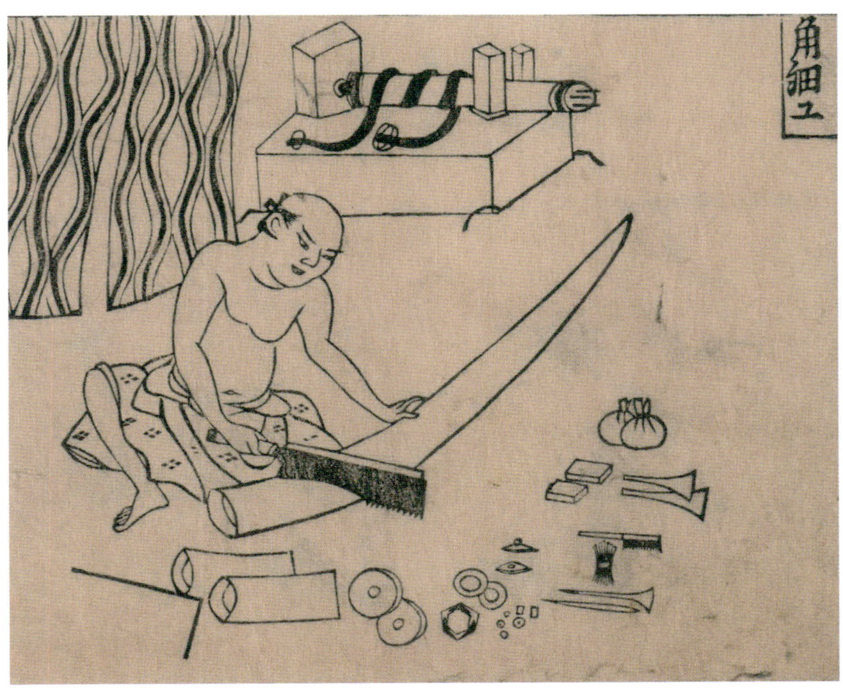

Ivory worker from *Jinrin kinmō zui (Illustrated Instructions for Proper Behaviour)*, vol. 5. Woodblock-illustrated book, 1690. From the collection of the National Diet Library, Tokyo.

contemporary carvers not only in Japan, but all over the world. Two contemporary netsuke are included in this book (pp. 104–105 and pp. 166–167), and illustrate that the tradition of carving netsuke continues to grow, with fresh interpretation and originality.

Materials for netsuke

Netsuke are made from many different materials. Among these, wood is traditionally the most widely used. About seventy percent of Japan is forested, and there is an abundance of different kinds of tree, due to the varied climates from the north to the south of the country. For example, boxwood (J. *tsuge*) has a pale and creamy natural colour (see p. 48), while ebony (J. *kokutan*) is black (p. 132). Other woods used for netsuke include Japanese cypress (J. *hinoki*), cherry, persimmon and bamboo, and these can additionally be stained or painted, sometimes making it difficult to identify precisely what kind of wood has been used. Elephant ivory was a particularly popular material for netsuke. Because elephants were not native to Japan, throughout the Edo period their tusks were imported by Chinese and Dutch traders. Ivory is characterized by its creamy white colour and diamond-shaped grain. It can also acquire an attractive golden patina (a kind of tarnish on the surface) with age, use, handling and exposure to light. Stag antler was another favourite material, particularly among carvers working in the downtown Asakusa district of Tokyo in the late nineteenth century. Notwithstanding its irregular shape and spongy texture, they were able ingeniously to incorporate these disadvantages into the design with skill and imagination (see pp. 154–155). Metal netsuke were generally made by professional metalworkers who were not specialist netsuke carvers, and lacquer and ceramic netsuke were also made by lacquer and ceramic craftsmen. Many other organic materials were also used, such as tortoiseshell, boar's tusk, coral and amber. Among these materials, boar's tusk is especially characteristic for netsuke from Iwami province (modern Shimane prefecture), the dense forests of which provided habitat for this wild animal. Materials such as tortoiseshell, coral and amber are often used for inlaid eyes, but are less common for the main body material.

Subjects

Netsuke could take almost any form, including human figures, animals, plants and everyday objects; also mythical creatures and other fantastical subjects. They provide a fascinating glimpse into Japanese popular culture of the late Edo period, featuring themes from daily life, legend and the world of the imagination. Foreigners – Chinese, Dutch and South Sea Islanders – were always the subject of great curiosity, and native Japanese were also generally represented with a winning sense of humour. From the seventeenth century onwards, many illustrated printed books came to Japan from China. The great variety of Chinese legends, historical episodes and exotic motifs they contained provided a rich source of designs for netsuke carvers. Animal motifs were also popular, especially the twelve animals of the twelve year zodiac cycle. The appropriate animal was worn at the New Year – a tiger for the year of the tiger, and so on – or a man would choose the animal of his birth year. The emergence of a more naturalistic style of painting, exemplified by the

Maruyama-Shijō school of Kyoto and Osaka during the late eighteenth century, exerted a strong influence upon the creation of netsuke. The majority of the netsuke which accurately and realistically depicted animal and plant subjects came from this period. In the case of *manjū* netsuke, their flatter, plainer surfaces were well suited to reproducing pictorial scenes from contemporary ukiyo-e prints, either engraved or carved in relief.

Netsuke carvers and production centres

Since Tokugawa Ieyasu (1542–1616), the first shogun of the Tokugawa shogunate, moved the centre of government to Edo from the ancient capital of Kyoto in 1603, this has been the principal city of Japan. By the eighteenth century, Edo became one of the largest cities in the world, with a population of over one million. It was home to a sophisticated urban populace and men as well as women sported the latest fashion accessories. It was therefore natural that Edo attracted many skilled craftsmen and it became the most important centre for the production of netsuke in the early nineteenth century. Lacking ancient artistic traditions, the city's crafts tended to be more original, sometimes exhibiting more humour than other centres. The other main cities – Osaka as the great commercial hub and Kyoto, the ancient cultural centre – continued to produce netsuke. Ōhara Mitsuhiro (see pp. 44–45 and 160–161) and Kaigyokusai Masatsugu (pp. 128–129 and 138–139), both active during the nineteenth century, were the greatest netsuke carvers of the Osaka region. As represented by the famous carvers Masanao (pp. 96–97 and 136–137) and Okatomo (pp. 118–119 and 124–125), Kyoto became especially noted for animal netsuke with a soft, restrained quality and realistic style. Apart from the traditional, urban areas of netsuke production, a number of other regional cities and castle towns emerged, such as Nagoya, Tanba, Hida, Iwami and Hakata, partly as a result of abundant supplies of local materials (see map on p. 18).

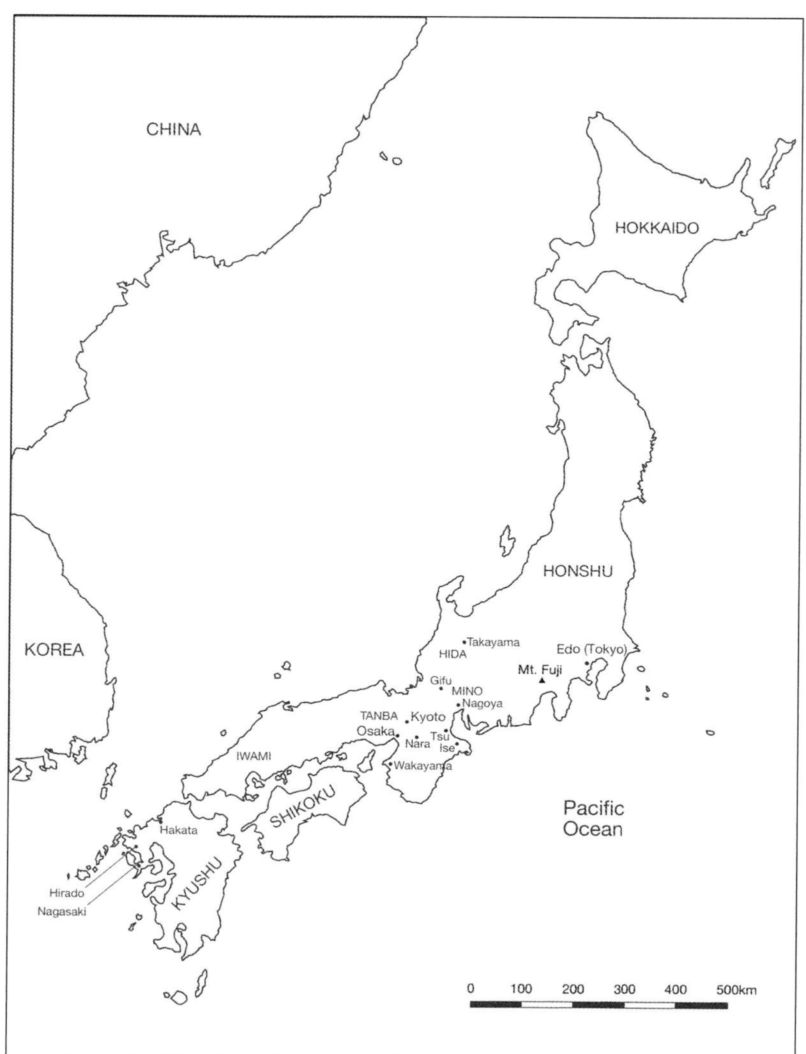

Map showing netsuke production centres in Japan during the Edo period (1615–1868). Artwork created by Morohashi Kazuko.

The netsuke collection in the British Museum

The backbone of the British Museum's netsuke collection was formed by
Sir Augustus Wollaston Franks (1826–1897), who was Keeper (chief curator)
of British and medieval antiquities and ethnology at the British Museum from 1862
to 1896. Franks spearheaded the expansion of the Museum's collection into works
from Asia. Although he never travelled to Japan, through his private wealth and
scholarly connections, Franks was able to acquire a total of 870 netsuke from the
1860s onwards, together with a substantial collection of Japanese ceramics.
Among his most important pieces are many early unsigned tall figure netsuke made
in wood and ivory, and one of the stars of the Museum's holdings, the ivory netsuke
of a sleeping rat by Masanao of Kyoto (see pp. 108–109). Another important part
of the collection was given by Professor John (1907–1984) and Mrs Anne Hull
Grundy (1926–1984). Mrs Grundy collected netsuke, supported by her husband,
and donated a total of 680 pieces, together with a fine *inrō* collection, from 1978
to 1984. In 1912 Mrs Juliet Seymour Trower gave 16 of the best netsuke, which
her husband, the prominent collector Mr Harry Seymour Trower (1843–1912) had
acquired since 1876. These included netsuke by the eccentric makers Sanshō
and Tsuji and (pp. 48 and 58–59). The bequest in 1945 by Oscar Charles Raphael
(1874–1941) included about 170 netsuke. Raphael collected a good number of
early figures, but also a few pieces by late netsuke carvers, among them the two
magnificent carvings by Kōseki (pp. 88–89 and 101).

Two netsuke books have previously been published by the British Museum.
The first, by Richard Barker and Lawrence Smith in 1976, selected 404 of the best
and most interesting netsuke from the collection, categorized by the main areas of
netsuke production. The second, by Victor Harris in 1987, described and illustrated
over 600 netsuke from the Hull Grundy collection, showing a wide diversity of
types and arranged by subject. In 1994, the exhibition *Treasured Miniatures:
Contemporary Netsuke* was held first at the British Museum and then at the Los
Angeles County Museum of Art, in which the works of twelve foreign and thirty-
three Japanese carvers were displayed. This was the first time that such a
comprehensive exhibition of contemporary netsuke had been staged internationally.

The human form

During most of the Edo period (1615–1868), Japan adopted a policy of relative national isolation and so foreigners – Chinese, Dutch and South Sea Islanders – were always the subject of great curiosity and they were portrayed with set characteristics. Native Japanese were also represented with a sense of humour. Many illustrated printed books which were imported from China also provided a rich source of Chinese legends, historical episodes and exotic motifs.

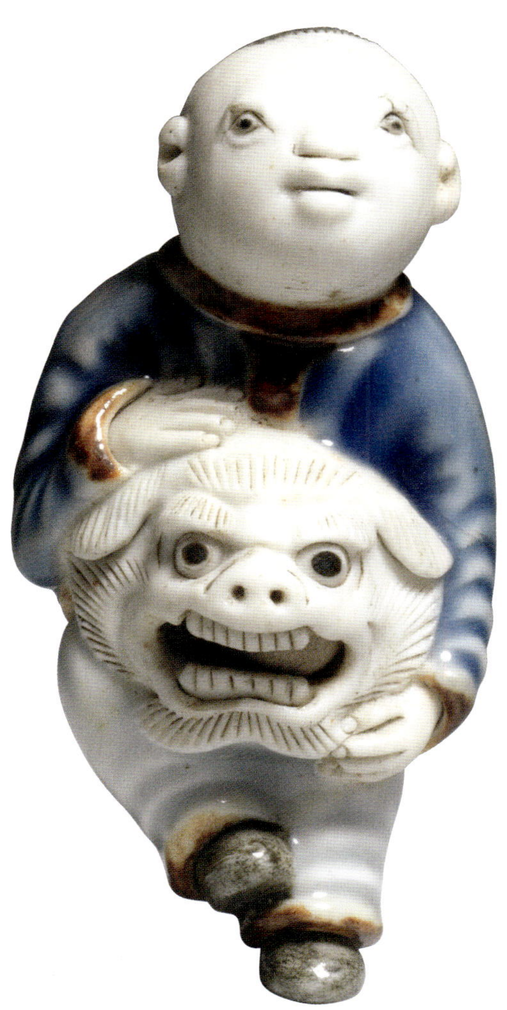

Chinese boy holding a lion mask

This netsuke of a dancing Chinese boy is made entirely of porcelain, with the head of the boy, hands and the lion mask in bisque, and the body and feet highlighted with underglaze cobalt blue and iron oxide glaze. Porcelain netsuke are less common than those in ivory or wood, but there are quite a few examples in the British Museum's collection. The netsuke was fired in the Mikawachi area kilns of Hizen province (current Saga prefecture) in Kyushu, the southern island of Japan. The official kiln of the Hirado clan was located there, and the area's kilns generally produced fine white porcelain, for both the domestic and European markets, from the later part of the seventeenth century to the present day. Chinese boys (*karako*) are a motif frequently encountered in Hirado ware. A mask of a Chinese lion (*shishi*) is used for a dance known as *shishi-mai*, performed at festivals all over Japan, especially at the New Year. The porcelain ball inside the mouth of the mask is moveable, and would reflect the wearer's movements.

A similar netsuke, with a muted iron oxide glaze on the lion mask, is illustrated in Lawrence 1997, p. 110, pl. 80. Another similar glazed white porcelain netsuke is held in the collections of Chhatrapati Shivaji Maharaj Vastu Sangrahalaya, formerly the Prince of Wales Museum of Western India, Mumbai, 22.1716.

—

Unsigned
Hirado ware, Mikawachi kilns
Partially glazed porcelain, early 1800s
H. 5.5 cm
British Museum Franks1462+
Given by Sir Augustus Wollaston Franks

Dutchman holding a cockerel

During most of the Edo period (1615–1868), Japan adopted a policy of relative national isolation. Dutch merchants were the only Europeans permitted to live in Japan, and they were confined to Dejima, a small man-made island in Nagasaki Bay. It would have been rare for a Japanese person to see a foreigner, so the Dutch became the object of great curiosity and a perfect subject for netsuke carvers. Woodblock prints of Dutchmen also became popular in the late eighteenth century (see right). Most Dutchmen were portrayed with set characteristics: a large nose, curly red hair, long buttoned-up coat and wide-brimmed hat, and were often accompanied by South East Asian servants. This type of netsuke was only created for a short period of time during the second half of the eighteenth century. In Dejima, the Dutch cultivated a small botanical garden and kept domestic animals such as fowl. The ivory Dutchman pictured here holds a fighting cock; the sport was a popular entertainment at that time.

This netsuke was previously published in Barker and Smith 1976, p. 157, fig. 355.

—

Unsigned
Ivory, about 1780
H. 11.8 cm
British Museum F.558
Given by Sir Augustus Wollaston Franks

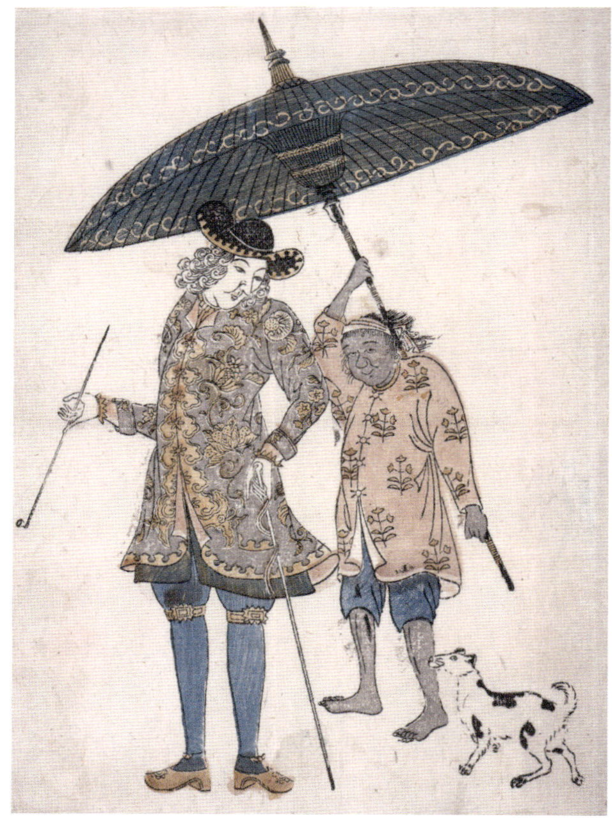

Dutchman taking a walk with his dog while a Javanese servant holds an umbrella. Unknown artist, colour woodblock print, *Nagasaki-e*, late 1700s. 32.2 x 22.9 cm. British Museum 1951,0714,0.17.

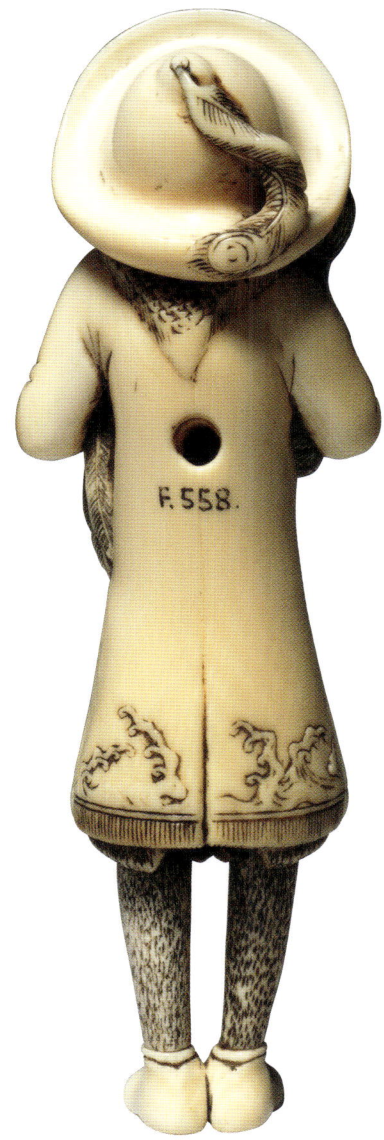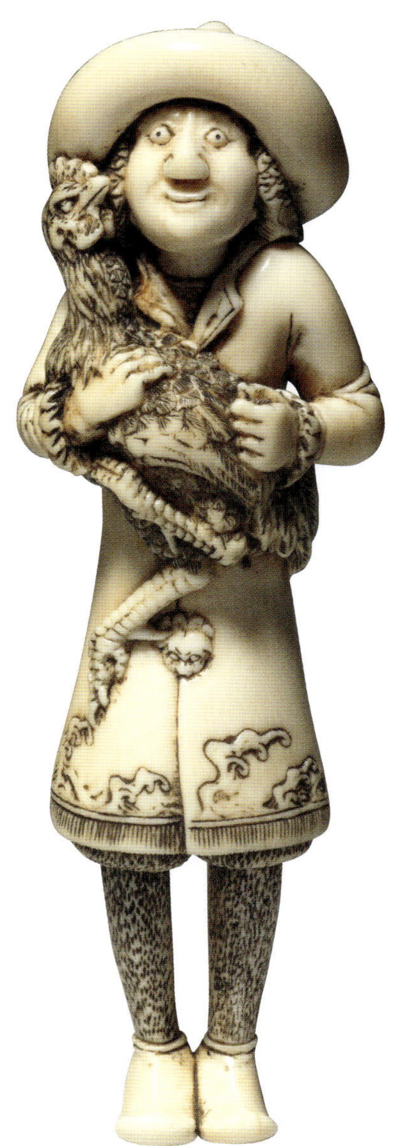

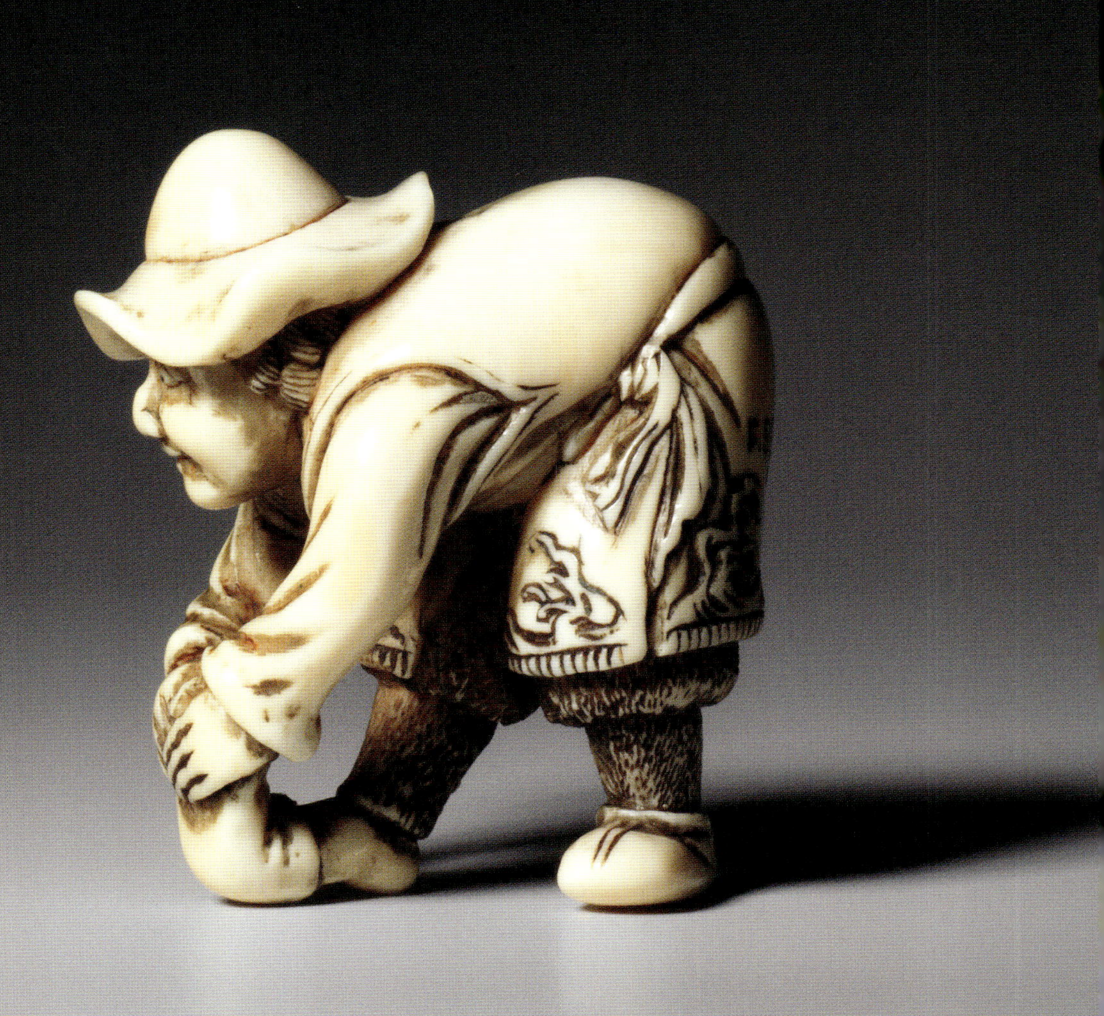

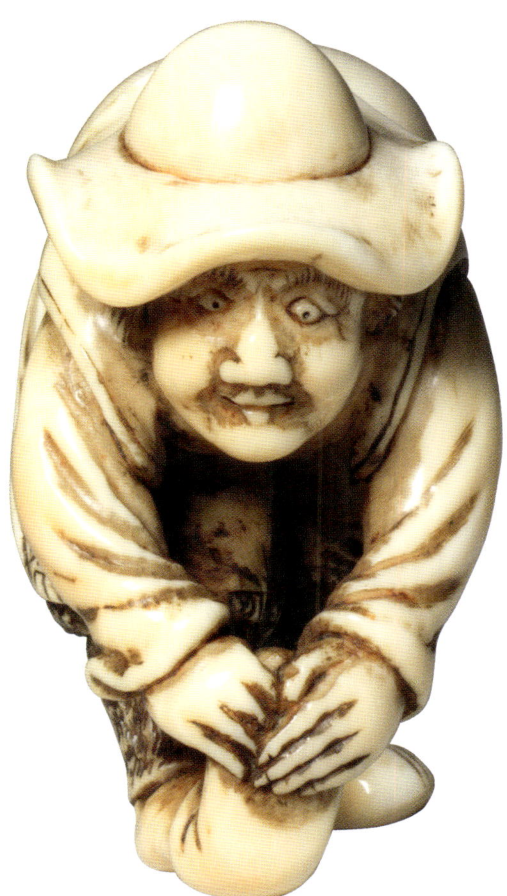

Dutchman grasping his shoe

A Dutchman bends over to grasp his shoe. He might be trying to remove an annoying stone. Looking straight ahead, he has a somewhat anxious expression. European footwear must have appeared as quite a curiosity to the Japanese who wore sandals and still customarily remove their shoes when indoors. This Dutchman also sports exotic patterned trousers and a large floppy hat. The body is deliberately contorted to make the overall shape of the netsuke into an effective toggle.

A similar netsuke in wood, signed Tsuji, is illustrated in Moss 1996, no. 27.

—

Unsigned
Ivory, about 1780
H. 4.3 cm; w. 4.1 cm
British Museum F.559
Given by Sir Augustus Wollaston Franks

South Sea Islander

Just as the Japanese were fascinated by the Dutch, so other exotic foreigners were also a source of great curiosity and were depicted in netsuke with inventive humour. Until the beginning of the seventeenth century there was considerable trade between Japan, South East Asia, particularly Luzon, the largest island in the Philippines, and the South Pacific. Exports from Japan were mainly silver and copper, and imports included Chinese silks and other textiles, as well as sugar, coral, incense, ivory and exotic woods from or transported via South East Asia.

In this netsuke, a man dressed in a loincloth stands to attention, bent slightly backwards with his fists held stiffly behind him, so that the arms provide the necessary hole for the cord, or *himotōshi*. The dark polished surface and his muscular legs are in keeping with other fantasic depictions of South Sea Islanders dating to the Edo period (1615–1868). A typical image appears in the printed book *Morokoshi kinmō zui* (*Illustrated Encyclopedia of China*) by Tachibana Morikuni (1679–1748), first published in 1719 (see right). The text records that people from the 'South Western Islands', or *Sōshiki koku*, have skin like black lacquer.

This netsuke was previously published in Barker and Smith 1976, p.140, fig. 302.

—

Unsigned; attributed to Miwa I
Fruitwood, about 1780
H. 11.9 cm
British Museum F.569
Given by Sir Augustus Wollaston Franks

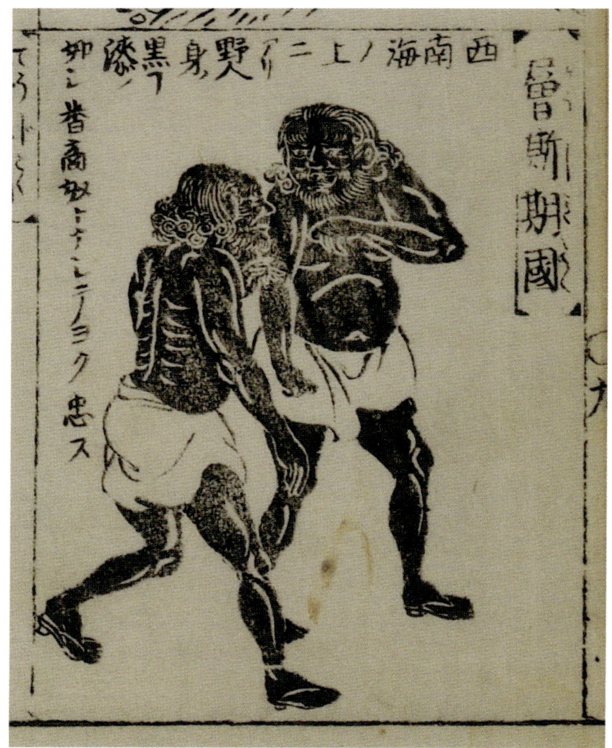

People from *Sōshiki koku*, from Tachibana Morikuni, *Morokoshi kinmō zui* (*Illustrated Encyclopedia of China*), vol. 5. Woodblock-illustrated book, 1719 (reprinted 1802). 25.5 x 18 cm (covers). British Museum 1915,0823,0.26.1-5.

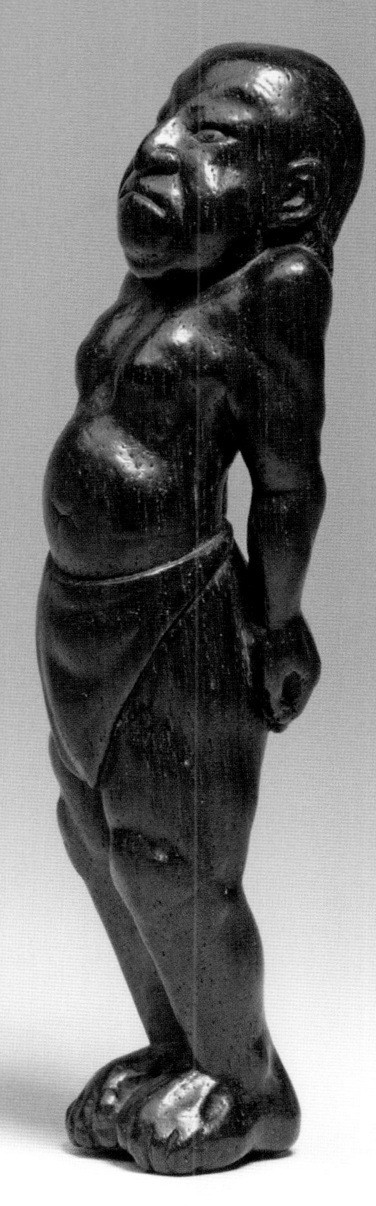

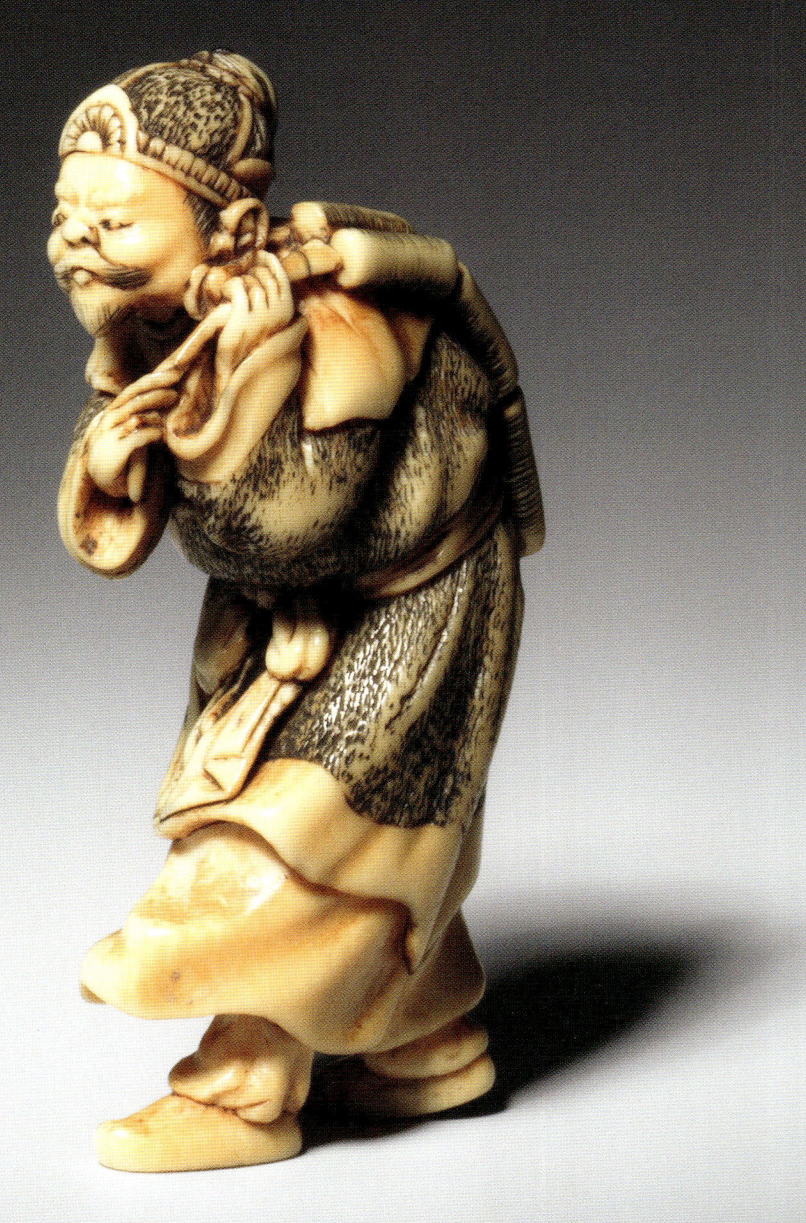

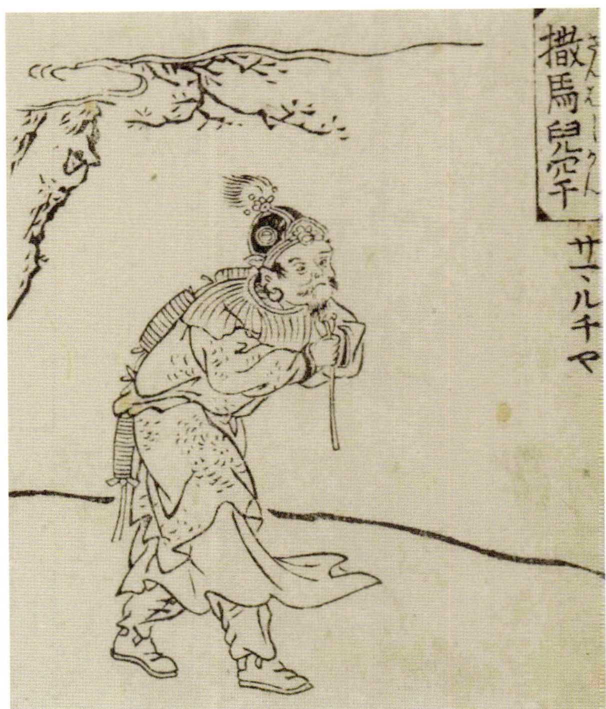

A merchant from Samarkand, from Tachibana Morikuni, *Morokoshi kinmō zui* (*Illustrated Encyclopedia of China*), vol. 4. Woodblock-illustrated book, 1719 (reprinted 1802). 25.5 x 18 cm (covers). British Museum 1938,1008,0.7.1-5.

Central Asian merchant

A Central Asian merchant carries heavy strings of coins over his shoulder, while a strong breeze blows from behind. The design for this compelling netsuke was taken from the woodblock-illustrated book *Morokoshi kinmō zui* (*Illustrated Encyclopedia of China*) by Tachibana Morikuni (1679–1748), first published in 1719 (see left). In the illustrated book, the merchant is recorded as coming from Samarkand, in present-day Uzbekistan. Samarkand is one of the oldest cities in Central Asia, celebrated for its central position on the Silk Road, the renowned trading route between China and Europe. From the seventeenth century onwards, printed books circulated widely in Japan at affordable prices, providing a wealth of visual information and a rich source of designs for netsuke carvers.

This netsuke was previously published in Harris 1987, p. 29, fig. 43.

—

Unsigned
Ivory, about 1850
H. 5.9 cm
British Museum HG.248
Given by Professor John and Mrs Anne Hull Grundy

Sleeping Chinese sage

Since netsuke were often used in combination with *inrō* (see pp. 188–189), it is natural that lacquer netsuke were sometimes made by *inrō* artists, creating a harmonious matching set. This netsuke is an excellent example of the carved red-lacquer technique known as *tsuishu*. The technique was introduced into Japan from China during the Kamakura period (1185–1333), essentially imitating Chinese lacquer of the Song (960–1279) and Yuan (1279–1368) periods. The technique involves the application of around twenty extremely thin base layers of lacquer before the craftsman could embark upon creating the surface decoration. In this example, a Chinese sage (a person of profound wisdom) dozes comfortably while wrapping his hands around his head and crossing his legs. His gown is elaborately decorated with Chinese patterns and his long beard streams over his chest.

Further information about the provenance of this netsuke can be found in W. L. Behrens; illustrated in Joly 1912, reprinted 1966, no. 799, pl. XIX.

Unsigned
Lacquered wood, about 1800
w. 4.3 cm
British Museum 1945,1017.631
Bequeathed by Oscar Charles Raphael

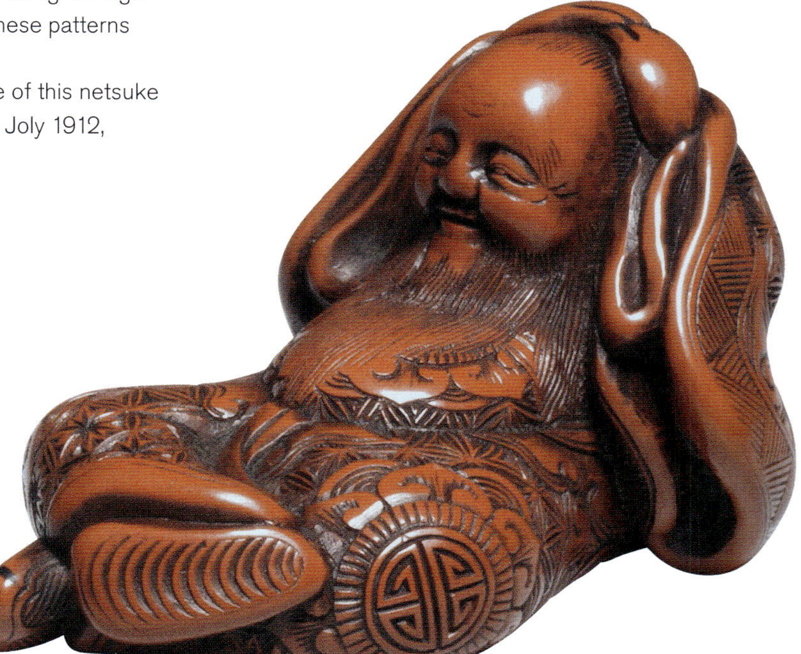

Japanese couple making love

Netsuke makers occasionally chose themes that were
erotic in nature, and they concealed these titillating carvings
within or under innocuous-looking exteriors. Here we have
a classic box (*hako*) netsuke that separates into two parts
and can be enjoyed in private as a pocket-sized amusement.
The box opens to reveal a couple embracing passionately
under a quilt decorated with a stylized floral pattern in gold
and red lacquer. The woman's hair is elegantly coiffured and
secured with a comb, and her legs are tightly wrapped
around her lover's back. Her closed eyes and delicately
pointed toes reveal the pleasure of the moment. Although
the man's face is concealed, their genitals are clearly visible
from one specific angle. Two small clasps and a line of
repair in gold lacquer on the lid reveal how much this
netsuke was used and treasured.

This netsuke was previously published in Buckland 2010,
p.24, fig. 2, and Clark et al (eds) 2013, p. 495, fig. 160.

By Masanao of Kyoto
Partially lacquered ivory, Kyoto, late 1700s
w. 4.9 cm
British Museum 1945,1017.675
Bequeathed by Oscar Charles Raphael

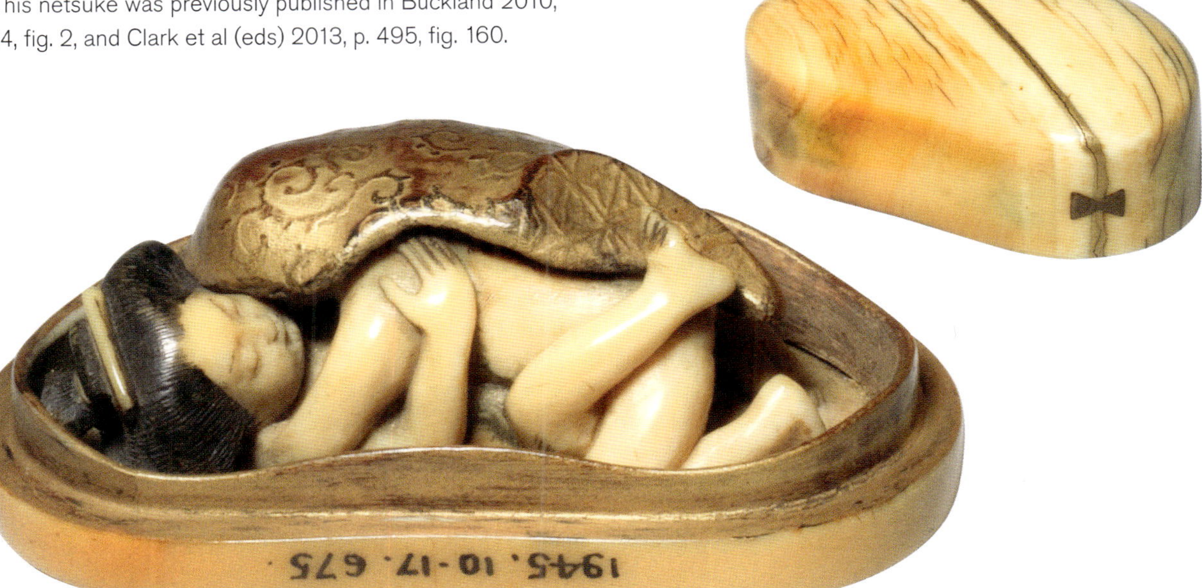

Man pulling a face

A man scares a child by pulling a face and rolling his eyes up into his head. The child is crouching and covering his face with his hands in fear. Exaggerated facial expressions seem to have held a fascination for netsuke carvers, and various amusing faces can be found in the woodblock-Illustrated book, *Hokusai manga (Random Sketches by Hokusai)*, a series of fifteen volumes, published between 1814 and 1878 (see below).

—

Unsigned
Wood, early 1800s
H. 7 cm
British Museum 1945,1017.572
Bequeathed by Oscar Charles Raphael

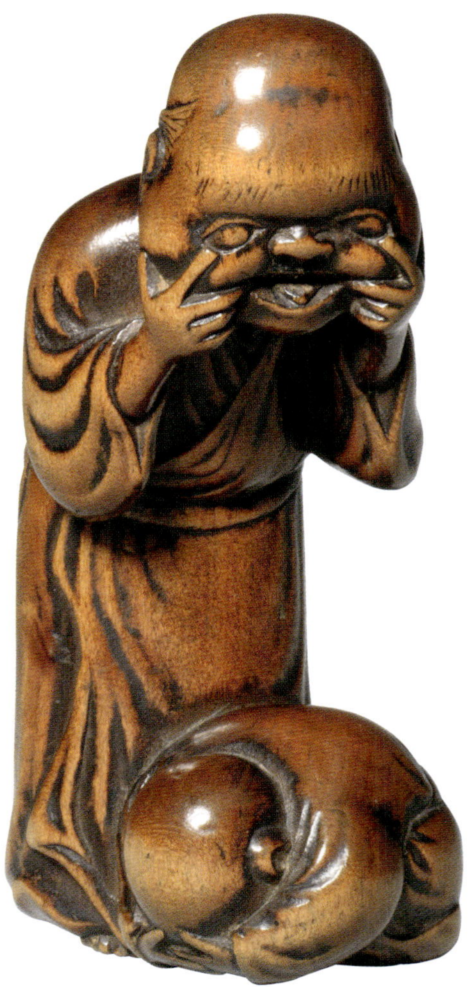

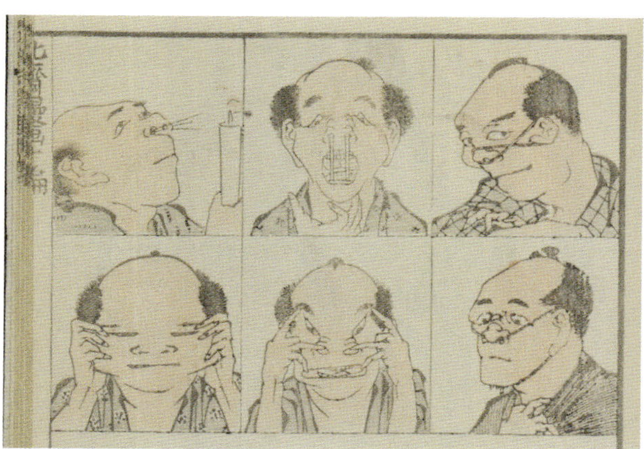

Various amusing faces, from Katsushika Hokusai (1760–1849), *Hokusai manga (Random Sketches by Hokusai)*, vol. 10. Woodblock-illustrated book, 1819. 23 x 16 cm (covers). British Museum 1979,0305,0.428.10.

Wood sculptor

A sculptor straddles a large block of wood and carves a projecting beam (*kibana*) with a hammer and a chisel. *Kibana* are ornamental finials, projecting from the upper sections of columns, and have no functional use. They often depict animals, mythological creatures and plants. Here the sculptor carves the head of a *baku*, a 'dream-eating' creature whose open-mouthed ferocity is startling to behold.

Because Japan is a country rich in varied woods, this has historically been one of the main materials used for carving Buddhist sculpture, and for the construction of buildings such as temples and shrines. A list of craftsmen illustrated in the volume *Saiga shokunin burui* (*Various Classes of Artisans in Coloured Pictures*), published in 1770, reflects what was admired during the mid-Edo period (1615–1868). The volume mentions that some craftsmen, such as woodworkers and swordsmiths, claimed ancient lineages and possessed prestigious craft skills with special status. Socially, craftsmen ranked higher than merchants, although their standard of living was not necessarily high during the Edo period.

—

Unsigned
Wood, about 1850
H. 5.5 cm; w. 5.1 cm
British Museum F.641
Given by Sir Augustus Wollaston Franks

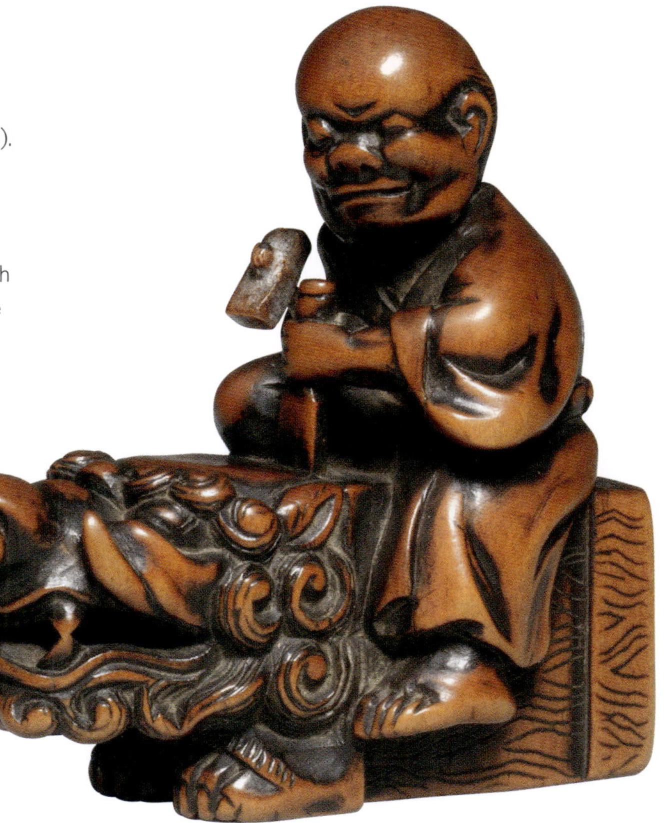

Stone-lifter

This netsuke appears to depict a blind masseur, clad only in a loincloth, squatting and grimacing from his attempt to lift a heavy stone. In this manner Japanese masseurs, who were more often than not blind, developed the muscles in their arms. However, what is actually depicted may be a man trying in vain to lift his enormously swollen scrotum and raise himself from the ground. In the Edo period (1615–1868), the disease *filarial elephantiasis* was endemic throughout Japan. The disease is transmitted by mosquitoes, producing parasitic worms and resulting in chronic swelling, most often noted in the lower torso, typically in the legs and genitals. In extreme cases, the genitals can reach to below the knees. An unfortunate victim of the disease is illustrated with unkind humour in *Hokusai manga* (*Random Sketches by Hokusai*) (see right). The subject was popular with netsuke carvers from relatively early on, and was often treated with ambiguity as to whether the object being lifted was a stone or an enlarged testicle.

This netsuke was previously published in Barker and Smith 1976, pp. 66–67, fig. 95, and Lazarnick (ed.), MCI, vol. 1, 1986, p. 79.

—

By Gesshō
Wood, about 1800
H. 5 cm
British Museum 1912,1012.7
Bequeathed by Harry Seymour Trower

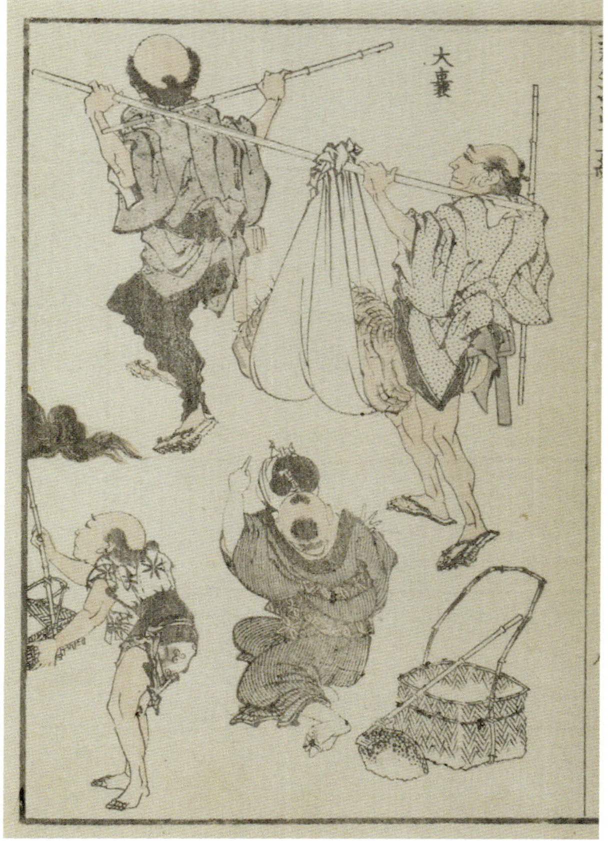

A man with an enormously swollen scrotum, from Katsushika Hokusai (1760–1849), *Hokusai manga* (*Random Sketches by Hokusai*), vol. 12. Woodblock-illustrated book, 1834. 23 x 16 cm (covers). British Museum 1979,0305,0.428.12.

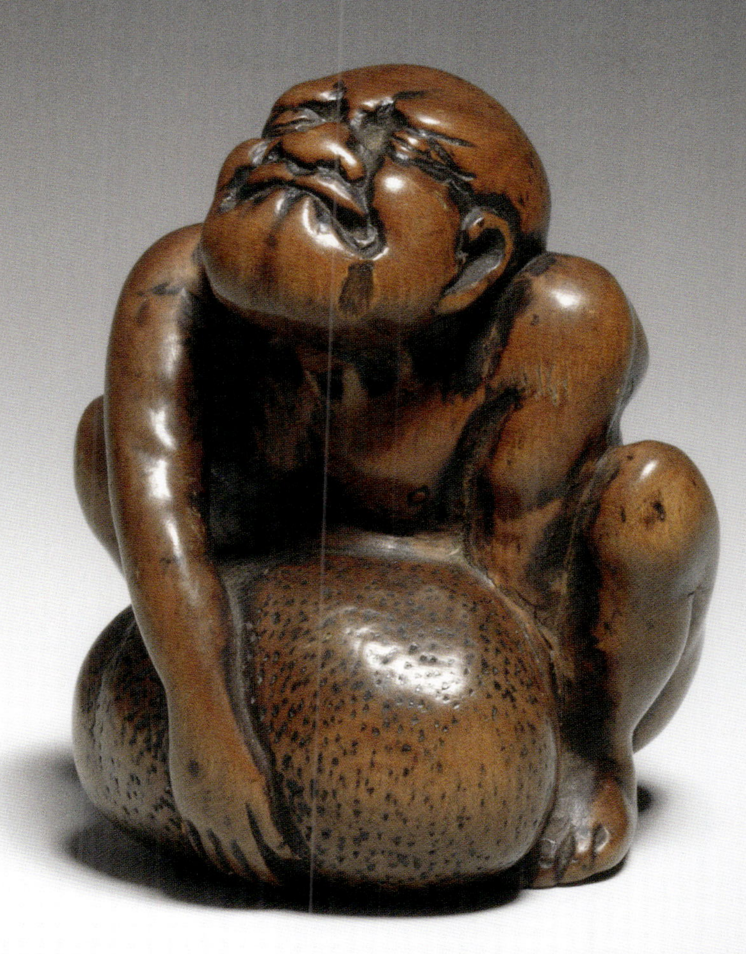

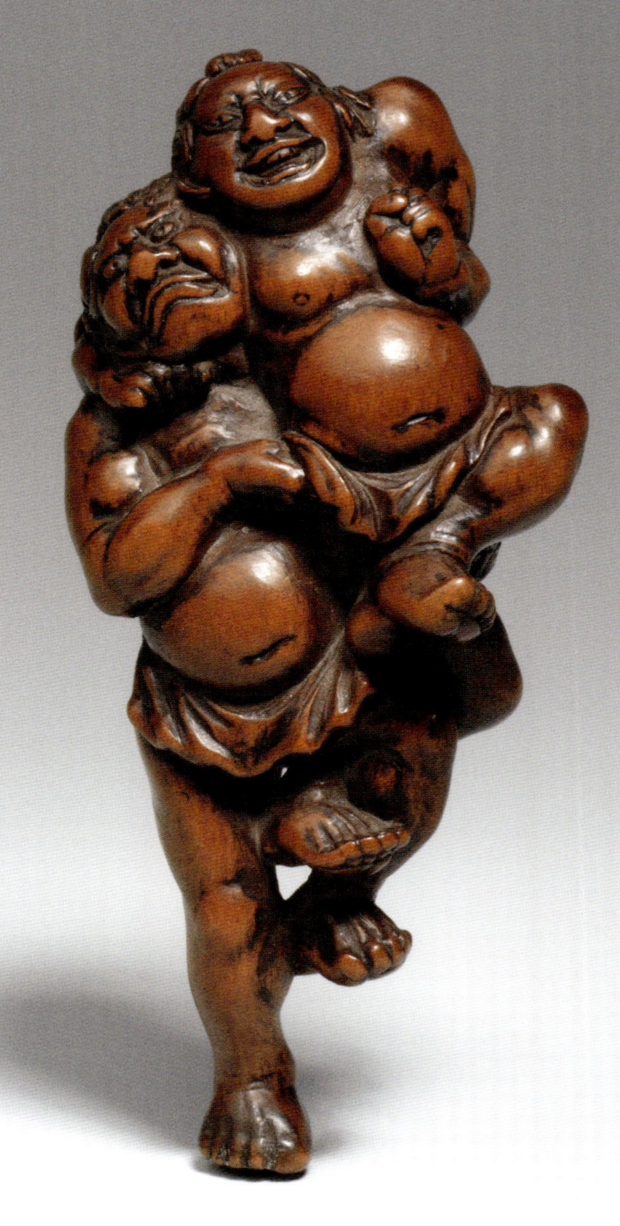

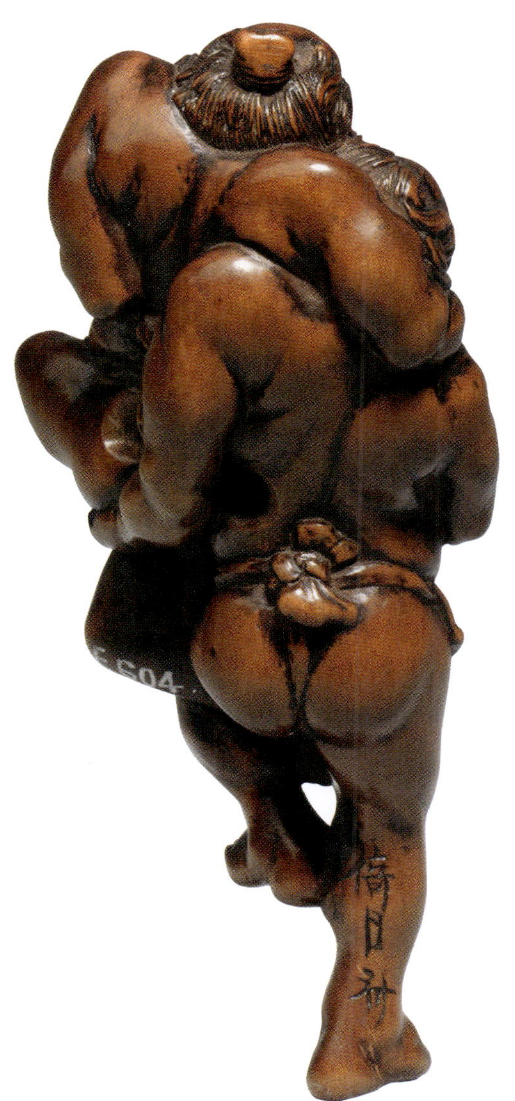

Sumō wrestlers

This netsuke represents a crucial moment in the combat of two fiercely grimacing sumō wrestlers, locked in the famous 'Kawazu' throw. The name of this winning technique is said to derive from a general of the Heian period (794–1185), Kawazu Sukeyasu (d. 1176), a sumō master. One day Sukeyasu fought against Matano Kagehisa (d. 1183), who lifted Sukeyasu up by his loincloth in order to throw him to the ground, thereby apparently winning the contest. However, Sukeyasu hooked one foot between his opponent's legs and wrapped one arm around his rival's neck, throwing Kagehisa off balance and actually securing victory. Here we see the uplifted wrestler rallying his last reserves of strength to win the match. Netsuke depicting wrestlers have always been popular on account of their dramatic, muscular and powerful expression, perhaps conferring these attributes to the wearer.

—

By Kijitsusai
Wood, about 1850
H. 8.2 cm
British Museum F.604
Given by Sir Augustus Wollaston Franks

Chinese couple playing a flute

This netsuke depicts the Chinese Tang emperor Xuanzong (AD 685–762) and his beautiful consort Yang Yuhuan (Yang Guifei, AD 719–756) playing a flute together, seated on an elaborately decorated throne. Yang Guifei was renowned for her beauty and skill at both dancing and playing music. Although she was initially the wife of the emperor's son, she became the emperor's favourite concubine during his later years. Under her sway, however, the emperor neglected his imperial duties and became addicted to a life of pleasure and debauchery, which ended in revolt by the discontented populace. Yang Guifei was killed and the emperor was forcibly retired. From the seventeenth century onwards, many illustrated printed books came to Japan from China. The great variety of Chinese legends, historical episodes and exotic motifs greatly influenced the development of netsuke, and were ultimately adopted as part of Japan's own heritage. Many parallels can be traced between the particular subjects of early netsuke and those of Chinese illustrated books and their Japanese editions (see right).

One of the oldest examples in the British Museum, this netsuke has acquired a beautiful golden patina with age.

This netsuke was previously published in Barker and Smith 1976, p. 152, fig. 339. Further information about its provenance can be found in W. L. Behrens; illustrated in Joly 1912, reprinted 1966, no. 1321, pl. XXIV.

—

Unsigned
Ivory, about 1700
H. 7.3 cm
British Museum 1945,1017.595
Bequeathed by Oscar Charles Raphael

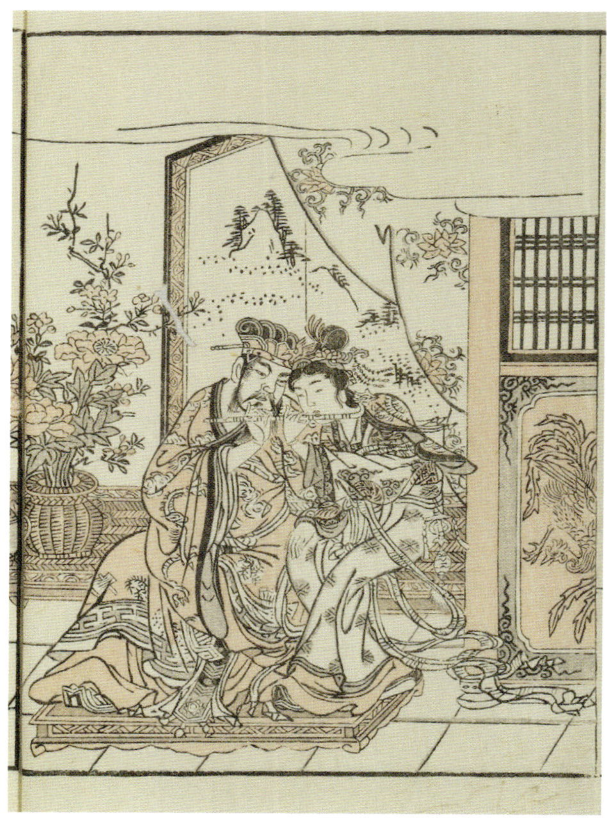

'Yang Guifei' (detail), from Toriyama Sekien (1712–1788), *Wakan jinbutsu kaiji hiken* (*Pictorial Comparisons of Figures of China and Japan*), vol. 2. Woodblock-illustrated book, 1777. 22 x 15 cm (covers). British Museum 1979,0305,0.128.2.

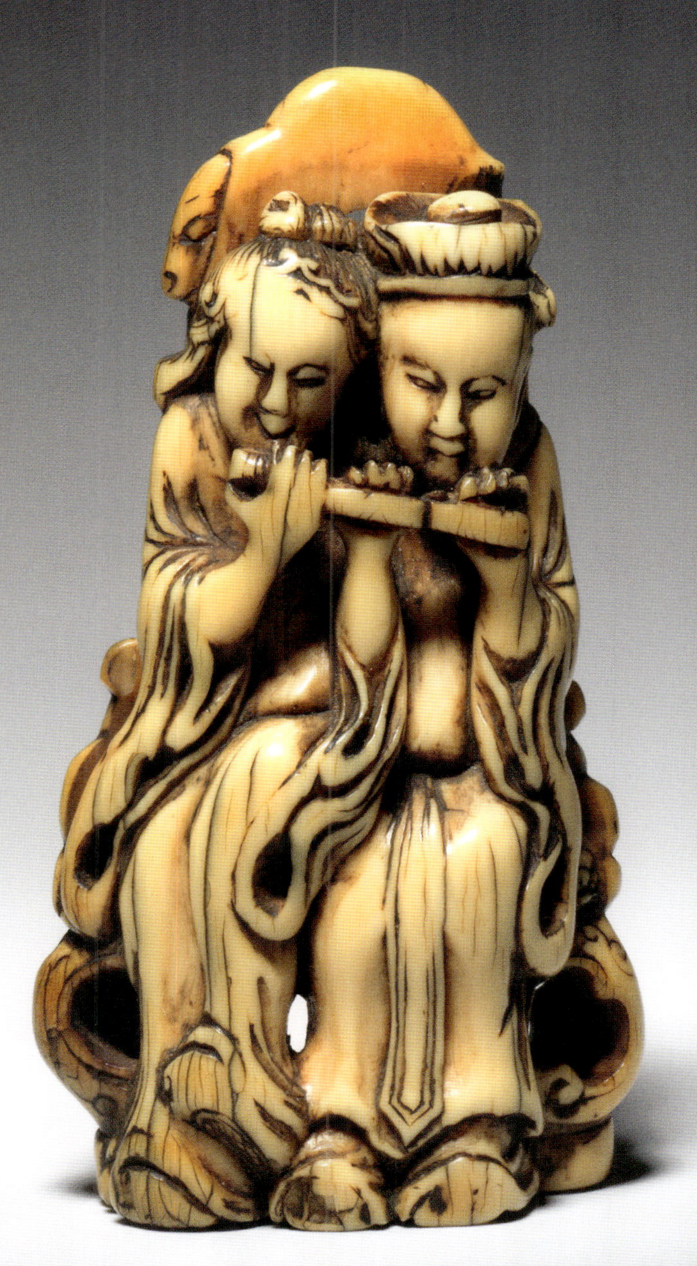

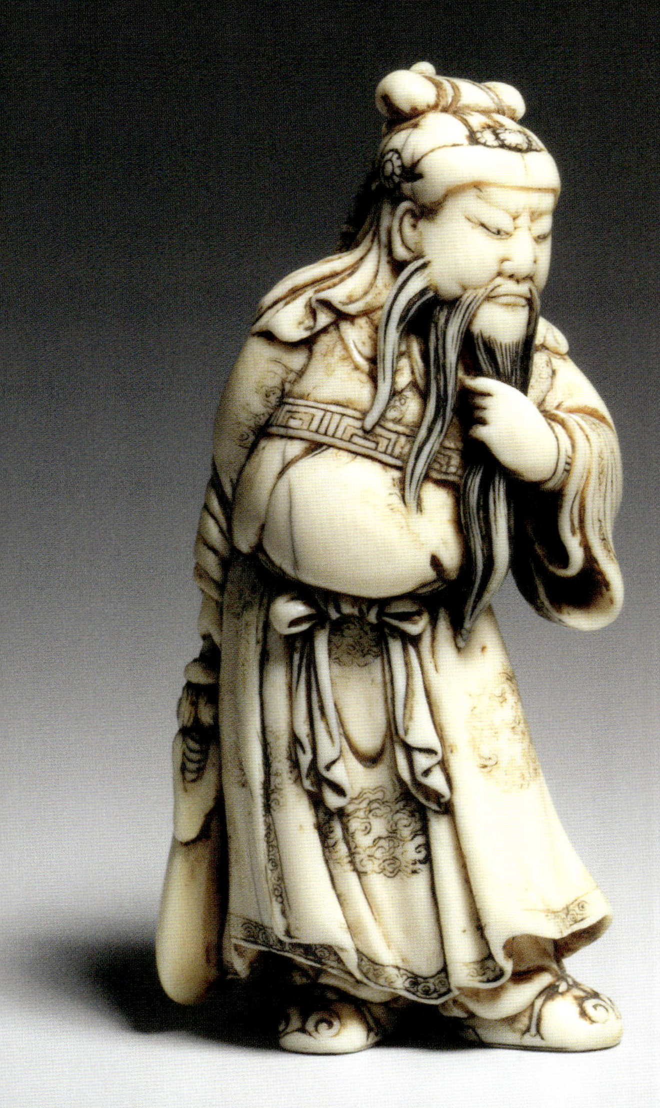

Guan Yu

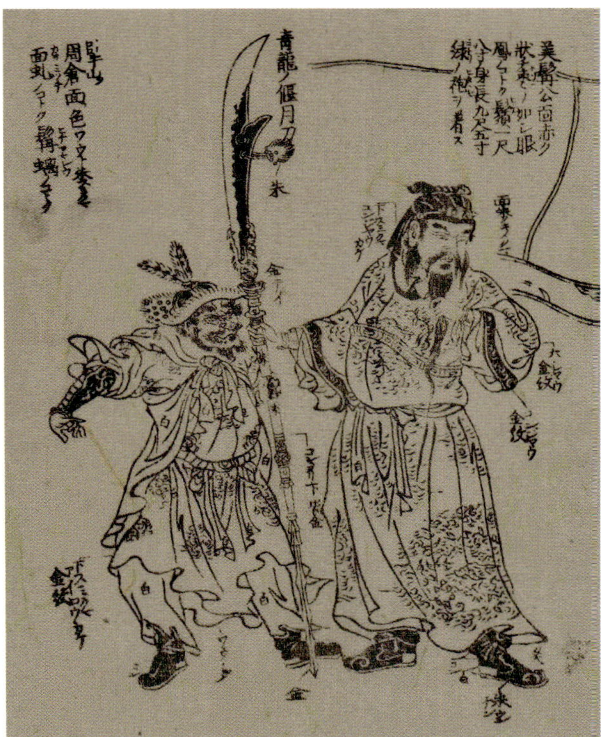

'Guan Yu', from Tachibana Morikuni, *Ehon shahō-bukuro* (*Treasure-bag Picture Book*), vol. 7. Woodblock-illustrated book, 1720 (reprinted 1770). 22.1 x 15.4 cm (covers). British Museum 1914,0528,0.4.1-10. Given by Mrs A. Moseley.

Guan Yu (J. Kan'u, d. AD 219) was a Chinese general and one of three great military heroes during the Han period (206 BC–AD 220). He played a significant role in the civil war that led to the collapse of the Han dynasty and the establishment of the state of Shu Han in the Three Kingdoms period (AD 220–280). Here he is shown as a warrior with a majestic appearance, stroking his long beard and holding a curved halberd (a type of weapon) behind his back. His robe is decorated with medallions of stylized dragons and clouds. The design for this netsuke was clearly taken from the Japanese woodblock-illustrated book, *Ehon shahō-bukuro* (*Treasure-bag Picture Book*) by Tachibana Morikuni (1679–1748), originally published in 1720 (see left). Worshipped as a god of war, Guan Yu was a popular subject for prints, paintings and netsuke throughout the Edo period (1615–1868).

There is a variant of this netsuke made of wood in the British Museum (F.691). It was not unusual for a carver or his school to repeat certain subjects, earning a reputation for excelling in that particular design.

This netsuke was previously published in Barker and Smith 1976, pp. 119–120, fig. 230, and Lazarnick (ed.), MCI, vol. 1, 1986, p. 10.

—

By Atokama
Ivory, late 1700s
H. 7.6 cm
British Museum 1912,1012.16
Bequeathed by Harry Seymour Trower

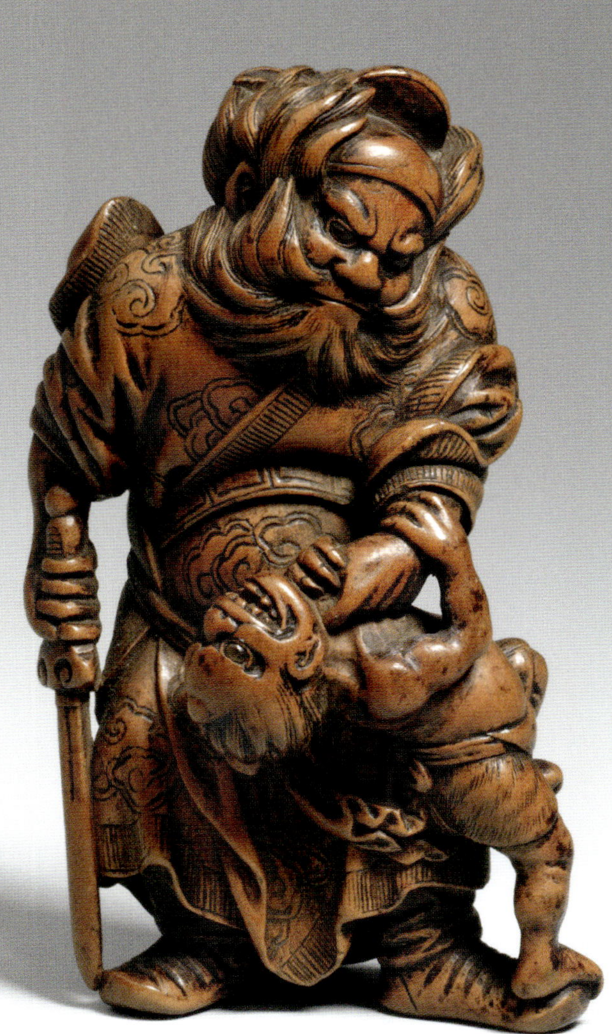

Shōki and a demon

Shōki (C. Zhong Kui), the Demon Queller, was
a legendary Chinese scholar of the Tang period
(AD 618–906). He is usually shown as a terrifying
bearded giant with a scholar's cap, carrying a heavy
sword. Here he shows off his power by holding a
demon, *oni*, by the throat as the demon throws
its head back in agony. In Japan, Shōki became
associated with the Boy's Festival which is held
on the fifth day of the fifth month. On that day,
Shōki's image is placed in a position of honour in
the household in order that the sons of the family
are protected from evil and grow up to be strong,
like him.

This netsuke was previously published in Barker
and Smith 1976, p. 68, fig. 99.

—

By Minkoku
Wood, with eyes inlaid in horn
Edo, about 1820
H. 6.8 cm
British Museum F.692
Given by Sir Augustus Wollaston Franks

Shōki and a demon

Here we have another version of the same subject (see previous page). Shōki (C. Zhong Kui), the Demon Queller, is of Chinese origin and became a favourite subject of Japanese artists – who often treated him with great affection and humour. It is not always inevitable that Shōki gains the upper hand in his eternal fight. Sometimes the demon (*oni*) wins by clinging to Shōki's back, climbing up on his hat or hiding in a tree. This netsuke depicts the other extreme, however. Shōki grips his rival's jaw to cross-examine him. His face appears so evil that the poor demon evokes our sympathy.

This netsuke was previously published in Barker and Smith 1976, p. 136, fig. 286 (but the plate number is 291).

—

Unsigned
Wood, mid 1700s
H. 6.3 cm
British Museum 1945,1017.619
Bequeathed by Oscar Charles Raphael

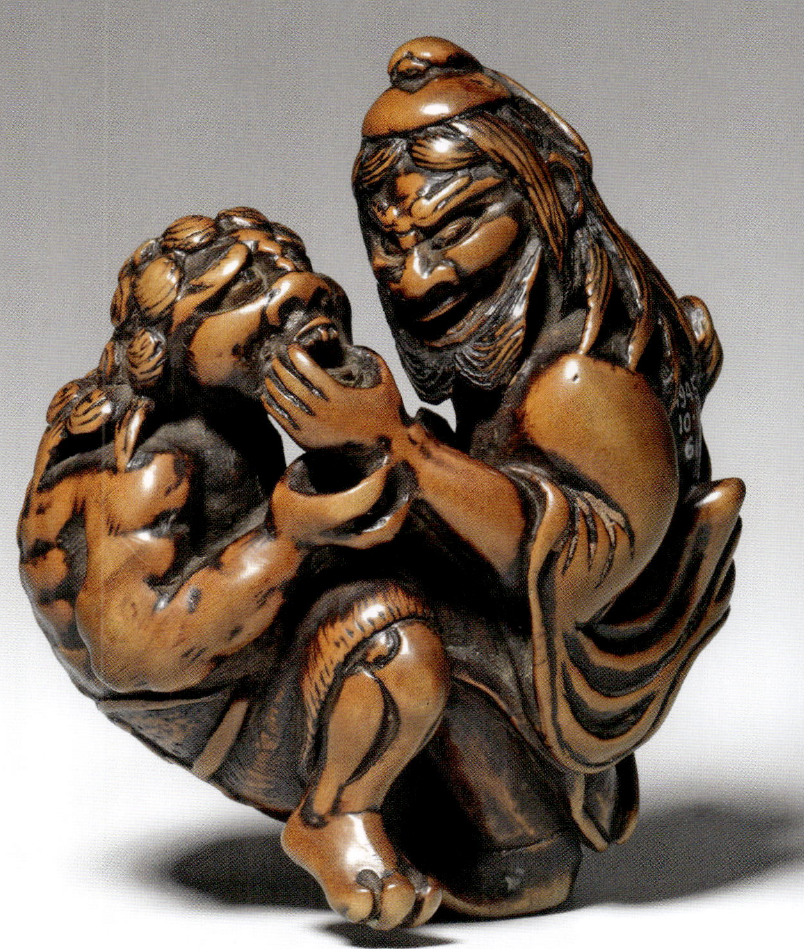

Daruma yawning

Daruma (Sanskrit *Bodhidharma*) was a sixth-century Indian monk, traditionally credited to be the founder of the Zen sect of Buddhism. Daruma is said to have spent nine years in deep meditation, seated facing the wall of a cave. Here, the monk stands yawning, as if awakening from his long contemplation. This humorous pose is called 'Daruma Yawning' (*Akubi Daruma*) and has always been a popular theme with netsuke carvers. Mitsuhiro, who was active in Osaka, is well known for his minutely detailed carvings. He worked mainly in ivory and often stained his ivory to a mellow shade of brown, which can be seen here in the folds of Daruma's robe. Also typical of his style is a fine incising and inked stippling (using a series of dots) of the surface in Daruma's black stubble and chest hair.

This netsuke was previously published in Barker and Smith 1976, p. 34, fig. 24.

—

By Ōhara Mitsuhiro (1810–1875)
Ivory, with eyes inlaid in dark horn, Osaka, mid 1800s
H. 5.2 cm
British Museum F.897
Given by Sir Augustus Wollaston Franks

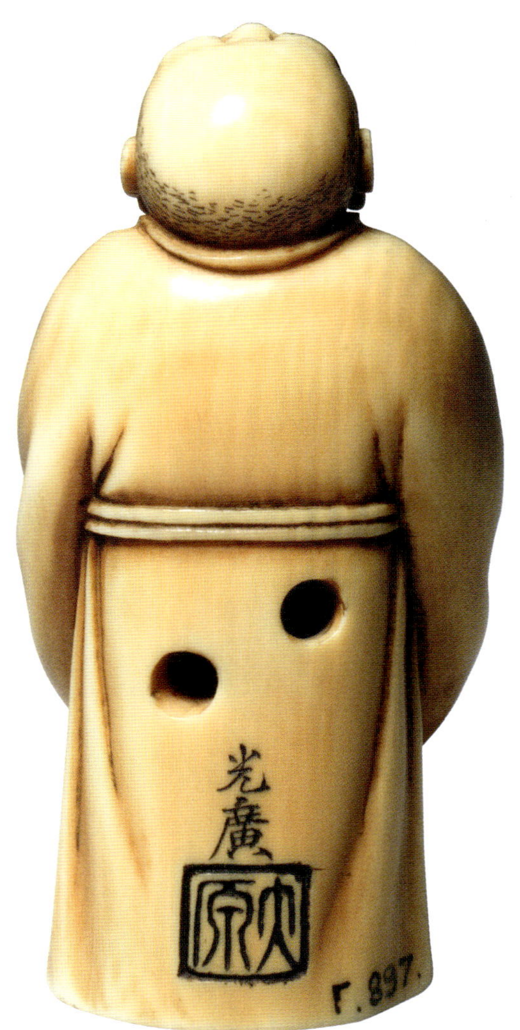

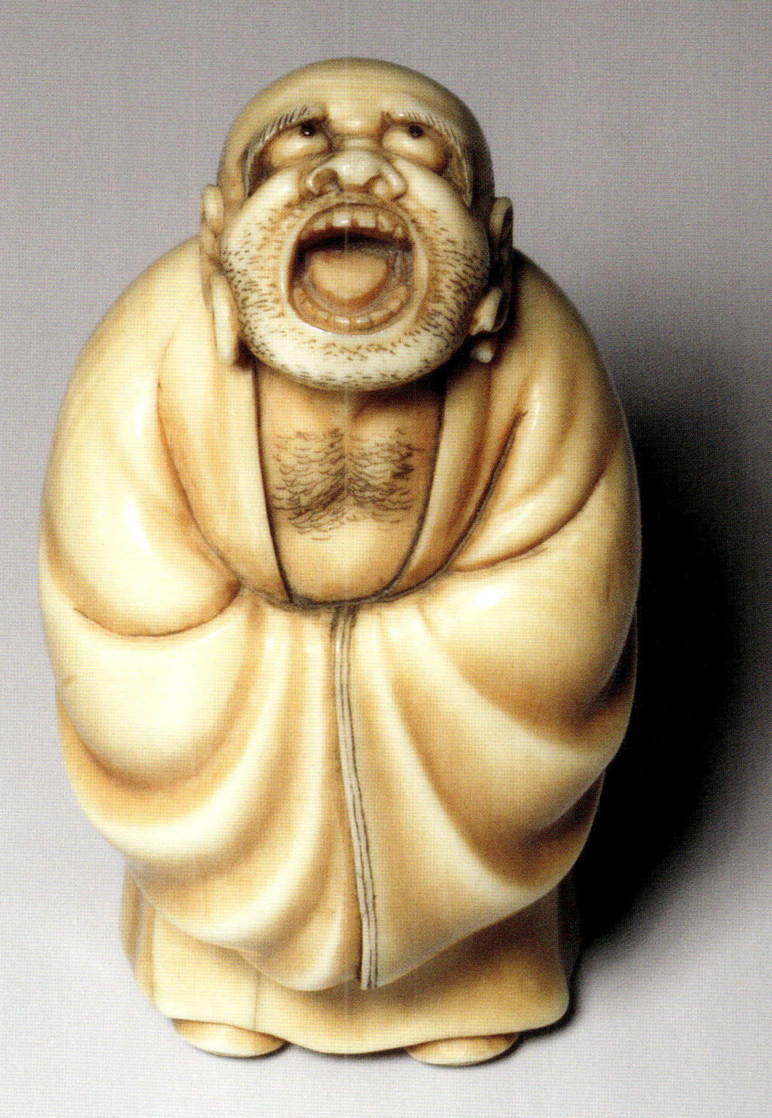

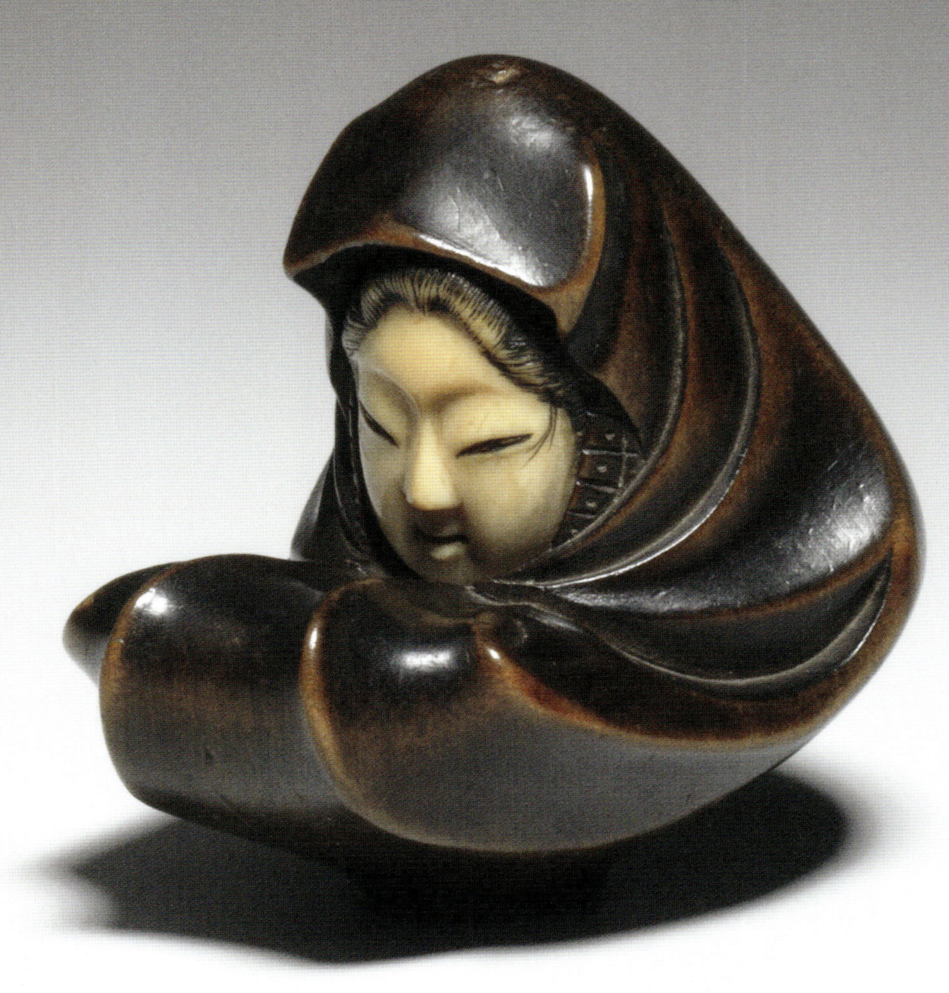

Woman as Daruma (Onna Daruma)

A courtesan has disguised herself as Daruma in a voluminous robe. Her face is inlaid with ivory and her hairline and features are delicately depicted with inked incised lines. Daruma is said to have meditated for nine years to attain enlightenment. Similarly, female sex workers typically had to endure ten years of indenture in their profession. So by association the word 'Daruma' became synonymous for 'sex worker' in Edo slang. In a broader sense, Zen philosophy had always challenged accepted thinking with a provocative mixture of sacred and profane. Following these traditions, the theme 'Woman as Daruma,' or 'Onna Daruma,' was depicted in many differnt media throughout the Edo period (1615–1868); not only in netsuke, but also in painting and woodblock prints (see left).

—

By Kikugawa
Wood, with face inlaid in ivory, Edo, mid 1800s
w. 4.2 cm
British Museum 1912,1012.14
Bequeathed by Harry Seymour Trower

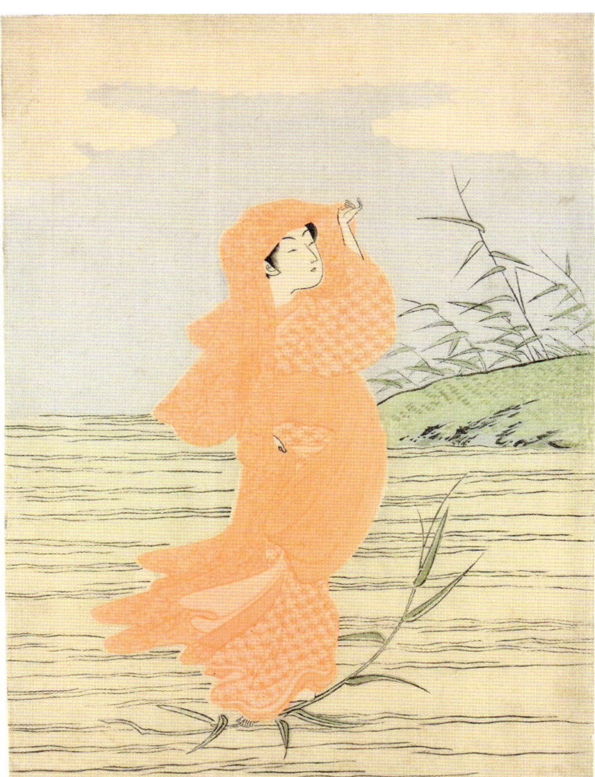

Courtesan as Daruma. Suzuki Harunobu (d. 1770), colour woodblock print, 1765–1770. 27.5 x 20.2 cm. British Museum 1945,1101,0.43. Bequeathed by Oscar Charles Raphael.

Arhat grasping a fly-whisk

Arhats (J. *rakan*, 'enlightened beings') were the original disciples of the historical Buddha and possessed supernatural powers, along with the Buddha's wisdom. Arhats are traditionally represented in groups of sixteen and sometimes even five hundred. In this example, the figure stands holding a fly-whisk, or *hossu*, a Buddhist implement used to chase away flies and dust. Importantly, the whisk was also believed to protect the wielder from earthly desire and distraction. This arhat has a frowning face, while attempting a somewhat comical feat. His tongue, which is made from ivory, juts out from his mouth attempting to touch the tip of his nose. His robe billows around him revealing his bare and emaciated chest. The carver, Sanshō, is said to have lived from 1871 to 1936, and is well known for his expressive and rather eccentric carvings. Most of his subjects are in human form, including street entertainers, labourers, legendary and religious figures. His figures are always treated with great humour, even absurdity, and sometimes they are even grotesque.

   This netsuke was previously published in Barker and Smith 1976, p. 41, fig. 41.

—

By Kokeisai Sanshō
Boxwood and ivory, Osaka, early 1900s
H. 8.7 cm
British Museum 1912,1012.6
Bequeathed by Harry Seymour Trower

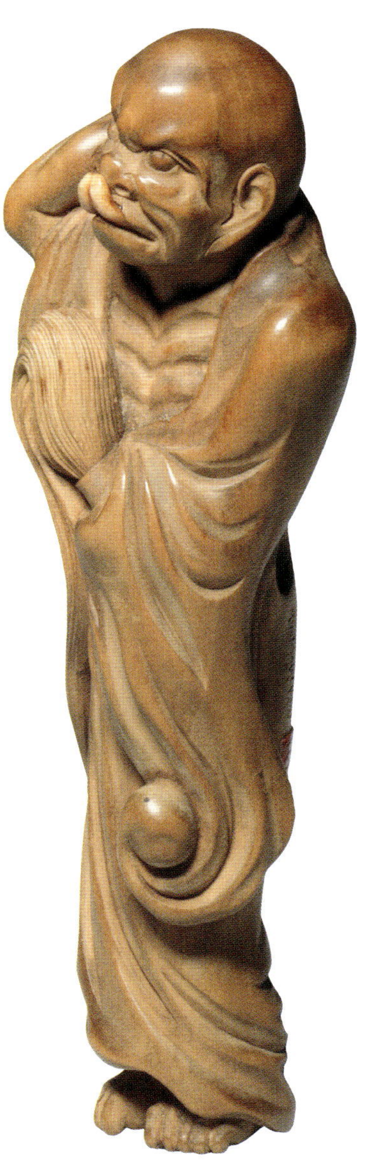

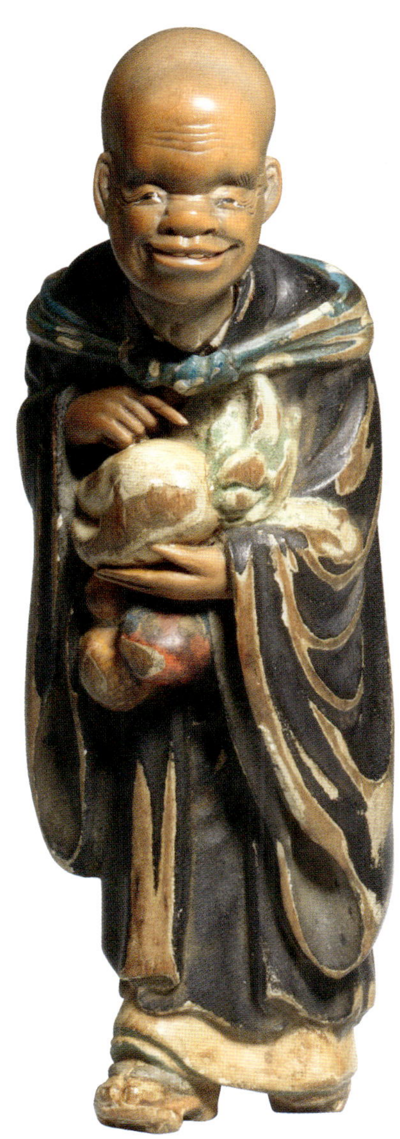

Takuan Sōhō holding a Japanese radish

Takuan Sōhō (1573–1645) is one of the most prominent monks in Japanese Zen Buddhism, renowned for his knowledge of arts such as calligraphy, painting, poetry and tea. He is credited with concocting the recipe for a type of pickled Japanese radish, still extremely popular today, which thereby carries his name, *takuan*. In this netsuke representation, the monk cradles a forked Japanese radish in his hands. He carries over his shoulders a wrapped parcel, and from his belt hangs a double-gourd water container and pouch. Although the netsuke is unsigned, it is typical of Sanshō to use unpainted boxwood for the head, hands and feet, and softwood, probably Japanese cypress (*hinoki*), painted with shell-white (*gofun*) and other pigments for the robed body. The latter is rendered using single-knife carving, or *ittōbori*, which helps delineate the folds and weight of the fabric.

—

Unsigned; attributed to Kokeisai Sanshō
Partially painted wood, early 1900s
H. 9.5 cm
British Museum 1912,1012.3
Bequeathed by Harry Seymour Trower

Niō arm-wrestling

Buddhist deities provided fertile subject matter for netsuke carvers, and they are often depicted in humorous situations. Here Niō, a pair of fierce guardian statues who stand either side of the gateway to a Buddhist temple, are shown arm-wrestling. Their muscular bodies tense as their contest reaches its climax. The same composition can be seen in the later woodblock-illustrated book, *Kachō sansui zushiki* (*Illustrations of Birds, Flowers and Landscapes*), published in 1866 (see opposite). It is conceivable that this printed version is derived from an earlier source, which also served as the inspiration for the netsuke. Here one Niō scents victory, while the other holds on desperately.

A similar netsuke signed by Higo Daijō is in the Museum of Fine Arts, Boston, 47.716. Another example is illustrated in Bandini, exhibition catalogue, 2013, p. 20, fig. 9.

This netsuke was previously published in Barker and Smith 1976, p. 128, fig. 257, and Lazarnick, vol. 1, 1981, pp. 463–464.

—

By Higo Daijō
Wood, late 1700s
w. 7.7 cm
British Museum 1945,1017.524
Bequeathed by Oscar Charles Raphael

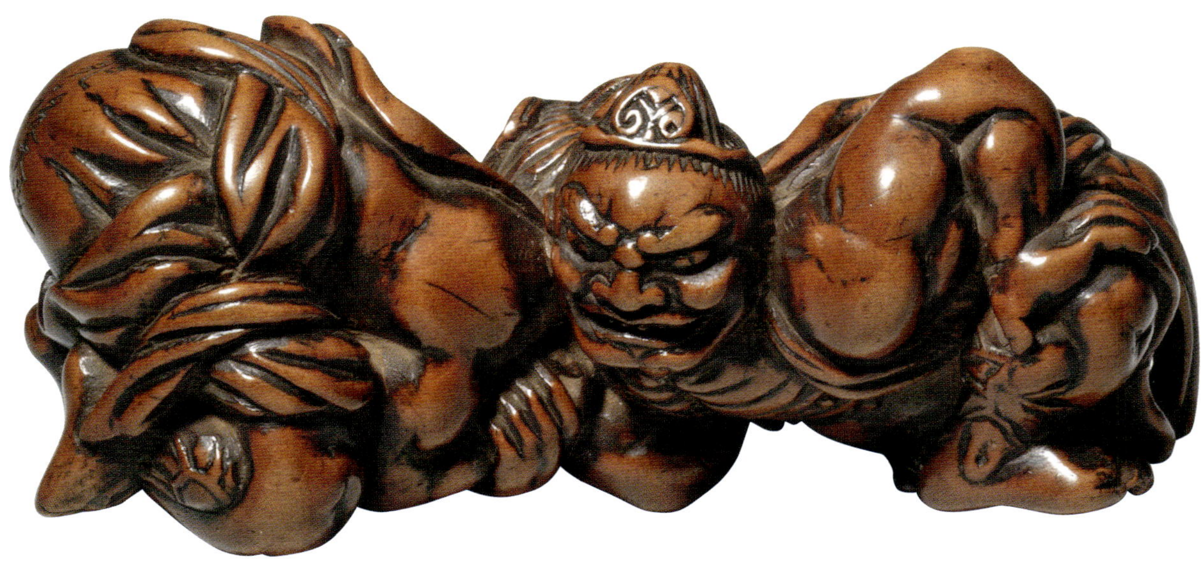

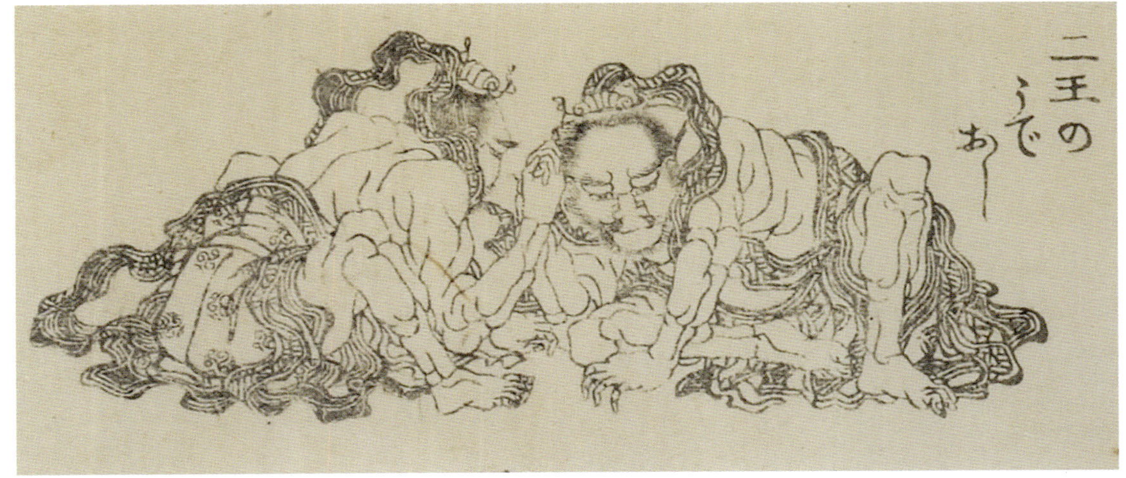

A design of Niō arm-wrestling, from school of Katsushika Hokusai, *Kachō sansui zushiki*
(*Illustrations of Birds, Flowers and Landscapes*), vol. 2. Woodblock-illustrated book, 1866.
12.3 x 17.7 cm. British Museum 1915,0823,0.129.

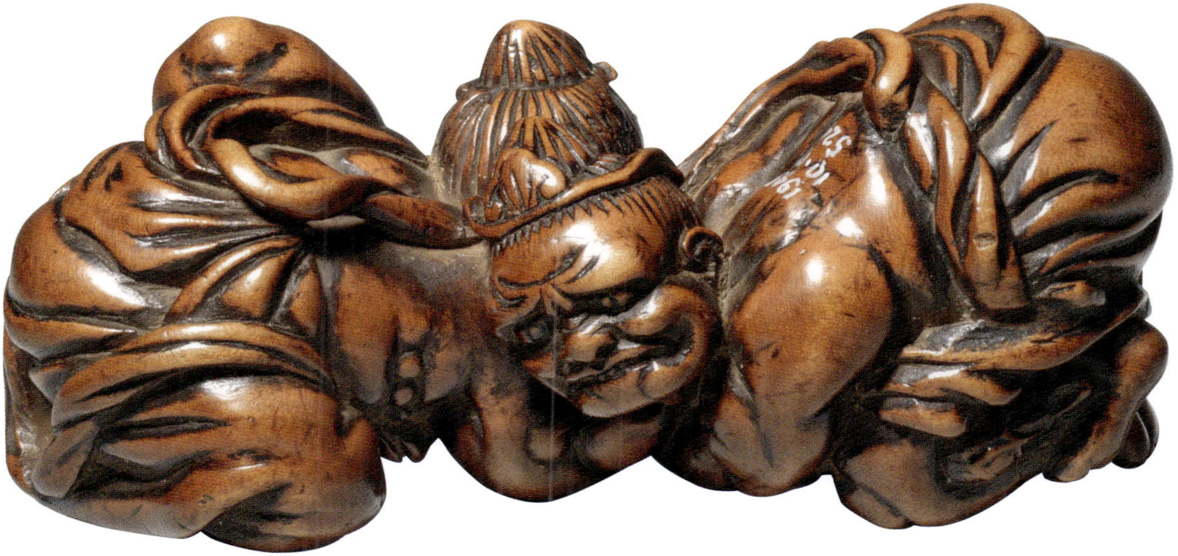

Handaka Sonja

Handaka Sonja is one of the sixteen arhats (J. *rakan*),
or disciples of the historical Buddha. He is credited with
supernatural powers and generally depicted with a bowl,
from which emerges a dragon or a rain cloud. Here he
holds the bowl aloft with his right hand and with the left
carries a sacred jewel, *tama*.

Naitō Toyomasa, born in Tanba province (present-day
Hyōgo prefecture), established a workshop specializing
in netsuke production and had a number of pupils.
According to documents which have been kept by a
descendant, he was appointed as the official carver to
the Lord of Sasayama in 1835. Because netsuke carvers
were regarded as being of lower status than the painters
commissioned by samurai or temples, it was quite rare
for them to receive official patronage.

Toyomasa's favourite material was wood, and many of his
works reveal a distinctive style of openwork carving which
incorporates swirling lines, as seen in this example. Here,
the beautifully carved scales of the dragon make a striking
contrast with the fluid swirling clouds. The openings in the
composition provide a natural hole for the cord to pass
through (*himotōshi*). Despite the complexity of the carving,
the netsuke sports an overall simple and compact shape.

This netsuke was also published in Barker and Smith
1976, p. 113, fig. 213.

—

By Naitō Toyomasa (1773–1856)
Wood, with eyes inlaid in pale horn, Tanba province
Early 1800s
H. 5.5 cm
British Museum 1912,1012.13
Bequeathed by Harry Seymour Trower

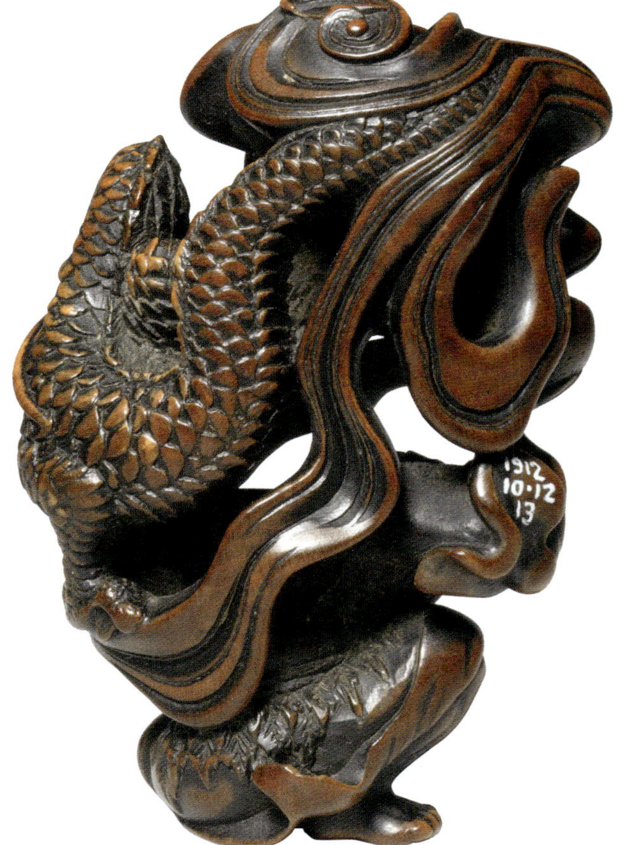

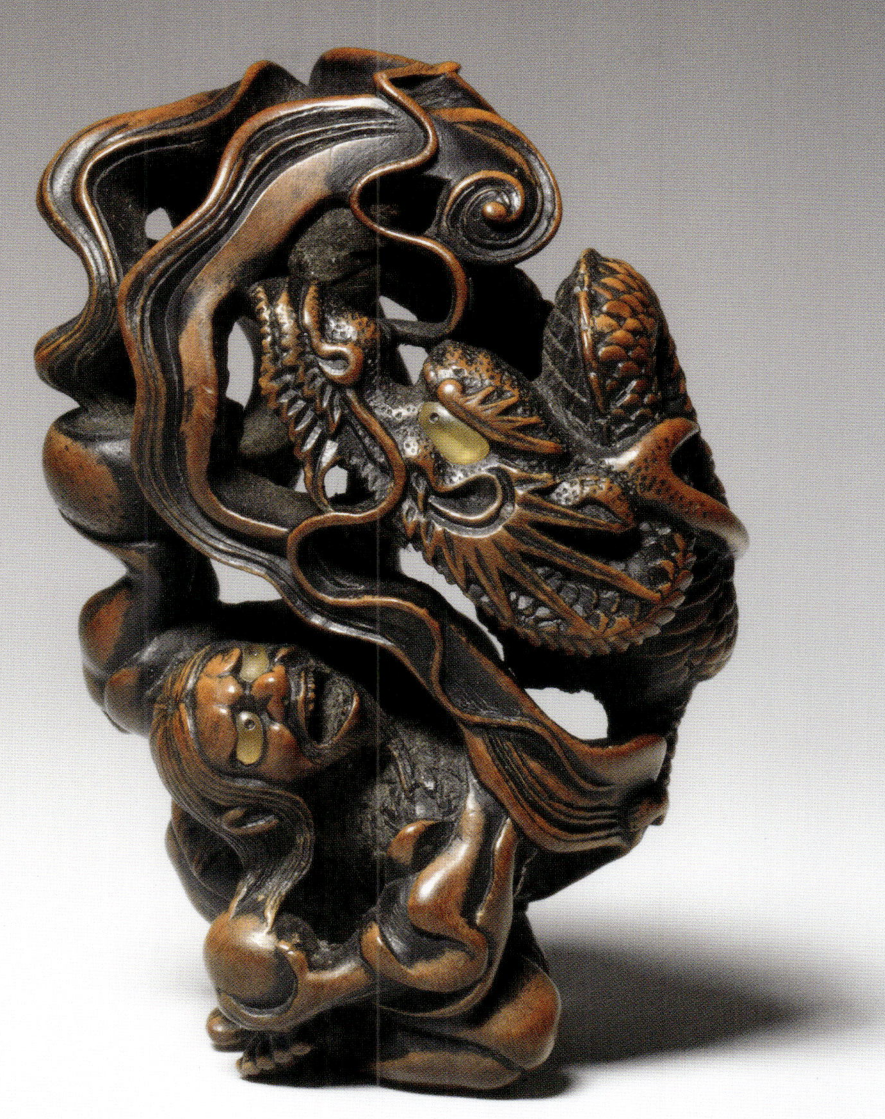

Handaka Sonja

This is another example of a netsuke depicting Handaka
Sonja (see also pp. 52–53), this time carved from a single,
large piece of ivory. Handaka Sonja crouches on one knee,
and holds a bowl with his right hand, from which a dragon
emerges. The robe is pulled down from Handaka Sonja's
left shoulder, and he seems to raise his left hand to scratch
the dragon's chin affectionately. Like a domestic cat, the
dragon turns up its head with pleasure and we can almost
hear it purr. The turning of such a ferocious beast into a
tame pet is an expression of Handaka Sonja's innate power,
as well as the artist's sense of playfulness.

—

Unsigned
Ivory, with eyes inlaid in metal, mid 1700s
H. 8 cm
British Museum 1930,1217.75
Bequeathed by James Hilton

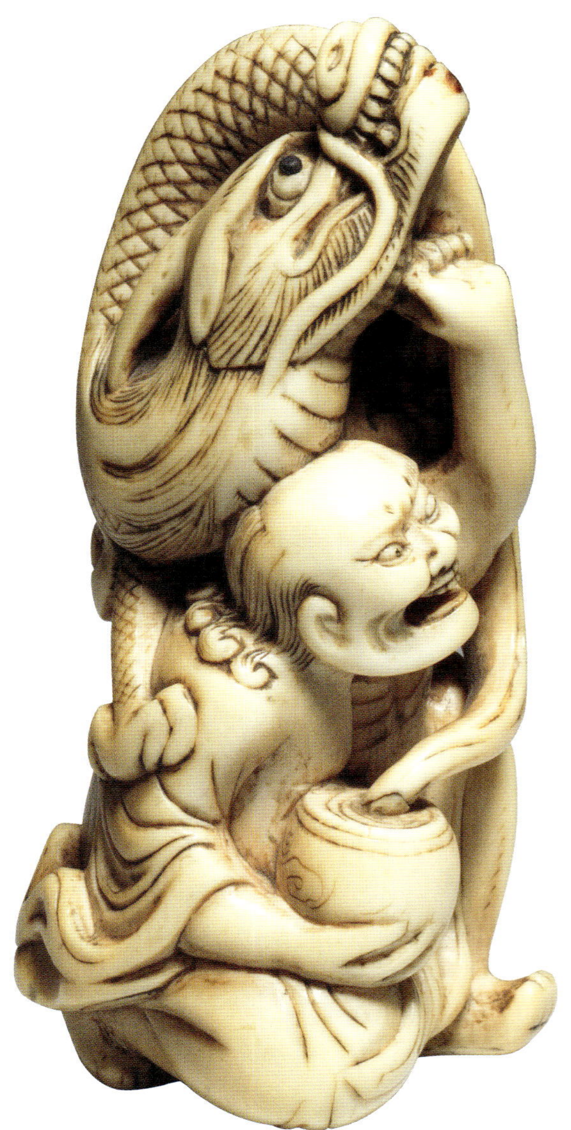

Immortals and others

Immortals or *sennin* are often portrayed in netsuke. The concept was taken from China but was particularly popular in Japan with immortals portrayed as holy and eccentric men, and occasionally women, who mostly lived in the mountains. Immortals are often depicted with long, flowing hair and a beard, carrying a staff, and dressed in a skirt of mugwort or artemisia leaves. The Seven Gods of Good Fortune or *Shichifukujin*, which are popular deities mainly of Buddhist origin, are also often carved in netsuke. The Seven Gods of Good Fortune are Benten, Bishamon, Daikoku, Ebisu, Fukurokuju, Hotei and Jurōjin.

Tenaga and Ashinaga

Tenaga (literally 'long arms') and Ashinaga ('long legs') are two legendary Chinese fishermen. Living on the seashore, they are said to cooperate in catching seafood that makes up most of their diet, and their favourite dish is octopus. Here they are working together to catch an octopus entangled around the long legs of Ashinaga, who wades into the sea. Tenaga, who is sitting on the shoulders of Ashinaga, stretches his long arm to catch the octopus and free his friend's legs.

This netsuke was previously published in Harris 1987, p. 28, fig. 40.

—

Unsigned
Wood, about 1780
H. 13.4 cm
British Museum HG.11
Given by Professor John and Mrs Anne Hull Grundy

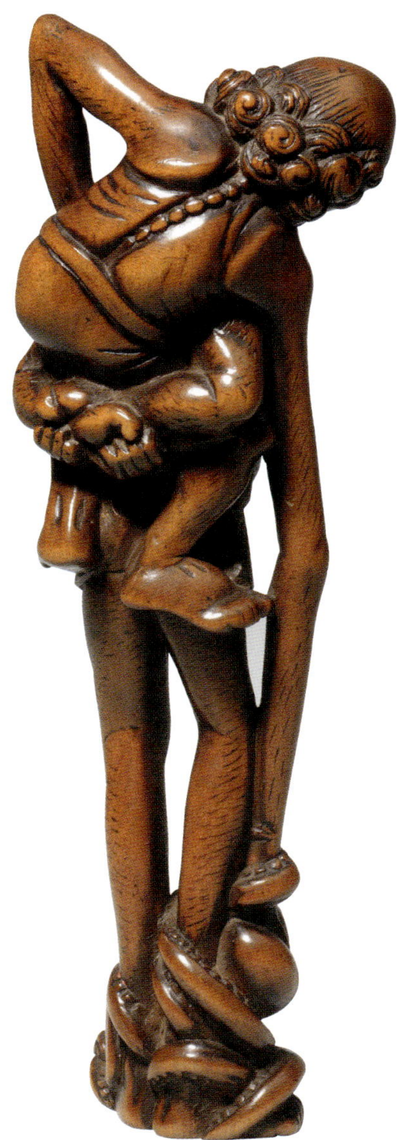

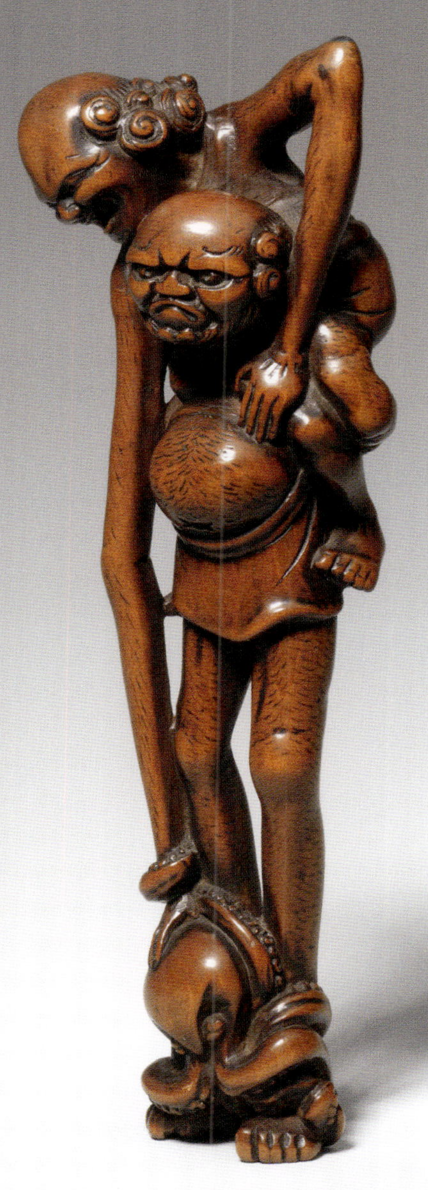

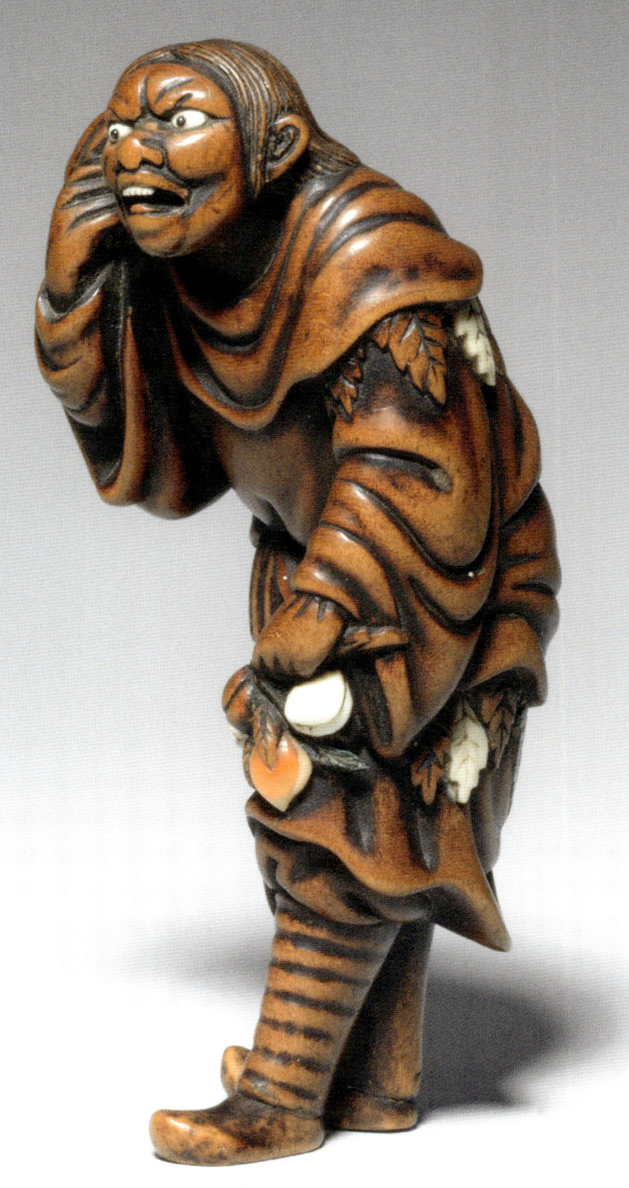

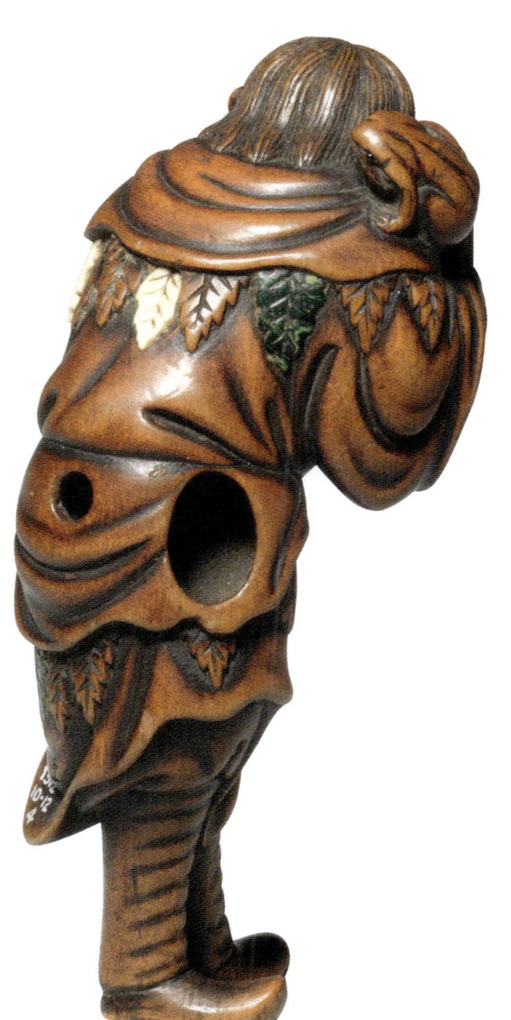

Gama Sennin

Gama Sennin is a legendary Chinese immortal, usually accompanied by a toad with three legs. The character of Gama is believed to have derived from a Chinese story of a travelling peddler of magical medicines, who had once transformed himself into a toad. Here, he holds the leg of his companion (the toad) which sits on his shoulder, and a cluster of peaches, a symbol of longevity, inlaid in ivory and agate, dangles from his other hand. The carver, Tsuji, who was active in Osaka in the late eighteenth century, created mainly figures of gods, deities and sages in wood. With his long hair parted in the middle, the immortal has an exotic face with big ears, accentuated by his eyes and teeth, which are inlaid in ivory. He is dressed in a robe with a cape, with mugwort leaves inlaid in ivory and probably malachite peeking out from underneath. Such inlays are unusual for this artist. Like most immortals carved by Tsuji, Gama Sennin wears leggings and shoes, otherwise uncommon in depictions of Chinese sages. The larger oval hole to conceal the knot of the cord is however a typical characteristic of the carver. Tsuji usually signed his works rather inconspicuously with the small single character of his name, here carved at the hem of the robe (see p. 207).

This netsuke was previously published in Barker and Smith 1976, p. 26, fig. 1.

—

By Tsuji
Wood, with details inlaid in ivory, semi-precious stones and horn, Osaka, about 1780
H. 8.2 cm
British Museum 1912,1012.4
Bequeathed by Harry Seymour Trower

Chinnan Sennin

The Chinese sage Chinnan (C. Chen Nan) is said to be able
to summon a dragon from a gourd or bowl and with it bring
rain. Like many other Chinese immortals or *sennin*, he is
shown as an angular old man with a ragged appearance.
Here the immortal floats on his large upturned hat, because
it was said that once he crossed a river in that manner when
there was nobody to ferry him across. While the figure is
illustrated in a printed book as a dignified character with a
distant expression on his face (see right), the immortal here
is depicted in a humorous fashion with his hand placed on
top of his head. In contrast to his emaciated chest, revealed
by the robe falling from his right shoulder, his stomach is
rather paunchy. He clutches a gnarled stick behind him,
while his left sleeve flaps in the wind. The waves swirl
and rise up like clouds behind him, ingeniously providing
a natural hole for the cord, or *himotōshi*.

This netsuke was previously published in Barker and
Smith 1976, p. 139, fig. 297.

—

Unsigned
Boxwood, late 1700s
H. 9.4 cm
British Museum 1945,1017.535
Bequeathed by Oscar Charles Raphael

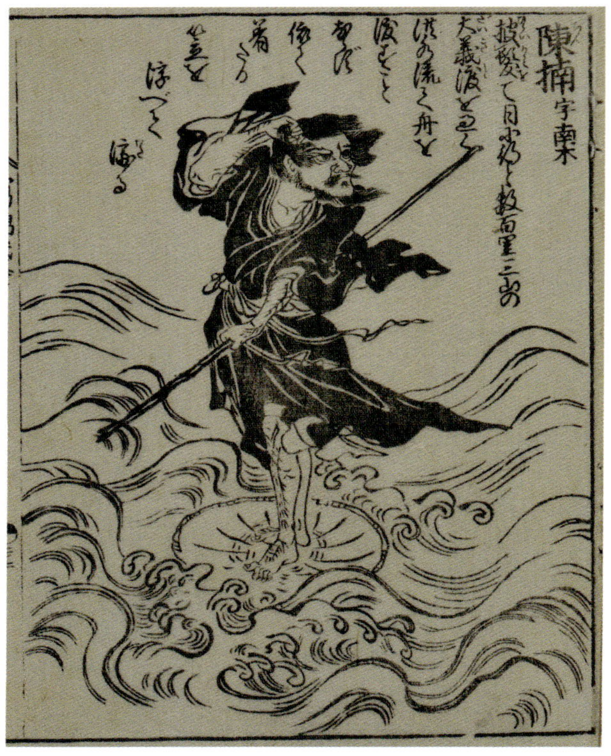

'Chinnan', from Tachibana Morikuni (1679–1748), *Ehon shahō bukuro*
(*Treasure-bag Picture Book*), vol. 7. Woodblock-illustrated book, 1720
(reprinted 1770). 22.1 x 15.4 cm. British Museum 1914,0528,0.4.1-10.
Given by Mrs A. Moseley.

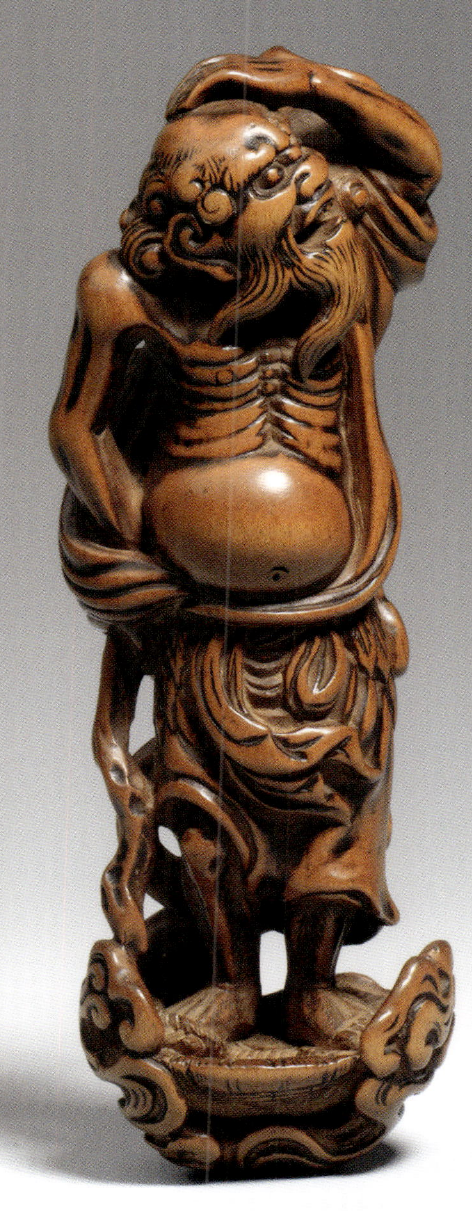

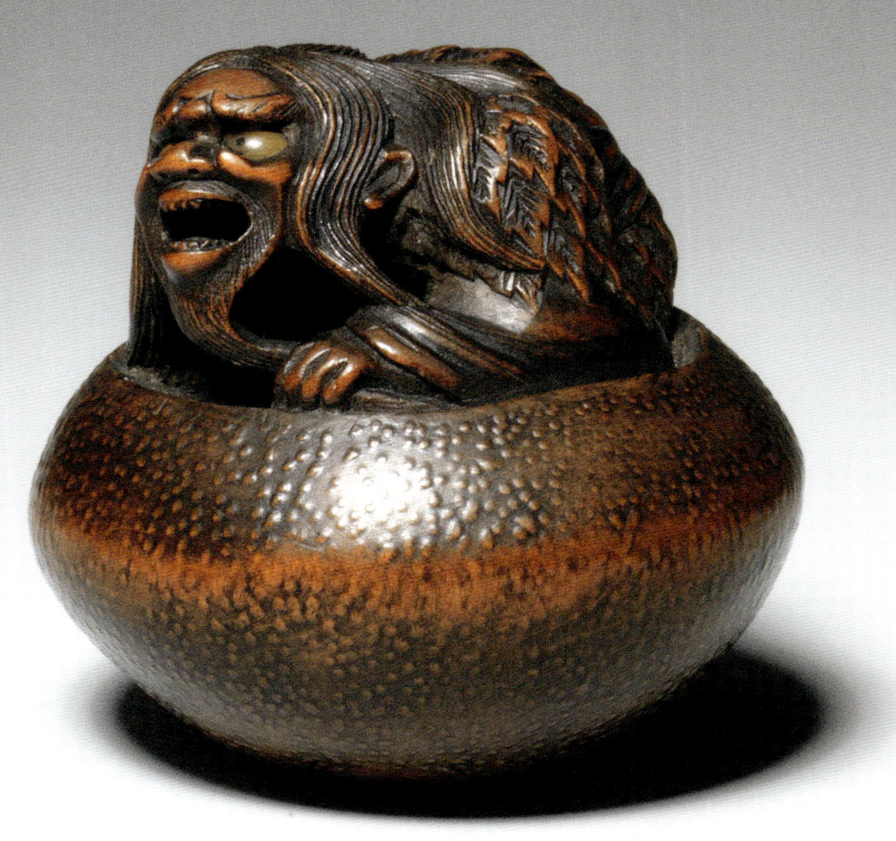

Kokō Sennin

Kokō Sennin is a Chinese immortal who is believed to retire
into his begging bowl at night. Here he wears a robe of
mugwort leaves as he nestles into the bowl. Carved details
are enhanced with a dark stain, and the eyes of the
immortal are inlaid in pale, translucent horn with tiny drilled
and inked pupils that are typical of the artist. The same
technique can be seen in his netsuke of Handaka Sonja
(pp. 52–3). The surface of the bowl is cleverly crafted by
using the technique known as 'raised carving', or *ukibori*,
usually employed for features in relief such as scales and
warts on fish and amphibians, veins on leaves and patterns
on kimono.

This netsuke was previously published in Barker and
Smith 1976, p. 112, fig. 211.

—

By Naitō Toyomasa (1773–1856)
Wood, with eyes inlaid in pale horn
Tanba province, early 1800s
H. 3.9 cm; w. 4.1 cm
British Museum F.900
Given by Sir Augustus Wollaston Franks

Ikkaku Sennin

Ikkaku Sennin was an immortal said to be of South Asian origin.
According to legend, he was born from a deer, and so he is
depicted with a single horn, often shown as a bump. The legend
relates that one day Ikkaku slipped in a rain puddle and became
so angry at the rain dragon that he punished the dragon by
imprisoning it in a cave, causing a terrible drought in the land.
Distraught at the drought, the local elders decided to send the
most beautiful woman, Princess Sendaramo, to tempt Ikkaku.
He found the princess by a stream and she asked him to carry
her across. While he carried her on his back, he saw her
beautiful face reflected in the water and fell instantly in love
with her. As a result, he lost all of his magical powers and the
rain dragon was released from its confinement. The story is also
performed as a Noh play, a form of Japanese classical drama.

In this netsuke the immortal, with a dried double-gourd
container hanging from his sash, carries the princess on his
back. His black shoes of dark wood contrast with the pale
colour of the rest of his body. He puts his right hand on his
shoulder, almost reaching out to her in a caring manner; in
response she places her hand close to his. Her hair is coiffed
in two bunches secured with a hair ornament, and the folds of
their robes flow elegantly. The carver is said to have also been
an expert manufacturer of artificial teeth, and adopted the name
Negoro from the style of lacquer with which he decorated his
works. The holes for the cord, or *himotōshi*, are cleverly hidden
under the robes.

This netsuke was previously published in Barker and Smith
1976, p. 127, fig. 250, and Lazarnick, vol. 2, 1981, p. 1030.

—

By Negoro Sōkyū
Wood, Osaka, mid 1700s
H. 7 cm
British Museum 1945,1017.664
Bequeathed by Oscar Charles Raphael

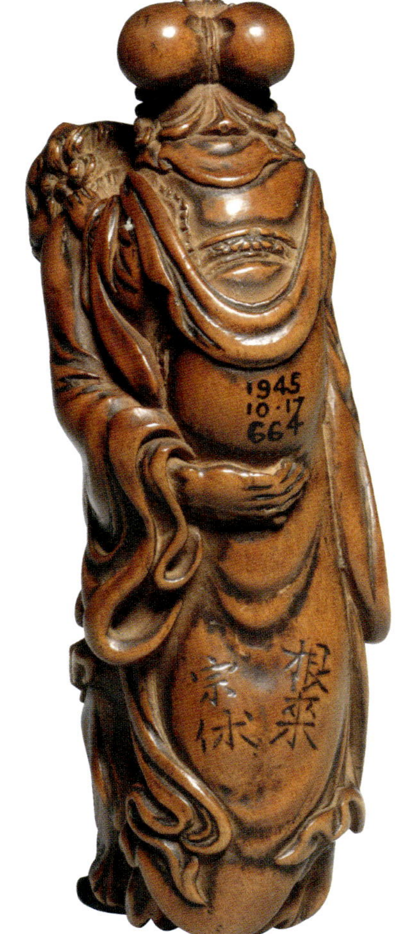

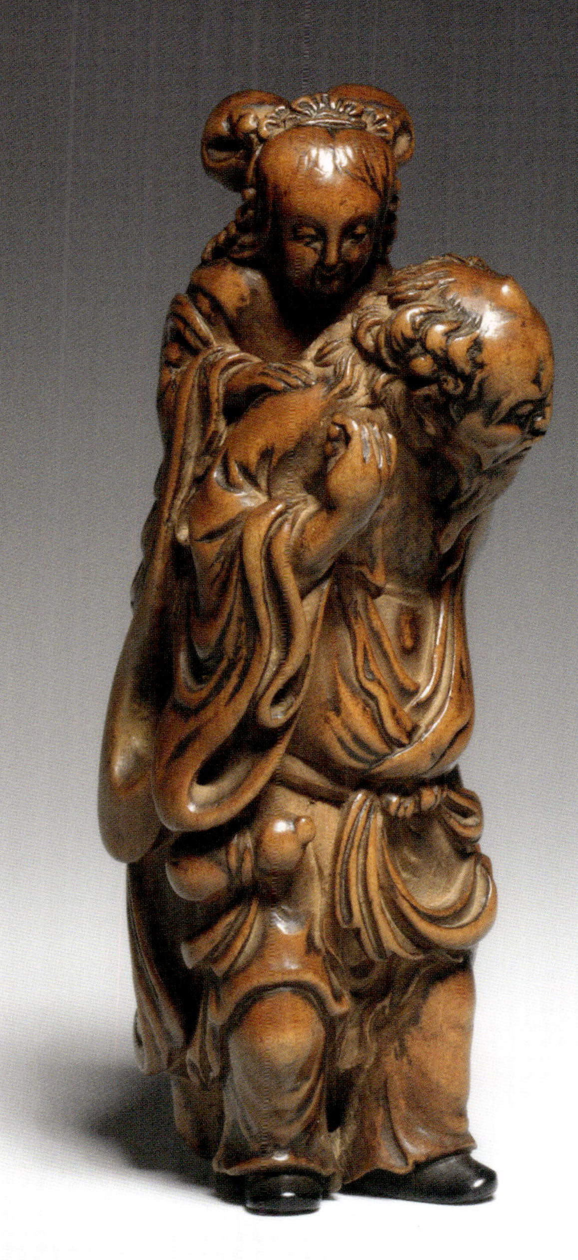

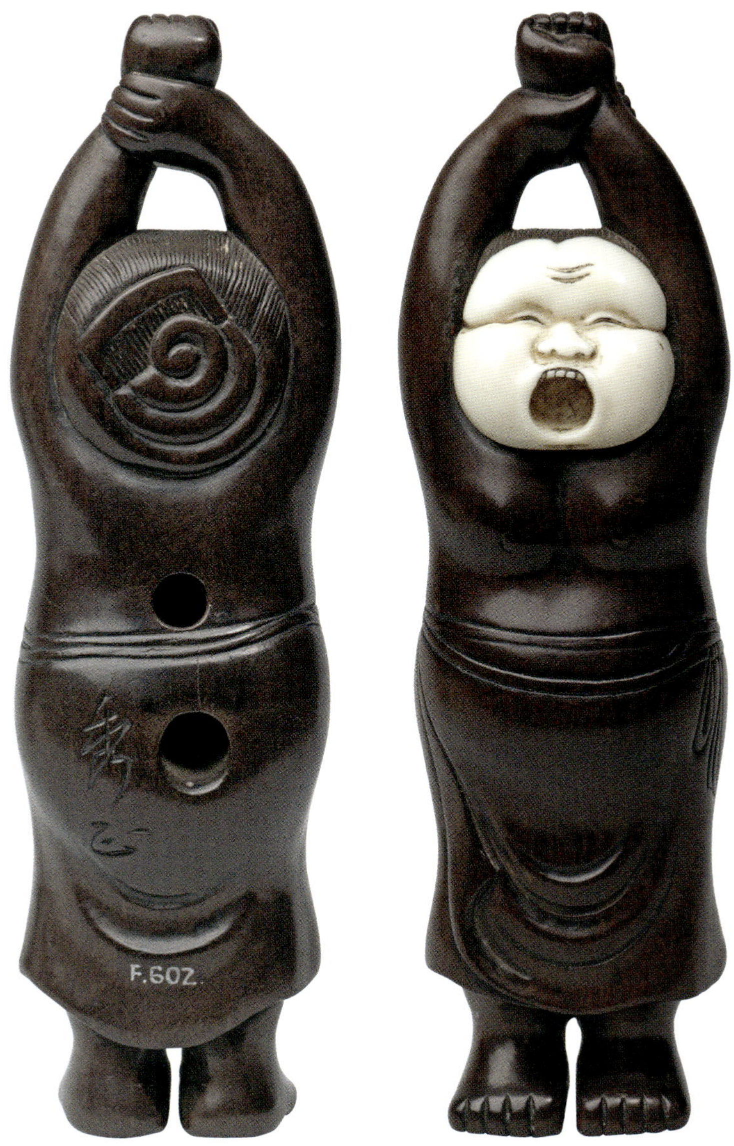

F.602.

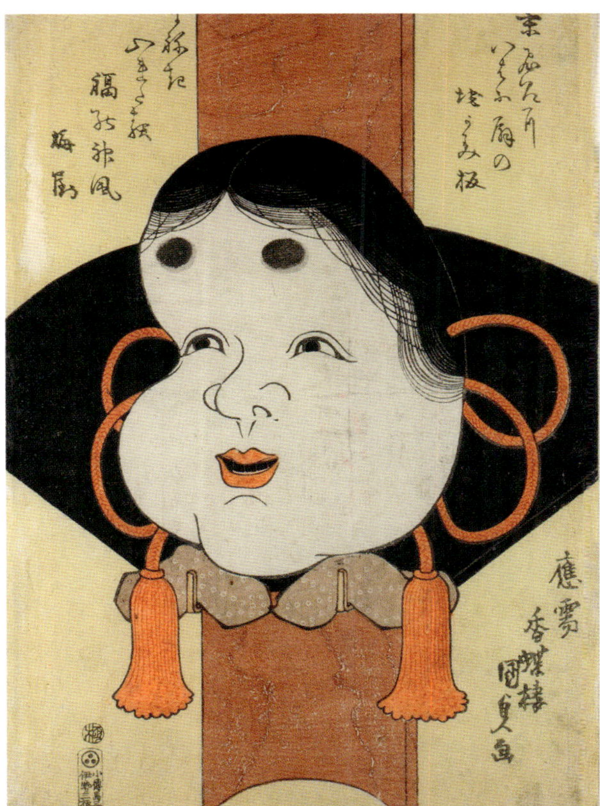

Mask of Okame on a fan-shaped lacquer board. Utagawa Kunisada (1786–1864), colour woodblock print, about 1830s. 35.9 x 25 cm. British Museum 1908,0718,0.49. Given by Sir Hickman Bacon.

Okame yawning

This netsuke's subject matter is a parody of 'Daruma Yawning' (*Akubi Daruma*), which is represented in another example in this book (pp. 44–5). Okame is said to derive from the Shintō deity, Ama no uzume, the goddess of mirth and good humour. According to a Japanese legend, the sun goddess, Amaterasu ōmikami, once hid in a cave, thereby plunging the world into darkness. The gods tried in vain to lure her out and finally Ama no uzume performed such a sexually provocative dance that the assembled deities burst into raucous laughter. This aroused the curiosity of Amaterasu, who then came out of the cave, thus restoring daylight to the world. Okame is a favourite subject for netsuke carvers with her round face, puffed-up cheeks, flat nose, small mouth and ever-present smile (see left). Here she stands, clad only in a skirt, with her mouth agape and hands clasped above her head. The ivory face is minimally but effectively incised to render the features, and contrasts well with the dark wood of her body. Her coiffure is particularly well detailed, with its spiralling bun held in place by a comb (*kushi*).

This netsuke was previously published in Barker and Smith 1976, p. 120, fig. 233, and Lazarnick (ed.), MCI, vol. 1, 1986, p. 148.

—

By Hidemasa
Wood, with face inlaid in ivory, early 1800s
H. 13.3 cm
British Museum F.602
Given by Sir Augustus Wollaston Franks

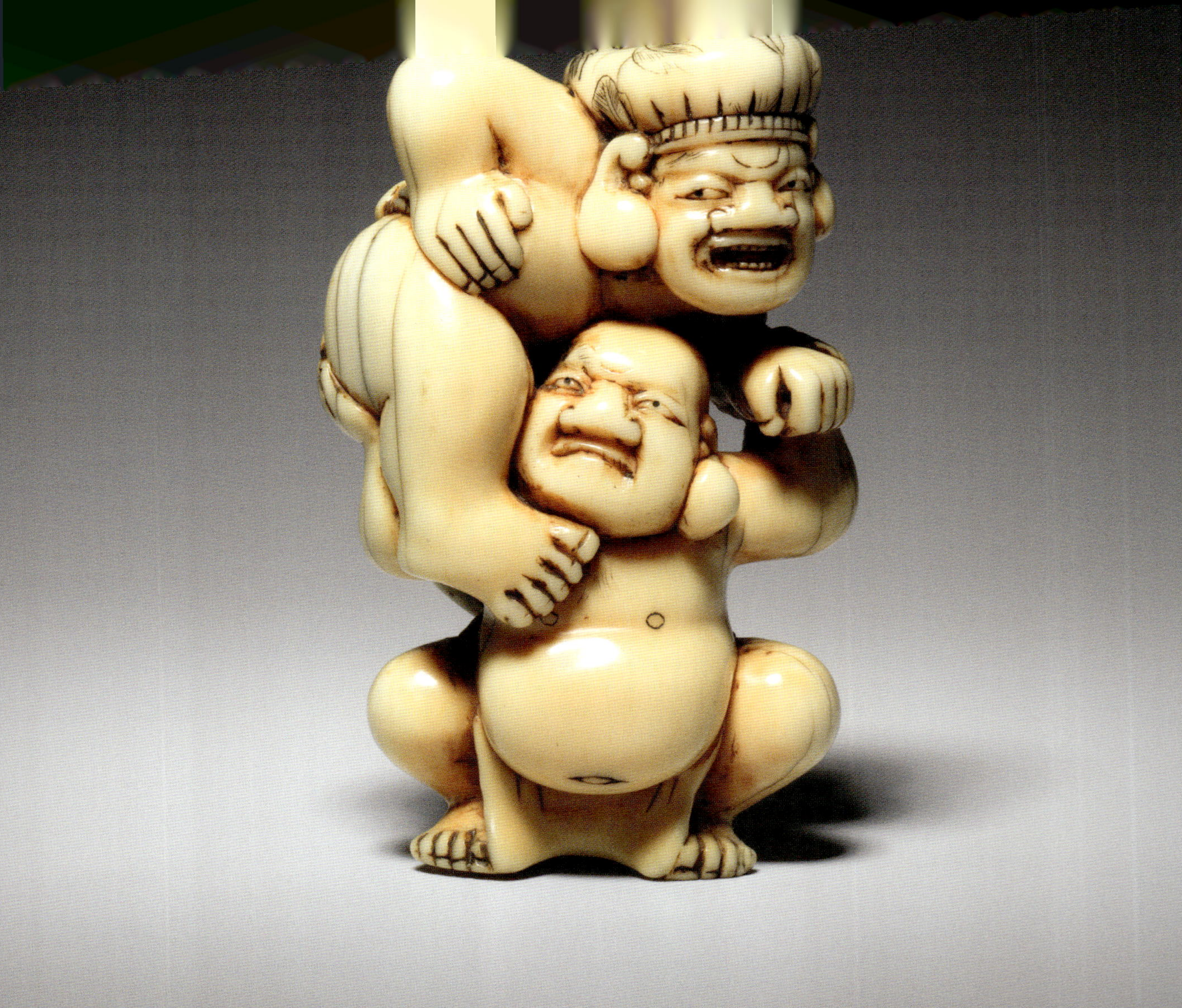

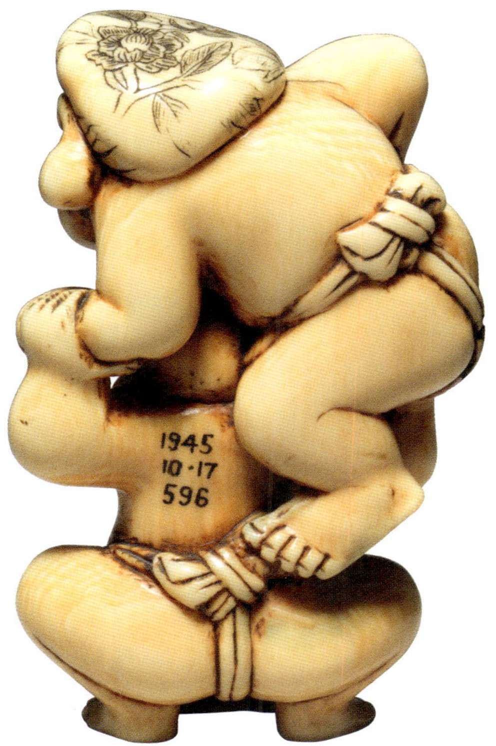

Daikoku and Hotei wrestling

The Seven Gods of Good Fortune, *Shichifukujin*, are probably the best known among the many characters of Buddhist origin who were adopted in Japan and became a popular subject for netsuke. Sometimes they are shown all together in a 'treasure ship' signifying abundant good luck (see p. 70), but here two of the deities, Daikoku and Hotei, are depicted as sumō wrestlers. Daikoku, wearing a flat cap with peony design, is held aloft by Hotei, who squats squarely on his feet. Both of them have the thick pendulous earlobes that signify good fortune. Daikoku is by origin the Hindu god Mahakala, and is usually shown with a bag of treasures and a magic mallet, with which he is able to grant wishes. Hotei is commonly portrayed as bald, obese and very cheerful, carrying a sack in which he stores precious treasures. Among the Seven Gods, Daikoku and Hotei are particularly associated with wealth and prosperity, and held a prominent place in popular worship among the rising merchant class from the middle of the Edo period (1615–1868). Throughout the Edo period, festivals were frequently held at shrines all over Japan, in which sumō wrestling competitions were dedicated together with prayers to the gods for plentiful grain harvests. This type of netsuke may have been commissioned by a merchant as a talisman.

This netsuke was previously published in Barker and Smith 1976, pp. 150–151, fig. 336.

—

Unsigned
Ivory, late 1700s
H. 6.9 cm
British Museum 1945,1017.596
Bequeathed by Oscar Charles Raphael

Hotei

Hotei, one of the Seven Gods of Good Fortune, was the most popular of the group. He sits here with his right knee drawn up, leaning against his treasure bag. He is jovial, and he doesn't seem to mind the front of his robe opening up and exposing his plump chest and belly. The netsuke was originally finished with gold lacquer over a brown and black lacquer ground, before the surface was almost certainly deliberately rubbed down so that the underlying colour shows through in irregular patches, creating an attractive contrast. The knot of his bag is removable and it is fitted on the inside with a lacquered ring, which cleverly serves as the hole for the cord, or *himotōshi*.

—

Unsigned
Lacquered wood, late 1700s
w. 4.3 cm
British Museum 1945,1017.545
Bequeathed by Oscar Charles Raphael

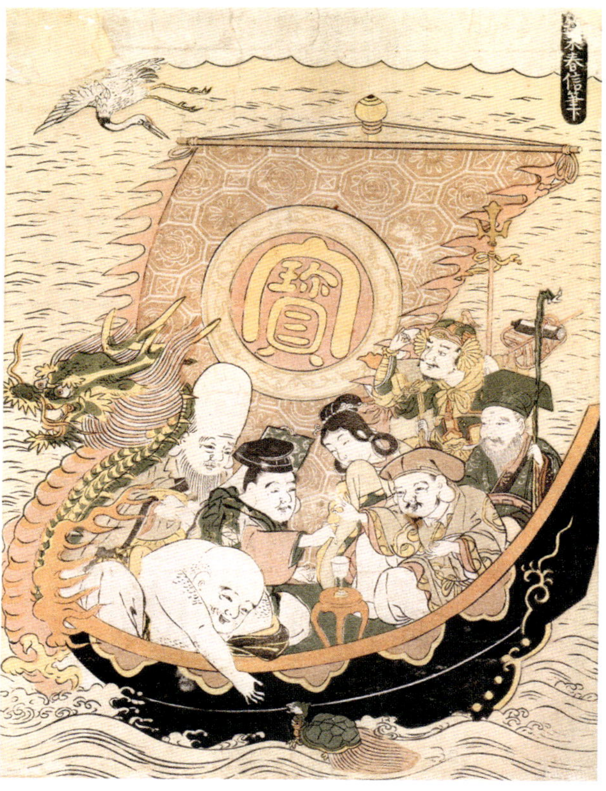

The Seven Gods of Good Fortune in their 'treasure ship'. Suzuki Harunobu (d. 1770), colour woodblock print, 1765–1770. 26.8 x 20 cm. British Museum 1907,0531,0.343.

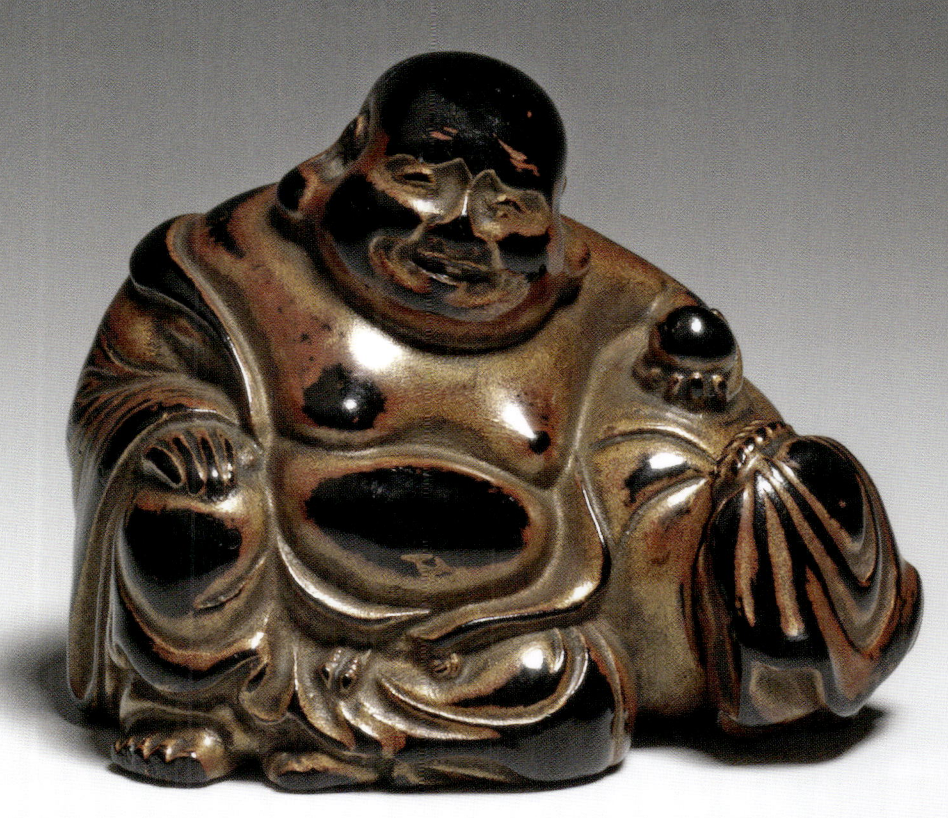

Fukurokuju

Fukurokuju, one of the Seven Gods of Good Fortune, is
the god of longevity, and is usually shown with a greatly
elongated cranium. He is sometimes accompanied by a
crane, which is also considered to be a symbol of long life.
In this example, the god has a jolly expression and appears
to be chuckling to himself. He is jumping and slapping his
uplifted knee, while holding a gnarled staff in his hand.

—

Unsigned
Wood, late 1700s
H. 8.4 cm
British Museum 1945,1017.624
Bequeathed by Oscar Charles Raphael

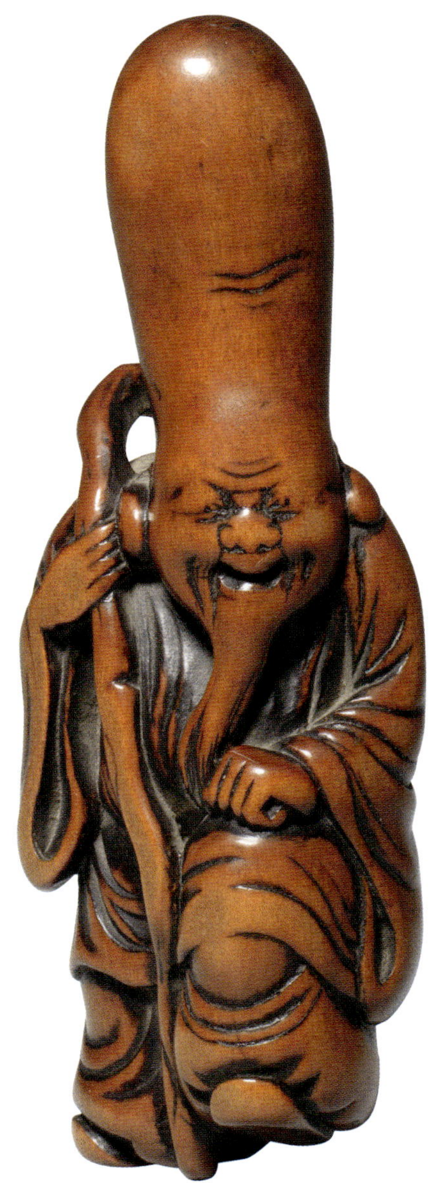

Ghosts and the supernatural

Numerous ghostly monsters (*bakemono*) and supernatural creatures populated the Japanese consciousness during the Edo period (1615–1868) and are still present in Japanese folklore. In netsuke, these ghostly creatures are often represented with a sense of humour, rather than the fierce expressions that they are normally known for. Through them we can catch a glimpse into the imaginary world of the Edo period.

Mermaid

The mermaid rests against the ground grasping a sacred
jewel, *tama*, with both hands close to her. Her tail, curling
back against her scaly body, forms the compact shape
which enables the netsuke to work effectively as a toggle.
Her long hair frames her delicately engraved face, details of
which are rendered in ink and a faint red colour to the lips.
Underneath, two small ventral fins are carved just below her
breasts. The earliest account of netsuke carvers, *Sōken
kishō* (*Strange and Wonderful Sword Fittings*) by Inaba
Tsūryū Shin'emon (1740–1786), first published in 1781,
illustrates the mermaid as a subject for netsuke. The design
in that book (see right) is a work by Unjutō Shumemaru,
a Shintō priest who lived in Osaka, not far from Wakayama
where Natsuki was active. Although there are minor
differences of detail, mermaids seem to have been a
popular subject in western Japan.

A different style of mermaid was carved by Ogasawara
Issai who was also active in Wakayama (ex-collection
Mrs Anne Hull Grundy, illustrated in Moss 1982, pp. 90–91,
fig. 61).

—

By Natsuki
Ivory, Wakayama, about 1790
w. 4 cm
British Museum F.761
Given by Sir Augustus Wollaston Franks

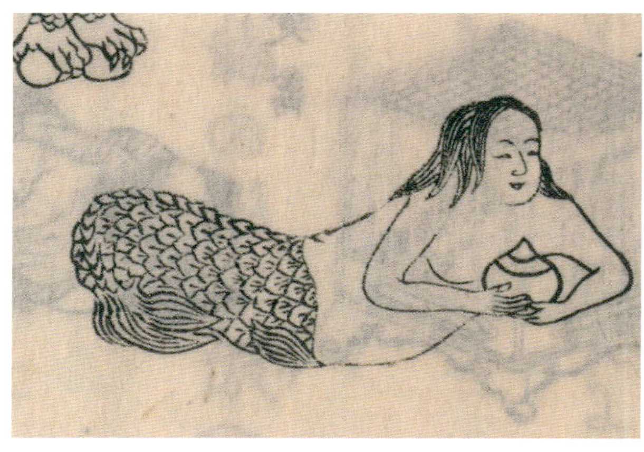

'Mermaid', from Inaba Tsūryū Shin'emon, *Sōken kishō* (*Strange and Wonderful
Sword Fittings*), vol. 7. Woodblock-illustrated book, 1781. From the collection
of the National Diet Library, Tokyo (840-38).

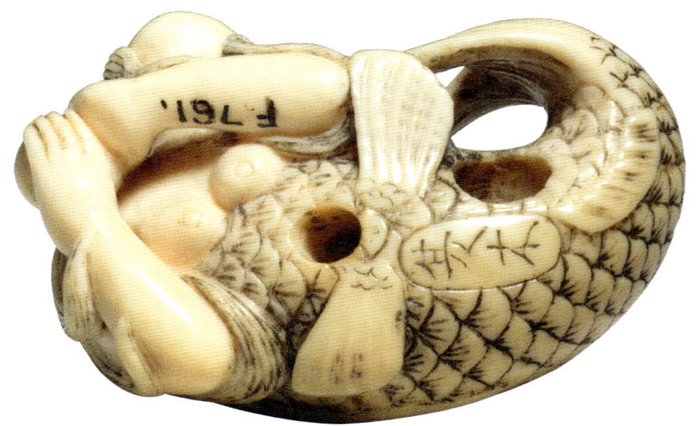

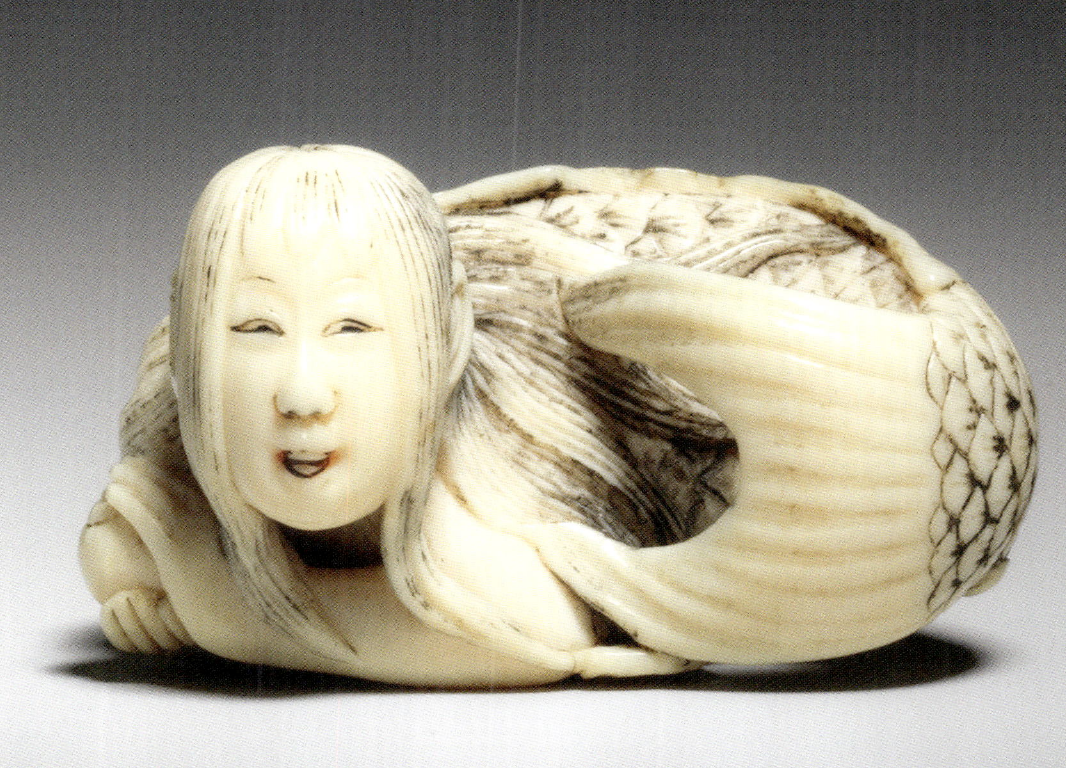

Mikoshi Nyūdō

Mikoshi Nyūdō is one of the many ghostly monsters of
Japan that are generally known as *bakemono*. This monster
is usually portrayed with a bald head and a jutting tongue.
Although there are many variations of this ghost story across
the different regions of Japan, the plots are roughly similar.
Essentially, when a person is walking alone at night, the form
of a monk suddenly appears. The ghost grows taller every time
the person looks up at it and gazing at it for too long invariably
results in death. In this netsuke the ghost rises above the
terrified man, with both hands raised and tongue sticking out.
The monster is depicted with the characteristic bald head with
engorged blood vessels clearly visible, and its inlaid eyes in
pale horn accentuate the impression of an unearthly being.
It is said that if you fall backwards while looking up at the
ghost, then your windpipe will be gnawed and you will be
killed. We do not know what will happen to this pitiable man,
but we can imagine that it is not a happy ending.

The subject of ghostly monsters has fascinated numerous
netsuke carvers. The famous set of illustrated books *Gazu
hyakki yagyō* (*Illustrated Night Parade of a Hundred Demons*)
by Toriyama Sekien (1712–1788), first published in 1776,
provided a major source for ghost netsuke. The books
illustrate a collection of ghosts, spirits, spooks and monsters;
many of which Sekien borrowed from earlier literature,
folklore and works of art.

This netsuke was previously published in Barker and
Smith 1976, pp. 142–143, fig. 306.

—

Unsigned
Wood, with eyes inlaid in pale and dark horn, late 1800s
H. 10.4 cm
British Museum 1912,1012.2
Bequeathed by Harry Seymour Trower

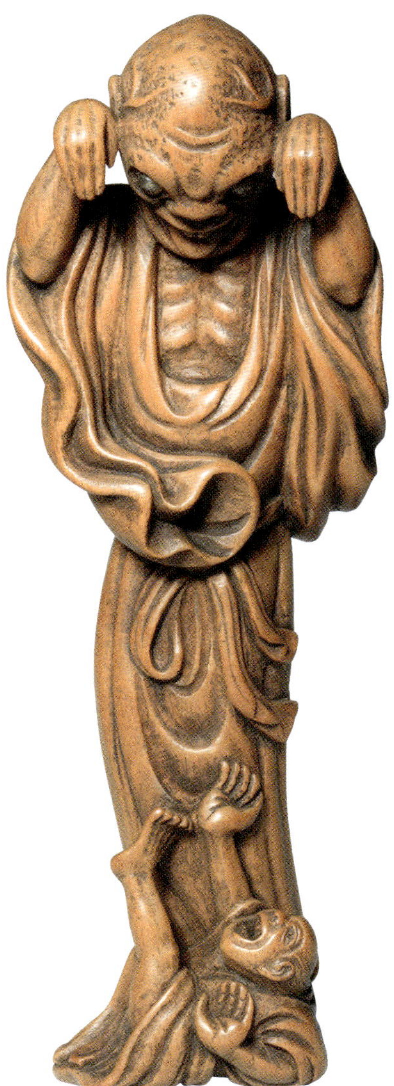

Crow Tengu with its young

The Crow Tengu, or Karasu Tengu, is a mythical creature
with the beak, wings and claws of a bird and the body of a
human. Tengu are believed to inhabit mountains, and are
sometimes regarded as spirits of the forests and mountains.
They are often depicted as ascetic mountain priests known
as *yamabushi*, practitioners of native mountain worship.
Here the Tengu wears a small round *yamabushi* cap and
robe with stylized cloud design. Although they are reputed
to steal children and eat them, this netsuke shows a Tengu
giving loving attention to its own young, cradling it between
its legs and enfolding it protectively in its wings.

—

Unsigned
Wood, about 1820
H. 4.5 cm; w. 4.3 cm
British Museum F.750
Given by Sir Augustus Wollaston Franks

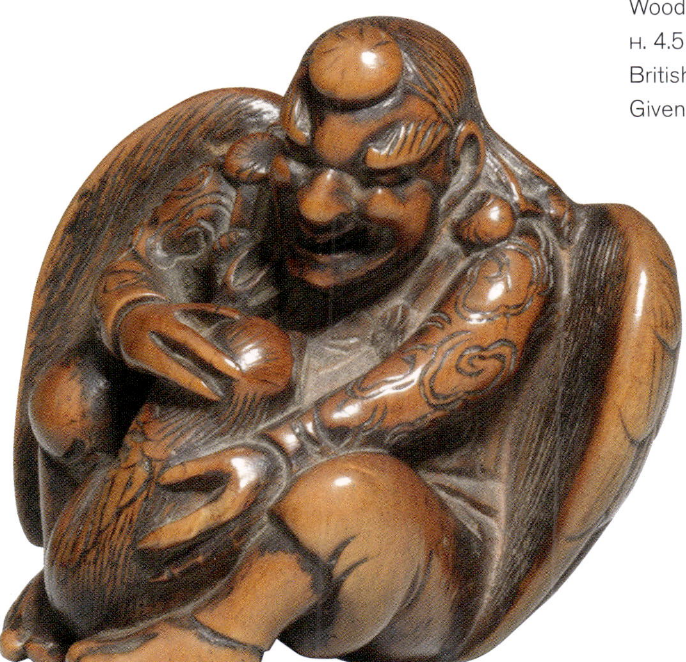

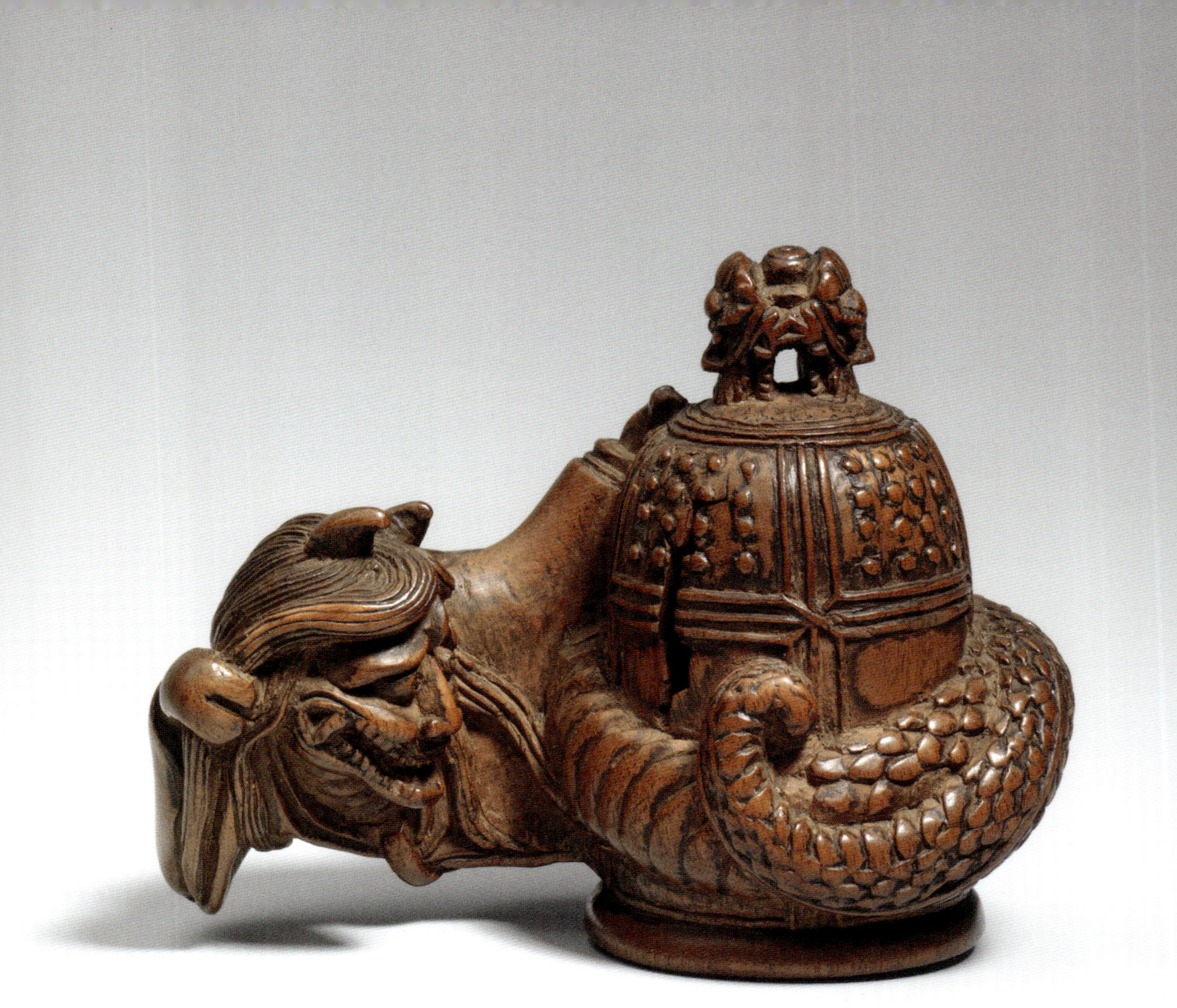

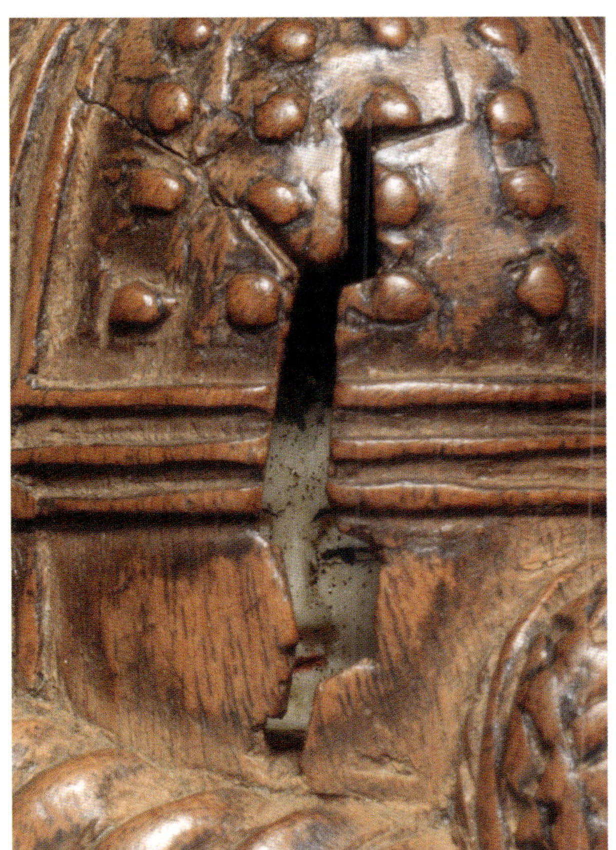

Kiyohime and Anchin

The subject of this netsuke is based on a legend of Dōjōji temple. Kiyohime was the daughter of an innkeeper who one night lodged a Buddhist monk, Anchin. He was on a pilgrimage to Kumano, in present-day Mie and Wakayama prefectures, which is still popular as a holy site, and a UNESCO designated world heritage site. Kiyohime fell desperately in love with Anchin but was rejected by him. Her unrequited love turned Kiyohime into a demonic serpent, with the face of a jealous female demon with two horns, known as Hannya. Kiyohime pursued Anchin, forcing him to take refuge under the great bell of Dōjōji temple. The story forms the plot of a drama made famous in both Noh and Kabuki theatre. In this netsuke, Kiyohime is coiling round the bell in which Anchin hides, and she is about to emit flames from her open mouth, the heat of which will consume the bell, the monk and Kiyohime herself. She peers through a crack created by damage to the bronze bell and inside the scared, ashen face of Anchin is visible. As a subject for netsuke, this affords carvers a wonerful opportunity to show off their skills in design and execution.

This netsuke was also published in Barker and Smith 1976, p. 108, fig. 199 (where it is wrongly numbered as F.887); Lazarnick (ed.), MCI, vol. 1, 1986, p. 517 (without image), and Lazarnick, vol. 1, 1981, p. 764.

—

By Minko
Wood, with the face of Anchin in painted ivory or horn
Late 1700s
H. 5 cm; w. 6.4 cm
British Museum F.882
Given by Sir Augustus Wollaston Franks

Reclining demon

Oni is the generic term for a Japanese demon. They are
portrayed with male characteristics and additional features
such as two horns, fangs, clawed hands and feet. In spite
of their propensity for misconduct, *oni* have been a
favourite subject of netsuke carvers, more often treated as
mischievous rather than evil. Here the *oni* lies on his elbow,
and stretches out his left arm to rest on his raised knee.
He looks up with an expression of boredom on his face,
his mouth agape revealing his sharp teeth. His hairy face
has large cheek bones with sunken eyes, and his heavy
eyebrows and hair flow backward and curl at the ends.
Although *oni* are usually represented wearing tiger-skin
shorts, this one sports only a skimpy undergarment with
key-fret pattern giving a comical appearance in contrast to
the muscular body. While the space between his outstretched
arm and body provides a natural hole for the cord (*himotōshi*),
the netsuke may also have been designed with the
secondary use of a rest for a writing brush, or *fudekake*.

This netsuke was previously published in Barker and Smith
1976, p. 136, fig. 288.

Unsigned
Wood, late 1700s
w. 9.9 cm
British Museum 1945,1017.649
Bequeathed by Oscar Charles Raphael

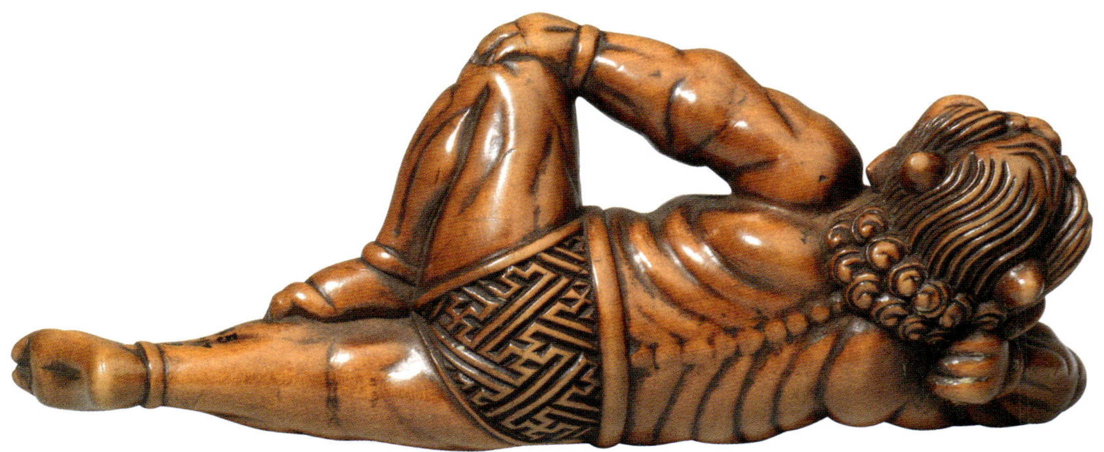

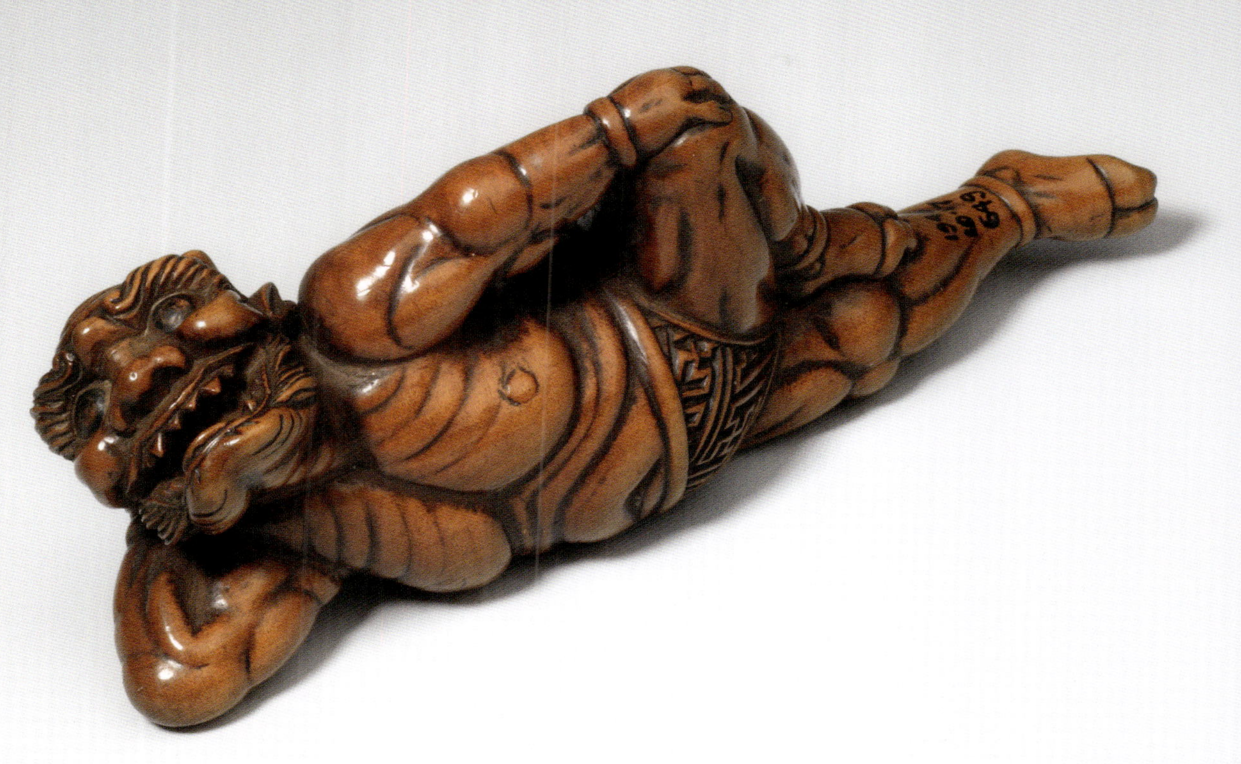

Hannya hiding under a kimono

Hannya is a female demon, once a beautiful woman who
has been transformed by jealous rage into demonic form.
She has horns, a gaping mouth and sharp fangs. She is
usually depicted wearing human clothes at the moment of
her transition from mortal to demon, as seen in this netsuke.
The subject of this netsuke may be based on the legend of
Watanabe no Tsuna (953–1025), one of the retainers of the
famous warrior leader Minamoto no Yorimitsu (948–1021)
(see right). One day Watanabe no Tsuna was sent by
Yorimitsu to carry a message to Ichijō, in present-day Kyoto
prefecture. On the way, near Modoribashi bridge, a beautiful
woman, Ibaraki, asked him to escort her home as the hour
was getting late and she was afraid. The warrior helped her
to mount his horse, whereupon she turned into a demon,
grabbing him by the hair. In defence he drew his sword and
cut off her arm, causing her to disappear.

In this netsuke Hannya attempts to hide her demonic
form with her kimono, which is draped over her head and
back. The kimono is beautifully lacquered in red and is
detailed with a chrysanthemum scroll design in gold lacquer.
She peeps out from beneath the kimono, her face half
visible with eyes inlaid in mother-of-pearl, with drilled pupils.
But her muscular bare clawed leg juts out of the robe and
the sharp claws of her hands rip at the kimono, revealing
her true identity.

This netsuke was also published in Barker and Smith
1976, p. 137, fig. 289.

—

Unsigned
Lacquered wood, with eyes inlaid in mother-of-pearl
Early 1800s
H. 9 cm
British Museum F.733
Given by Sir Augustus Wollaston Franks

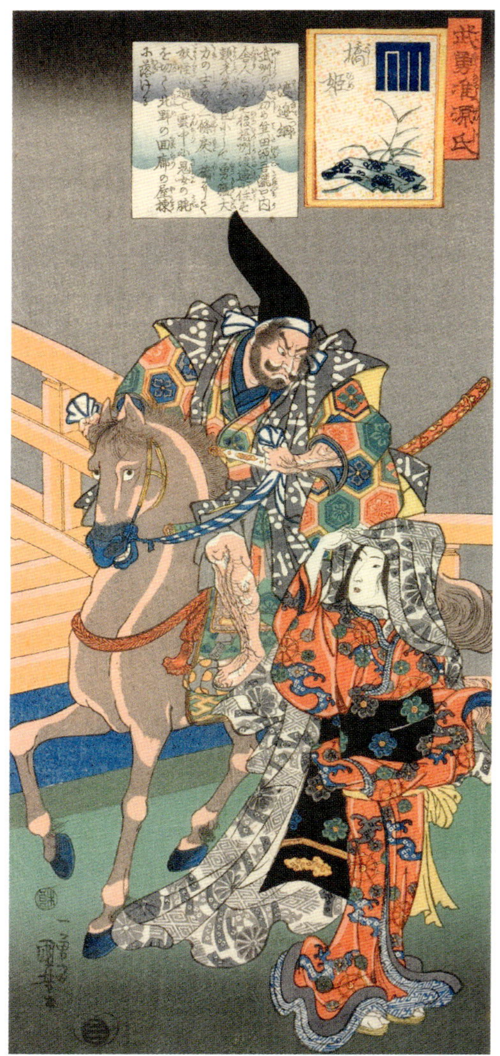

Watanabe no Tsuna, on horseback, encounters the demon woman Ibaraki at
Modoribashi bridge. Utagawa Kuniyoshi (1797–1861), colour woodblock print,
about 1843. 37.2 x 16.5 cm. British Museum 2008,3037.05504. Loaned by
the American Friends of the British Museum (Prof. Arthur R. Miller collection).

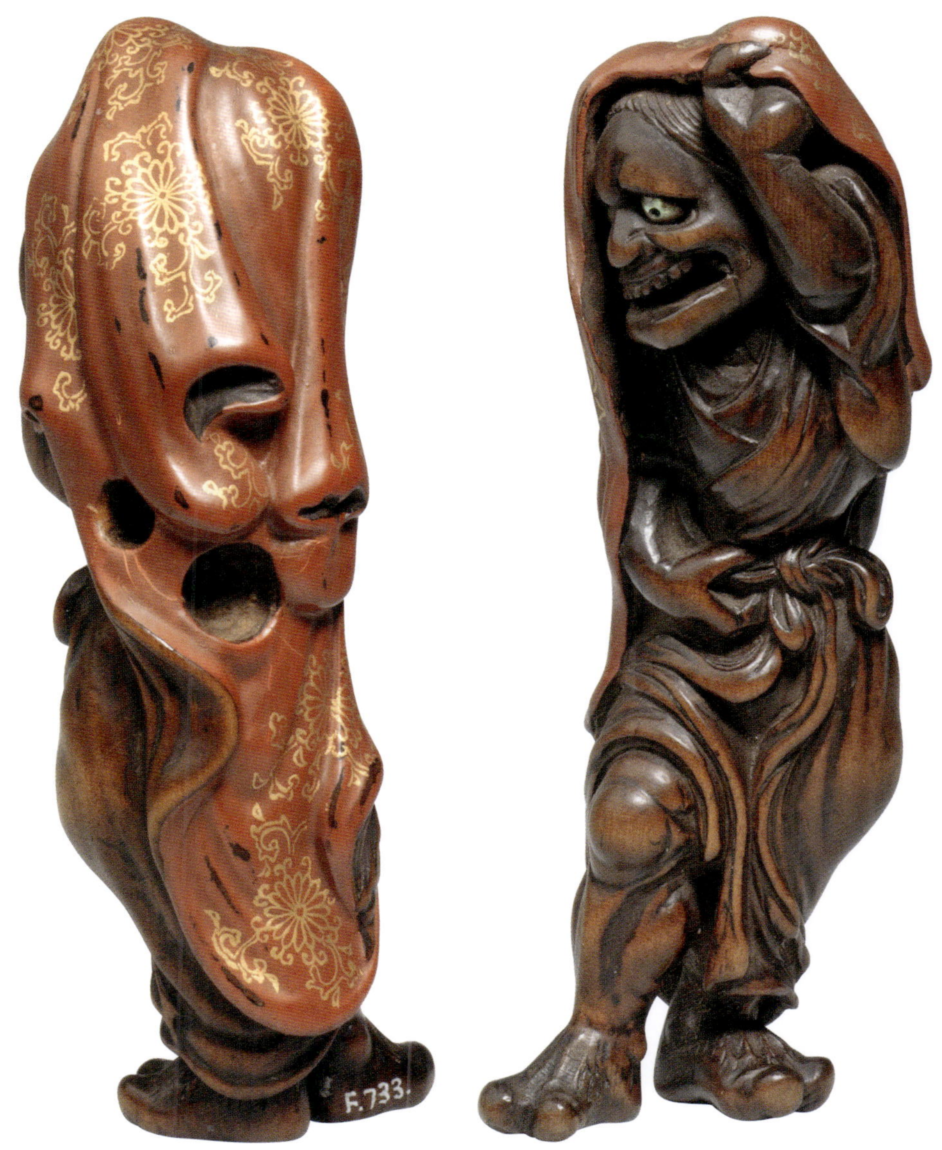

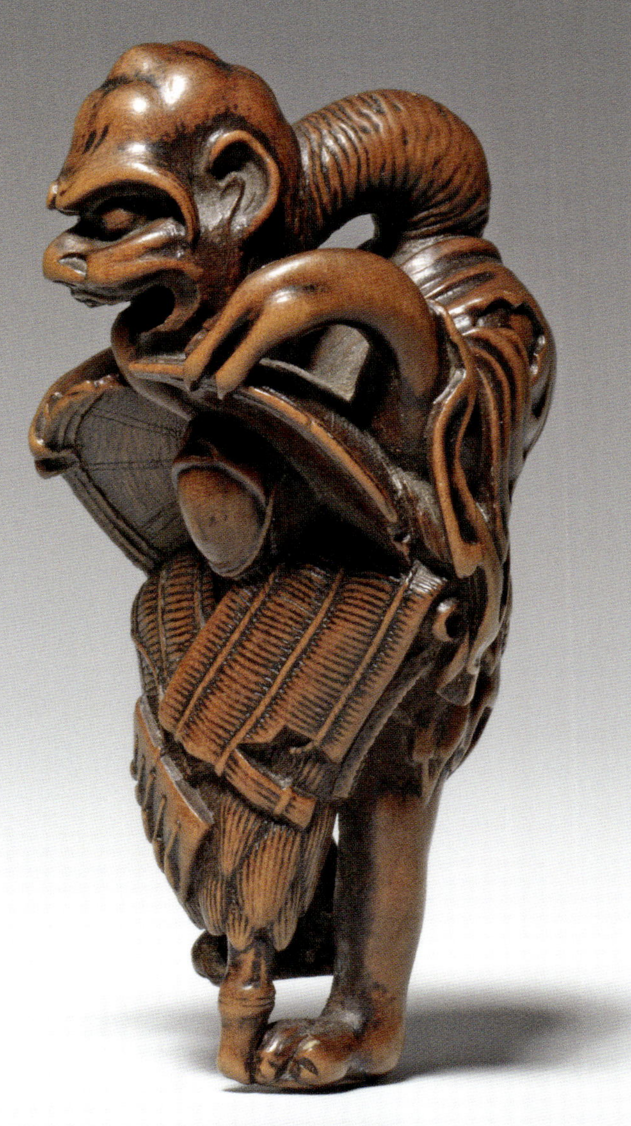

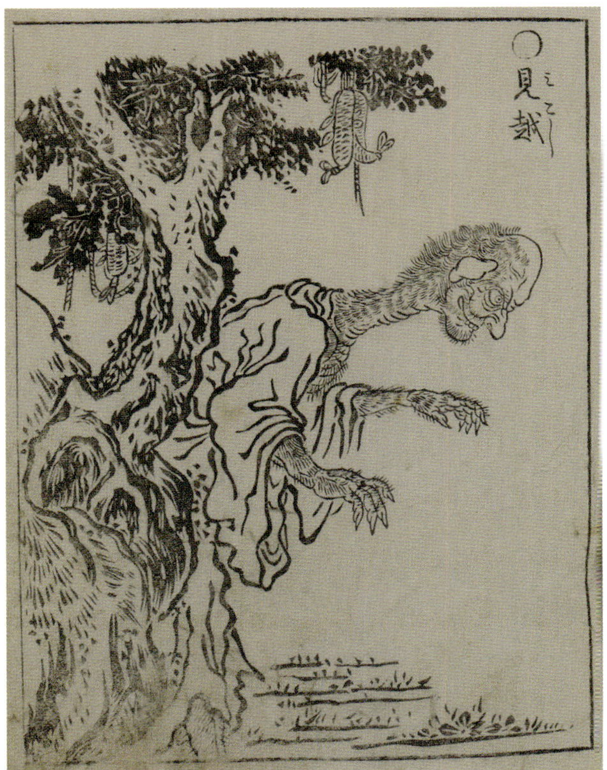

'Mikoshi', from Toriyama Sekien (1712–1788), *Gazu hyakki yagyō* (*Illustrated Night Parade of a Hundred Demons*). Woodblock-illustrated book, 1776. 22.7 x 16 cm (covers). British Museum 1915,0823,0.63.

Mikoshi Nyūdō and a scarecrow

This netsuke represents yet another appearance of Mikoshi Nyūdō (see pp. 76–77), this time with a long neck as illustrated in the famous set of illustrated books *Gazu hyakki yagyō* (*Illustrated Night Parade of a Hundred Demons*) (see left). Here the monster (*bakemono*) looms over a scarecrow, grasping the straw hat with its sharp claws. He intimidates the scarecrow by licking the top of its head with his long tongue. Wearing a tattered robe of mugwort leaves, the ghost has a bump on its head and a wrinkled neck snaking out from its collar. The scarecrow is made of straw matting over a wooden frame, with attached clappers, *naruko*, to frighten away the birds. Although little is known about the carver Sōshin, his netsuke are very individual with distinctive traits such as the dramatic eyebrows carved in exquisite high relief.

This netsuke was previously published in Harris 1987, pp. 24–25, fig. 15. Further information about its provenance can be found in W. L. Behrens, illustrated in Joly 1912, reprinted 1966, no. 387, pl. VIII.

—

By Sōshin
Wood, with eyes inlaid in dark horn, early 1800s
H. 5.6 cm
British Museum HG.245
Given by Professor John and Mrs Anne Hull Grundy

Mikoshi Nyūdō and a collapsed scarecrow

This netsuke depicts what occurred following on from the previous netsuke by Sōshin (see pp. 84–85). Here the scarecrow has collapsed and Mikoshi Nyūdō crouches over the straw hat and holds it close to him. The scarecrow is trapped under the hat and looks uneasy, still tortured by the ghost's pendulous tongue licking its face. Although the netsuke is unsigned (Sōshin rarely signed his netsuke), the ghoul has the characteristic eyebrows carved in high relief which are a recognizable feature of Sōshin's work.

This netsuke was previously published in Barker and Smith 1976, pp. 142–143, fig. 308.

—

Unsigned, attributed to Sōshin
Wood, with eyes inlaid in dark horn, early 1800s
H. 3 cm; w. 3.9 cm
British Museum 1945,1017.651
Bequeathed by Oscar Charles Raphael

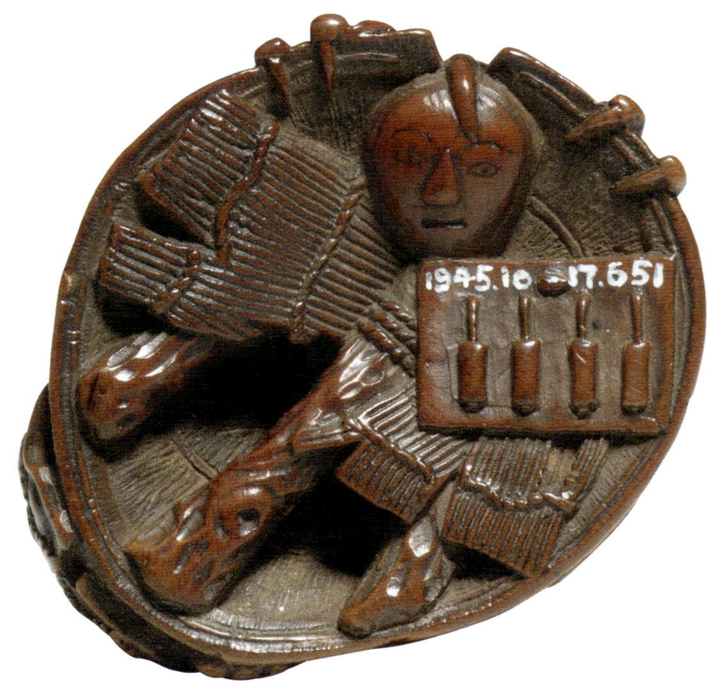

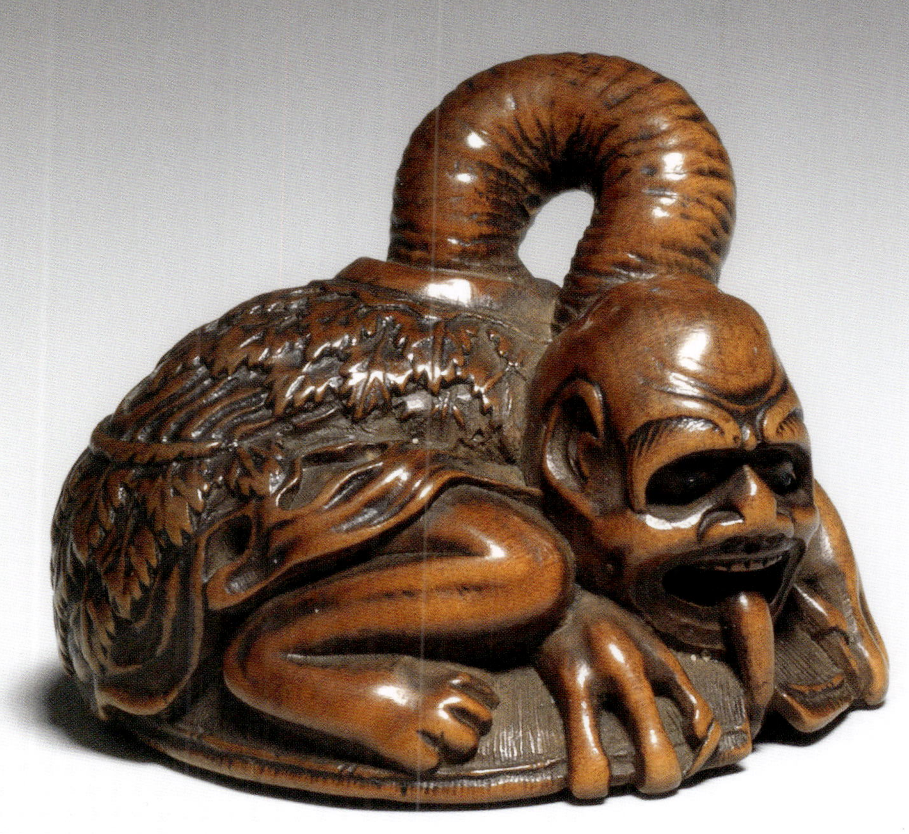

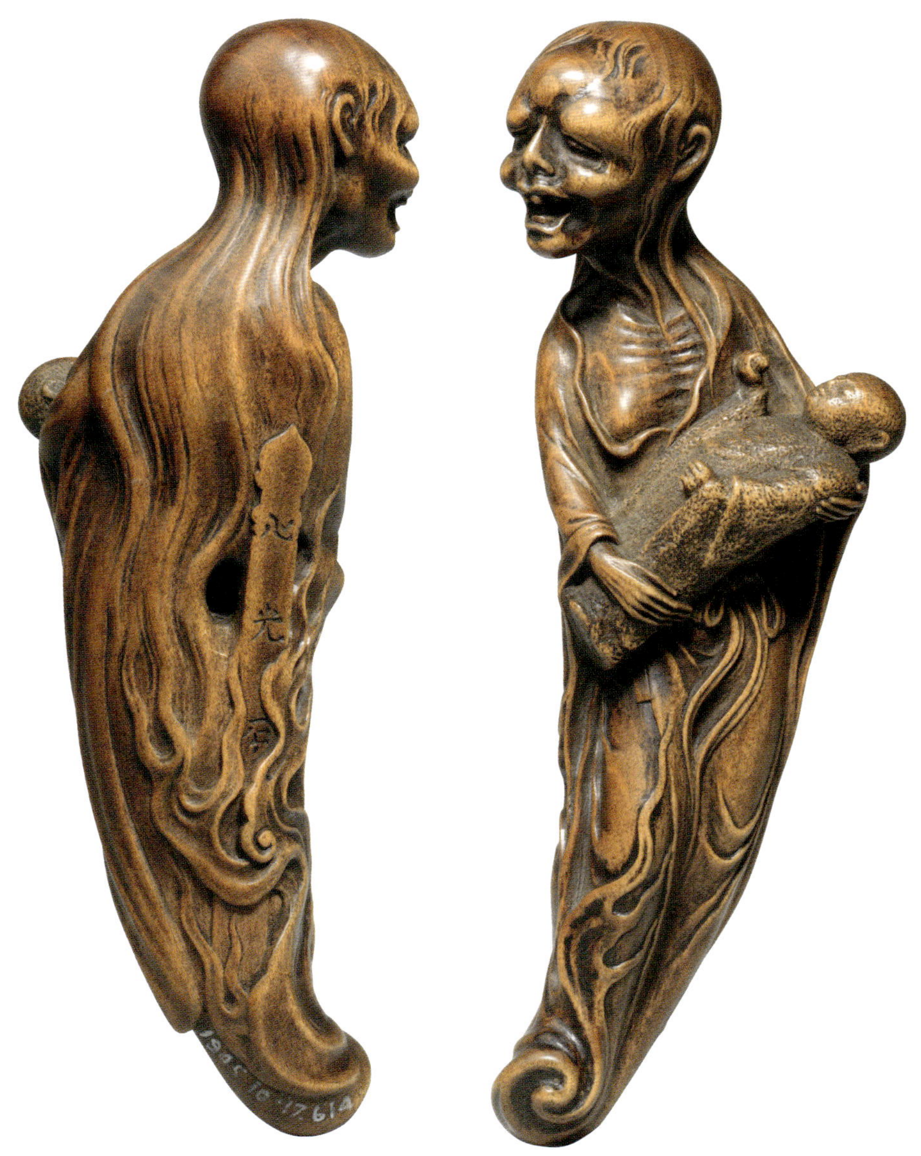

    Ghosts and the supernatural

By Naitō Kōseki (1871–1948)
Boxwood, Kyoto, early 1900s
H. 10.5 cm
British Museum 1945,1017.614
Bequeathed by Oscar Charles Raphael

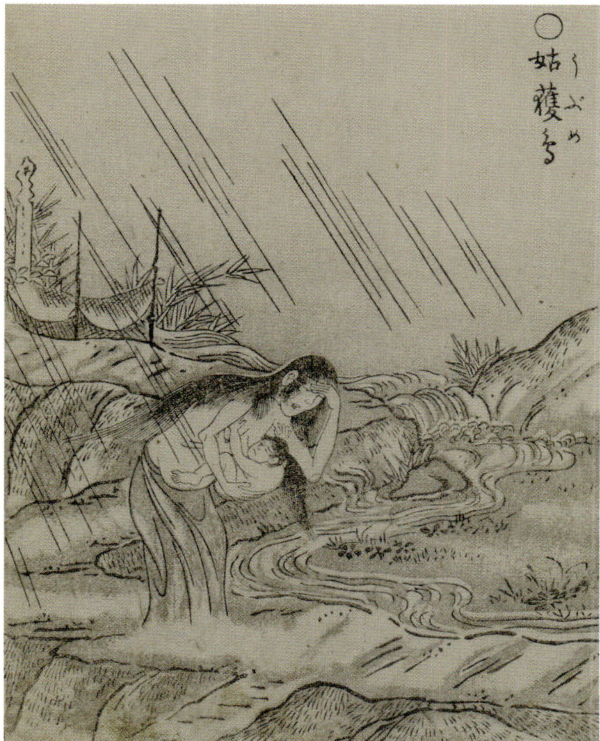

'Ubume', from Toriyama Sekien (1712–1788), *Konjaku zoku hyakki* (*Illustrated Hundred Demons of Now and Then*). Woodblock-illustrated book, 1776–1779. 22.7 x 16 cm (covers). British Museum 1915,0823,0.63.

Ubume holding Jizō

Ubume is the ghost of a woman who has died in childbirth and cannot find peace as she worries about her child (see left). Here she is depicted rising out of flames, holding in her arms a stone sculpture of the Bodhisattva Jizō (Sanskrit *Ksitigarbha*), a patron deity of children. In folk tales, she is said to implore passers-by to hold the infant for a while and then she disappears. The baby becomes increasingly weighty until finally it is too heavy to hold. It is then revealed to be not a human child, but rather a rock or a stone image of Jizō. In this netsuke, Ubume is shown with long straight hair which flows down her back, one breast exposed over sunken ribs. Her face is detailed with swollen eyelids, and her legs tapered at the end, as ghosts in Japan have no feet. The surface of the Jizō statue is cleverly treated by using a technique called 'stone roughening' (*ishime arashi*) to imitate the texture of stone. The signature is incised on a narrow wooden grave marker, or *sotoba* – usually placed behind a grave for the repose of the dead – and reads Shin Kōseki.

Kōseki, born after the Meiji Restoration of 1868 and resident in Kyoto, was a professional Buddhist sculptor. He was not a regular carver of netsuke, but created a few works at the request of Western collectors. His great skill acquired from the study of ancient sculpture fascinated collectors, and his carvings made for export helped introduce Japanese carving abroad. He was persuaded by the collector Oscar Charles Raphael (1874–1941), who visited Japan in the early twentieth century, to carve a few netsuke, of which two were included in Raphael's bequest to the British Museum (another is pictured on p. 101). These are the first recorded examples of netsuke made to order for a Western collector.

This netsuke was also published in Barker and Smith 1976, p. 64, fig. 89, and Lazarnick, vol. 1, 1981, p. 673.

Meditating skeleton

This eccentric netsuke portrays a skeleton in a meditative
pose with its hands clasped in prayer and feet placed
together. The netsuke employs an unusual combination
of materials, silver at the front and stag antler at the back.
The ribs of the skeleton carved in stag antler appear to form
a Chinese character, which may be the maker's 'signature'
– as yet undeciphered. The motif of a meditating skeleton
has been depicted in various artistic forms in Japan since
the Kamakura period (1185–1333), evoking the fleetingness
of life. A fascinating scroll painting of a skeleton meditating
and floating on or above waves by Maruyama Ōkyo (1733–
1795), founder of the Maruyama-Shijō school, is preserved
in Daijōji temple in Hyogo prefecture. Although there are
many interpretations of the subject, it might simply be a
humorous statement on the human fixation with earthly
life and the transitory nature of existence.

This netsuke was previously published in Harris 1987,
p. 34, fig. 76.

—

Unsigned
Silver set in stag antler, late 1800s
H. 4.2 cm; w. 4 cm
British Museum HG.290
Given by Professor John and Mrs Anne Hull Grundy

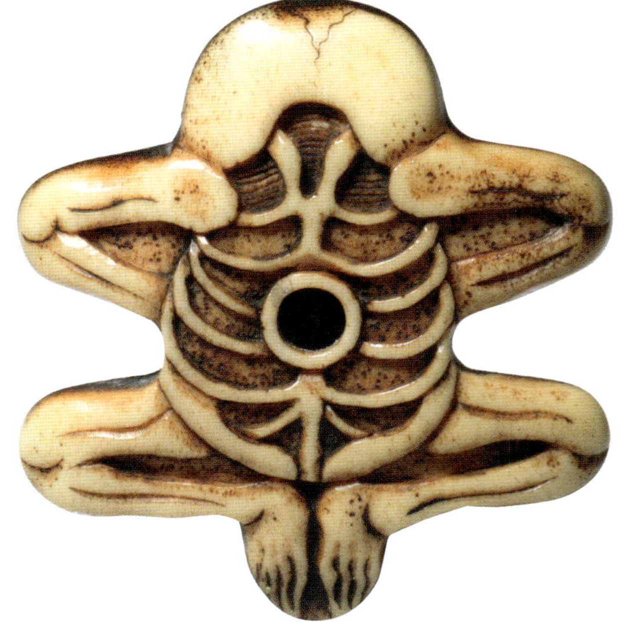

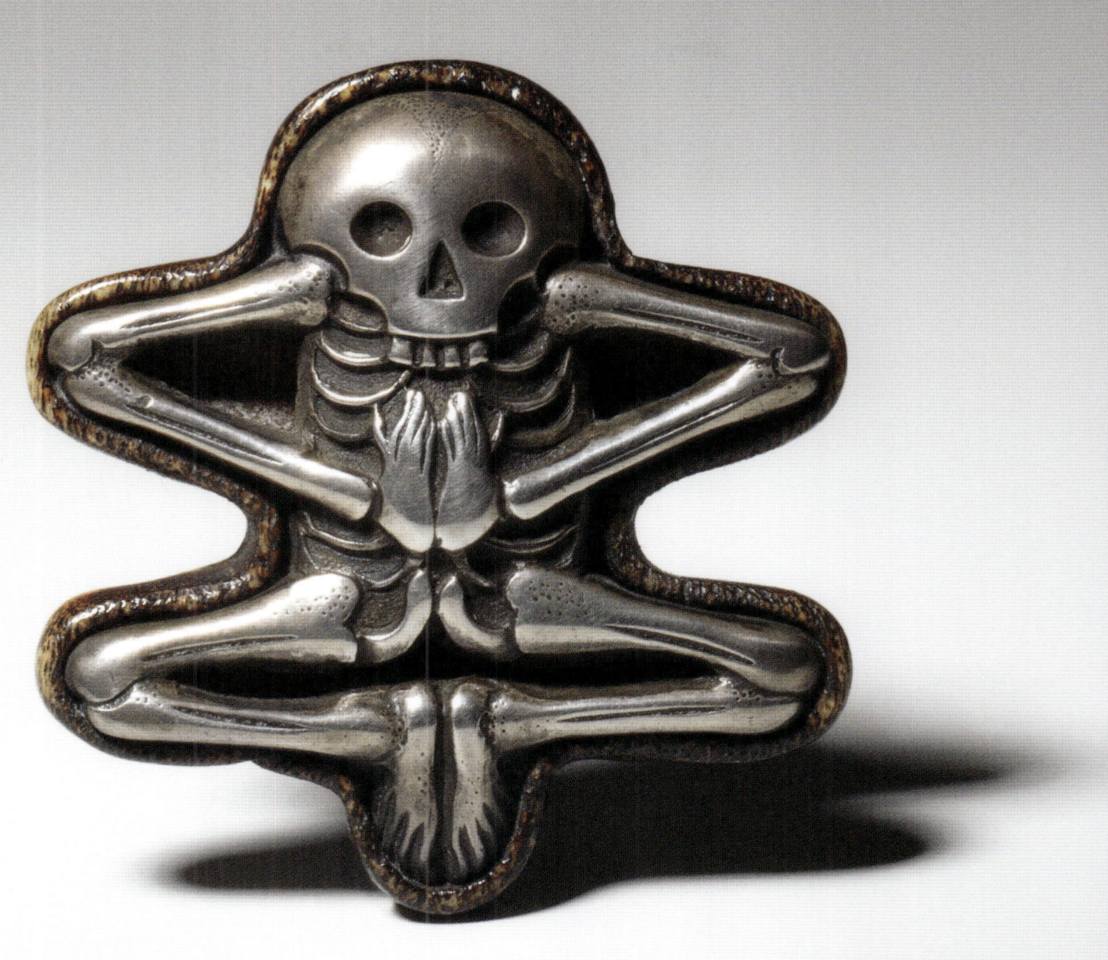

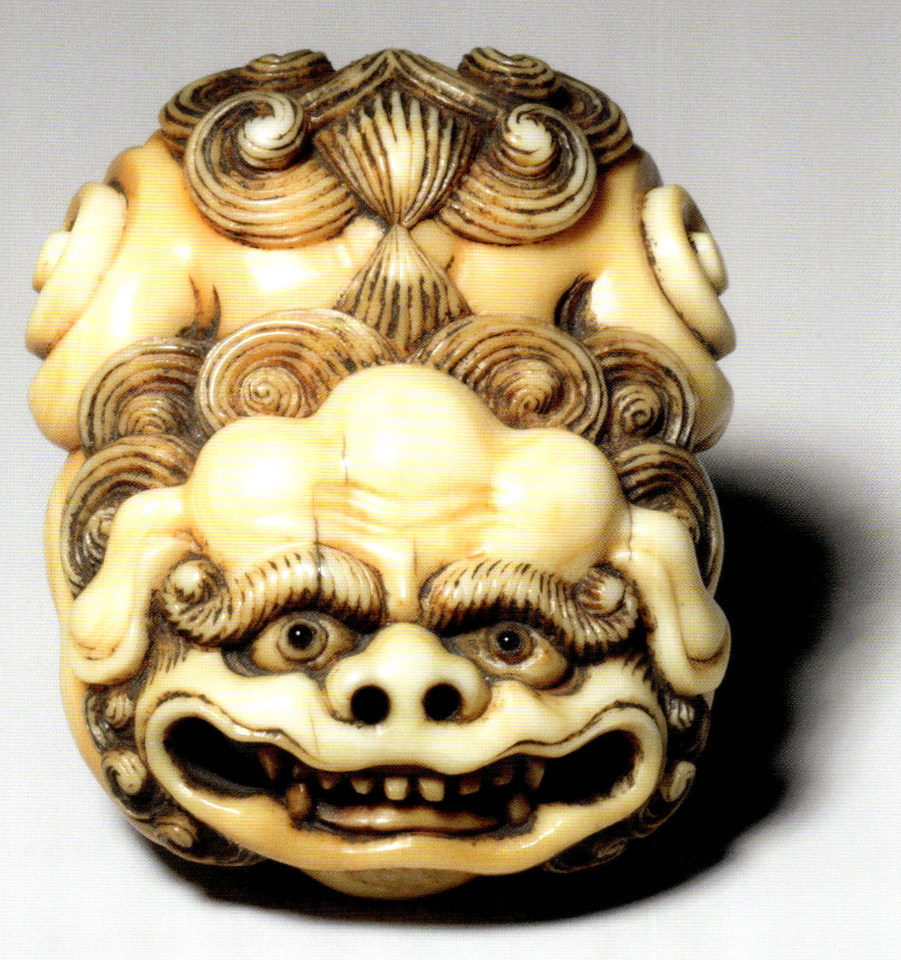

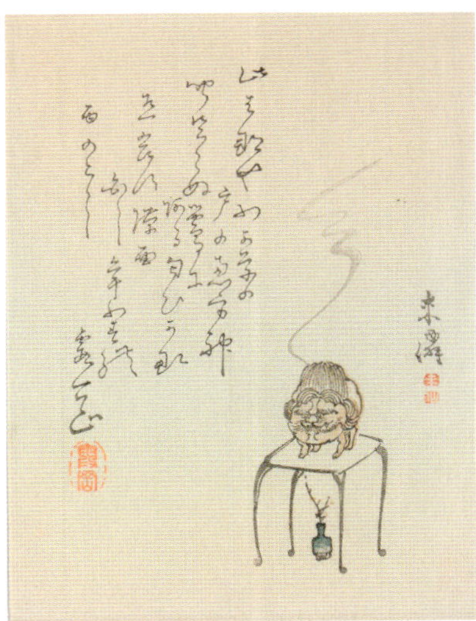

Incense burner in the shape of a Chinese lion. Raisen, colour woodblock print (*surimono*), late 1700s to early 1800s. 19.8 x 14 cm. British Museum 1980,1022,0.547.

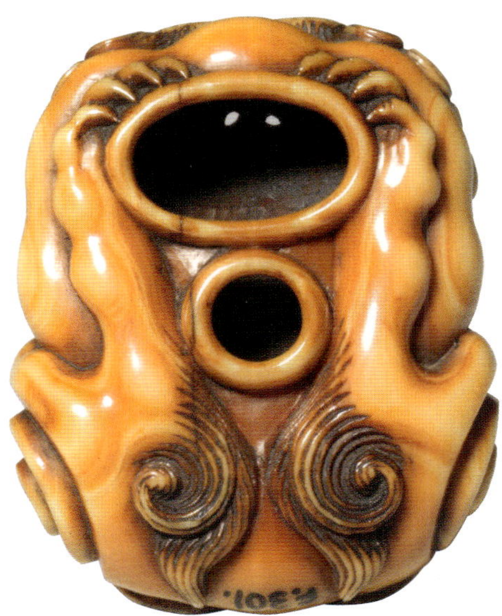

Chinese lion (*shishi*)

Shishi are lion-like mythical creatures introduced from China, where they were a common subject in the decorative arts. The imagery reached Japan together with Buddhism around the late sixth century AD. As lions were not indigenous to Japan, at first representations were based on Chinese images, but gradually *shishi* depictions took on a more distinctive native appearance. Like the Niō guardian statues (see pp. 50–51), a pair of *shishi* sculptures sometimes stands at either side of the gate to a shrine or temple, to ward off evil. These are generally depicted with fierce expressions, though in their netsuke guises they are more humorous. Here the *shishi* is rendered in a compressed form, which was perhaps simulating the shape of an incense burner (see left). Incense burners were made for use in temples, tea gatherings and also in private homes. They often take the form of an animal and in such cases they are usually designed to emit the incense smoke from the mouth. In this netsuke, the comical facial expression is emphasized by the deep-set eyes and the wide grinning mouth with sharp teeth. The mane and tail are richly carved in luxuriant relief, with convoluted tresses. The reverse shows two of the *shishi*'s legs enfolding the oval larger cord hole with its claws. The beautiful deep brownish-gold patina indicates age and wear. Although unsigned, the style of carving suggests an attribution to Rensai (see pp. 152–153 and pp. 182–183).

This netsuke was previously published in Barker and Smith 1976, p. 92, fig. 159.

—

Unsigned, attributed to Rensai
Walrus ivory, with eyes inlaid in dark horn eyes, Tokyo, 1870s
w. 3.8 cm
British Museum F.301
Given by Sir Augustus Wollaston Franks

Chinese lion (*shishi*)

This netsuke carved from rhinoceros horn depicts a mythical Chinese lion or *shishi* scratching its chin with its left hind leg. It sprawls on rocky ground and contentedly tips up its chin with mouth firmly shut. The pupils are inlaid in dark horn set within glass eyeballs. Any remnant of a fierce expression has now evaporated, and the *shishi* is here rendered as a familiar and loveable subject. Rhinoceros horn is only rarely used for netsuke. As examination of the base reveals, the material at the root of the horn attached to the skull is coarse and has a porous texture. Therefore that part of the horn is the toughest and most difficult to carve. However, it is also this area that boasts a beautiful two-tone colour, a translucent light shade nearer the rind and a greyish-black shade nearer the core. Nothwithstanding the difficulties of working it, Chinese craftsmen miraculously achieved minute and delicate relief carvings on the surface of rhinoceros horn. It was a popular material for carving in China. The earliest surviving rhinoceros horn objects date to the Tang period (618–906) and a few of these early Chinese examples are preserved in the Shōsōin Treasure House at Tōdaiji temple in Nara in Japan. In the Edo period (1615–1868), rhinoceros horns were imported to Japan and much prized as a herbal medicine, effective in preventing fever and smallpox. Tragically five species of rhinoceros are now close to extinction because of the continuing demand in Asia for their horns for use in medicines and for ornaments. Because of the expense of the raw material even in the Edo period, this netsuke must have been commissioned by a well-to-do patron.

This netsuke was previously published in Harris 1987, p. 39, fig. 110.

Unsigned
Rhinoceros horn with silver ring and eyes inlaid in glass
Early 1800s
H. 4 cm; w. 5.3 cm
British Museum HG.263
Given by Professor John and Mrs Anne Hull Grundy

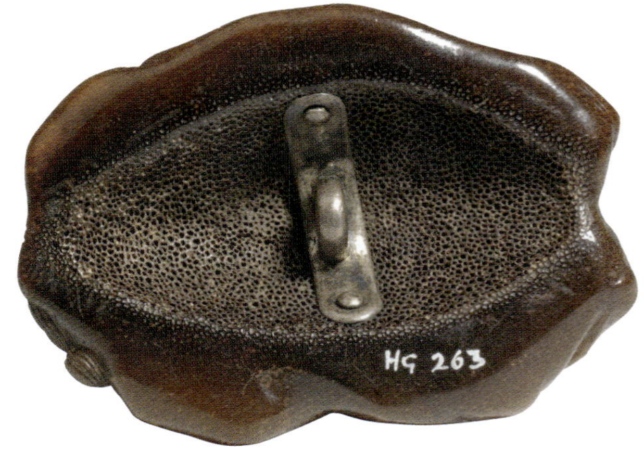

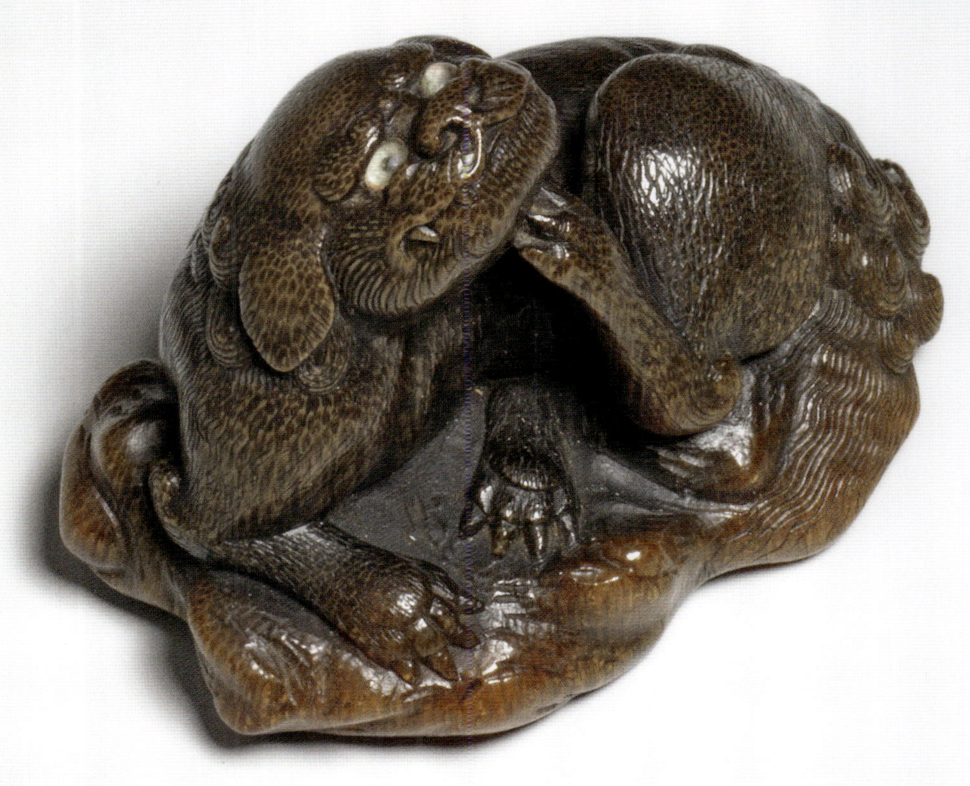

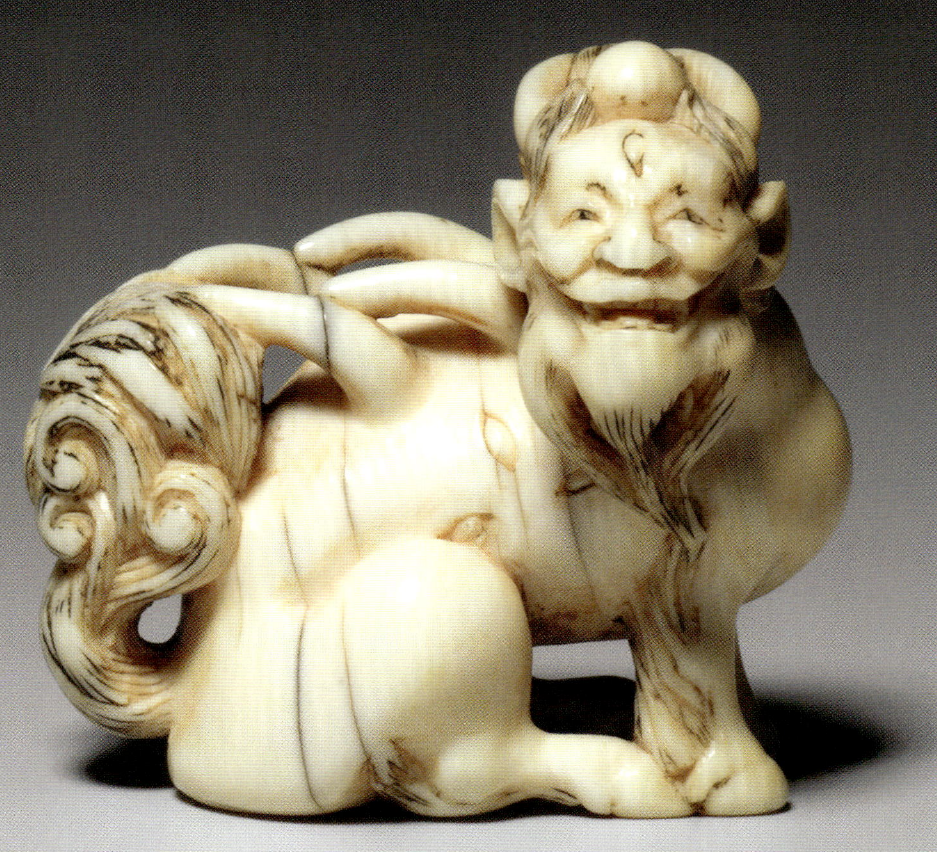

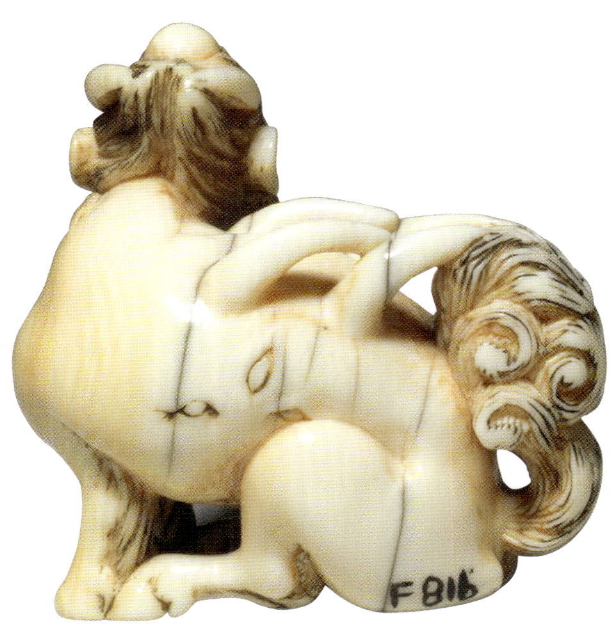

Hakutaku

This fabulous creature that originates from a Chinese legend is a rare subject for netsuke. Hakutaku (C. Bai Ze) are said to have the head of a man and the body of an ox, often with three eyes on each flank and horns on its back. Here the creature sits upright and alert with its head turning to the right. It has an additional eye on its forehead, a knot with two horns on its head and a luxurious but convoluted tail. According to legend, one day the Yellow Emperor (C. Huangdi), a legendary sovereign in ancient China, encountered the hakutaku during his journey to the east. The animal is said only to appear to leaders who are virtuous. Through its thorough knowledge of all kinds of evil supernatural creatures, it taught the emperor how to avoid and overcome them. This incident later helped him in dealing with disasters and diseases caused by demons. In Edo period (1615–1868) Japan, images of Hakutaku were believed to protect the wearer against danger and bad luck, and so they were carried while travelling and also put by the pillow while sleeping. This netsuke may well have been worn as such a talisman.

This netsuke was previously published in Barker and Smith 1976, pp. 42–43, fig. 44, and Lazarnick (ed.), MCI, vol. 1, 1986, p. 441.

—

By Masanao of Kyoto
Ivory, Kyoto, late 1700s
H. 3.6 cm; W. 4 cm
British Museum F.816
Given by Sir Augustus Wollaston Franks

Seated Kappa

Kappa are mischievous water creatures who live in ponds or rivers. They are said to have the body of a turtle, the head of a monkey and the limbs of a frog. They are also thought to attack humans when they are in the water. Kappa are generally depicted with a saucer-shaped cavity on the top of their head which contains a fluid vital for their life. In this netsuke, the kappa is represented as human-like, wearing a robe tied with a knotted rope at the back. There is a large depression on the top of its head, ringed with lanky straight hair. The kappa's face is depicted with bulging eyes, pointed ears and a mouth stretching almost from ear to ear. The face and parts of the limbs are stippled to resemble amphibian skin. Despite its fierce nature, the kappa is said to be quite polite. In the unfortunate event of encountering a kappa, one must bow; if greeted with a bow the creature will return it, thereby spilling the life-sustaining liquid kept in the hollow of its head and losing its magical powers. It is also believed that kappa propagate by throwing cucumbers, their favourite vegetable, into the water. This surely explains why cucumbers are still called 'kappa' in sushi restaurants in Japan today. Japanese children are frightened away from swimming in rivers by their mother warning them that a kappa will grab them and drown them in the water.

This netsuke was previously published in Barker and Smith 1976, p. 122, fig. 239, Lazarnick, vol.1, 1981, p. 485, and Lazarnick (ed.), MCI, vol. 1, 1986, p. 184.

—

By Hokushō (or Kitamasa)
Wood, with eyes inlaid in dark horn, late 1800s
H. 5.3 cm
British Museum F.747
Given by Sir Augustus Wollaston Franks

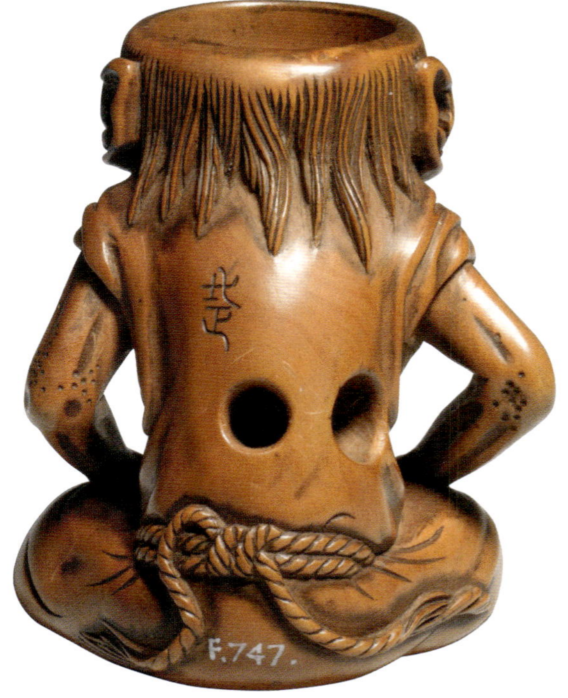

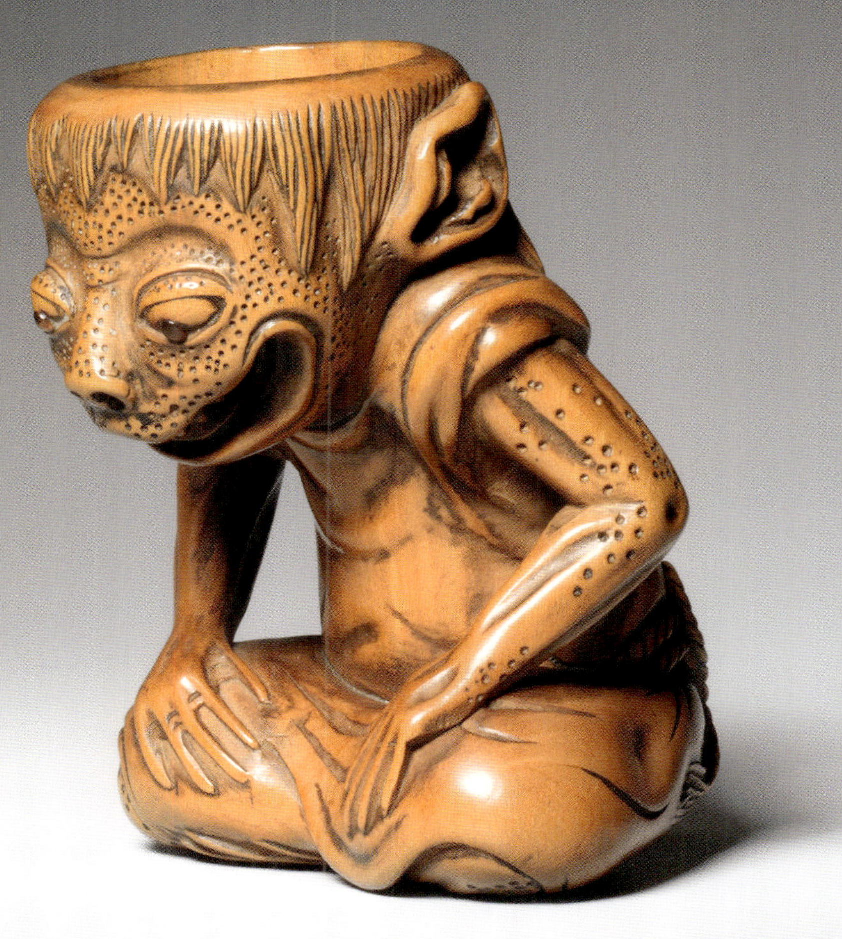

Masks

During the Edo period (1615–1868) theatre was quite popular among a broad spectrum of the populace, and masks were a common feature of many performances. Netsuke that represent some aspect of the performing arts often take the form of an actor, dancer or mask.

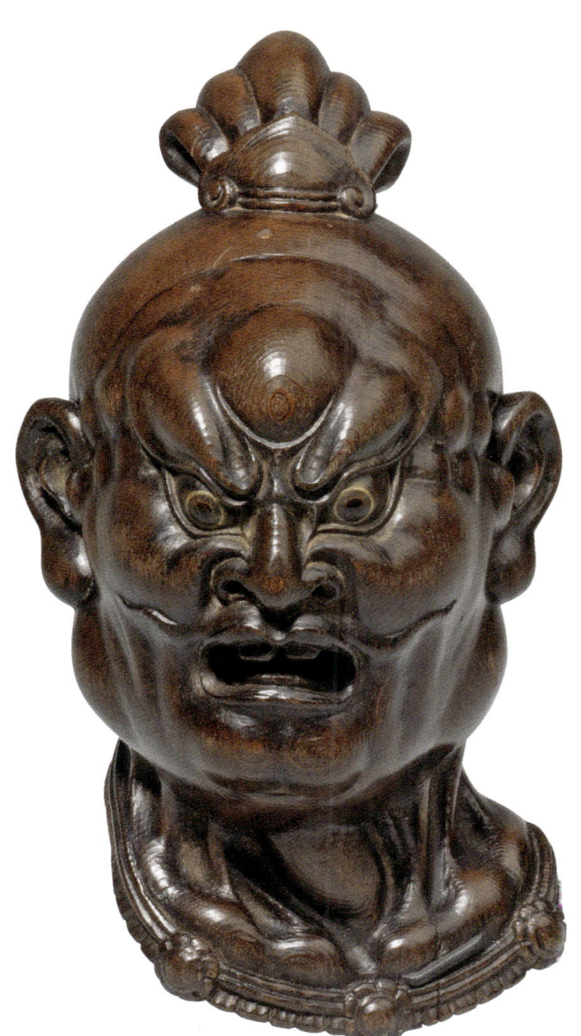

Head of a Niō

This arresting netsuke takes the form of the head of a
Buddhist Guardian King, a Niō, usually depicted as a pair
of statues stationed either side of a temple gate (see also
pp. 50–51). The figure placed to the right of the gate would
be sculpted with the mouth agape to form the sound 'A',
and the other figure with compressed lips forming the
sound 'Om' to the left. These are the first (A) and last (Om)
syllables of the Sanskrit language, symbolically representing
the beginning and end of all things. Here the head of a Niō
reflects the deity's violent power, with his mouth tensely
open and straining muscles vividly carved on the neck.
This powerful effect is enhanced by centring the natural
tree rings on the face, with larger rings radiating outwards.
The eyes are dilated in anger and highlighted in gold and
black lacquer. The netsuke is carved in the form of a mask,
and the reverse is hollow.

Kōseki was a sculptor of Buddhist images who diligently
studied many of the famous Buddhist sculptures from the
Kamakura period (1185–1333). He might have had in mind
the imposing Guardian Kings of Tōdaiji temple in Nara when
he carved this head. This is one of two netsuke carved at
the request of Oscar Charles Raphael (1874–1941) (the
other is pictured on p. 88).

This netsuke was previously published in Barker and
Smith 1976, p. 64, fig. 88, and Lazarnick, vol. 1, 1981, p.
672.

—

By Naitō Kōseki (1871–1948)
Japanese cypress (*hinoki*) with lacquered eyes
Kyoto, early 1900s
H. 9.5 cm
British Museum 1945,1017.530
Bequeathed by Oscar Charles Raphael

Demon mask

When the compelling demon mask is examined closely it becomes apparent that this stag antler netsuke employs carefully carved ornamental cloud scrolls to create the demon's face. Although the netsuke is unsigned, it can be attributed to the carver Ozaki Kokusai (1835–1894) on account of the eccentric design. Kokusai was active in the late nineteenth century in Tokyo. He worked in a distinctive and highly original style that is easily recognizable, employing many different types of scrolling and circular motifs in his designs. His favourite material was stag antler, which was also widely used by his fellow carvers working in the downtown Asakusa district of Tokyo. Although stag antler is readily available and is relatively inexpensive, it is a challenging material for netsuke carvers because of its irregular shape and somewhat spongy texture. The Tokyo carvers of this period were able ingeniously to incorporate these difficulties into the design with skill and imagination, creating forceful works such as the demon mask we see here.

Similar examples are illustrated in Joly 1912, reprinted 1966, no. 211, pl. VII, and in Bandini, exhibition catalogue, 2013, pp. 96–97, fig. 193.

This netsuke was previously published in Barker and Smith 1976, p. 91, fig. 151.

—

Unsigned, attributed to Ozaki Kokusai (1835–1894)
Stag antler, Tokyo, late 1800s
H. 4.4 cm; W. 4 cm
British Museum F.351
Given by Sir Augustus Wollaston Franks

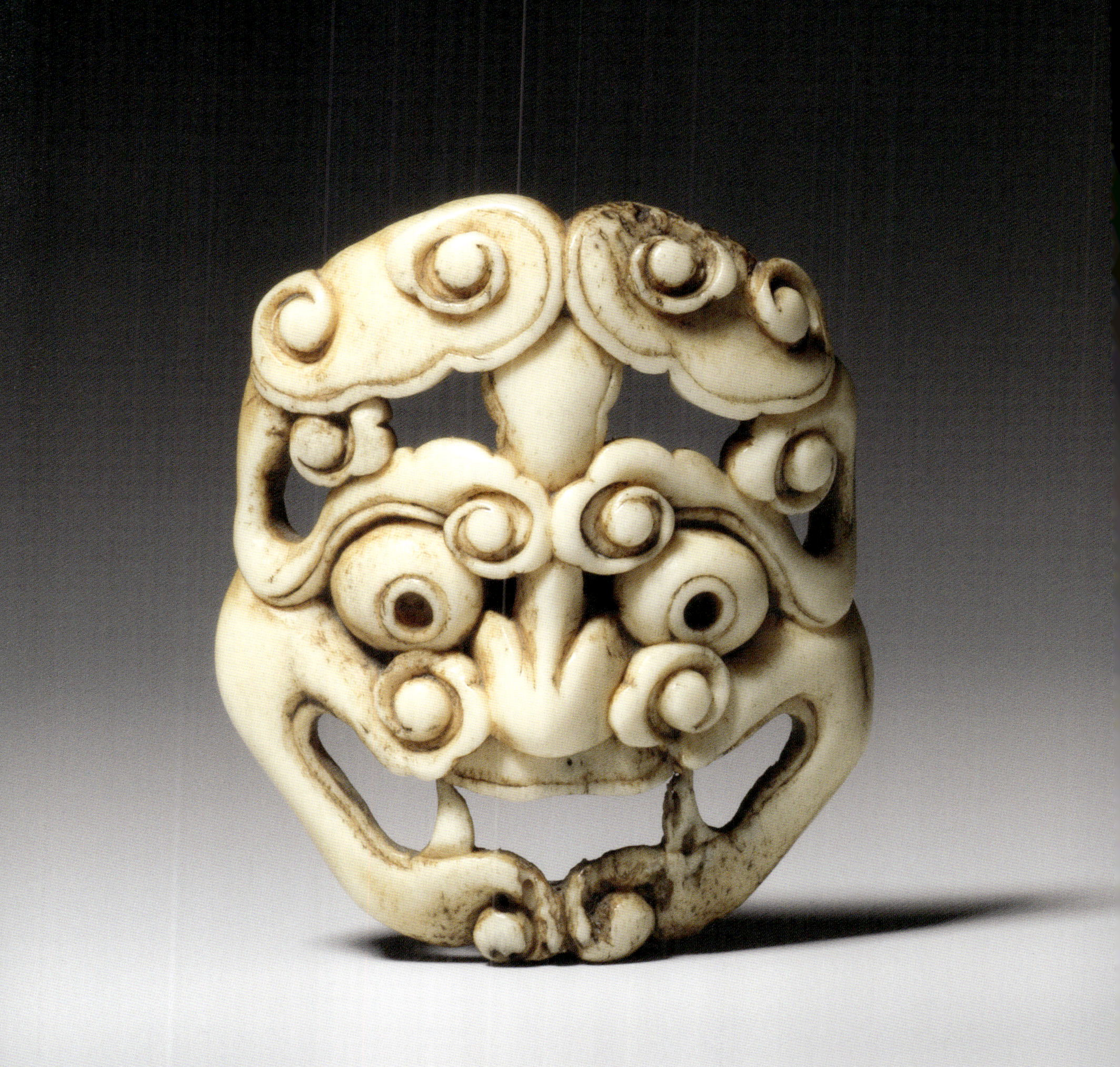

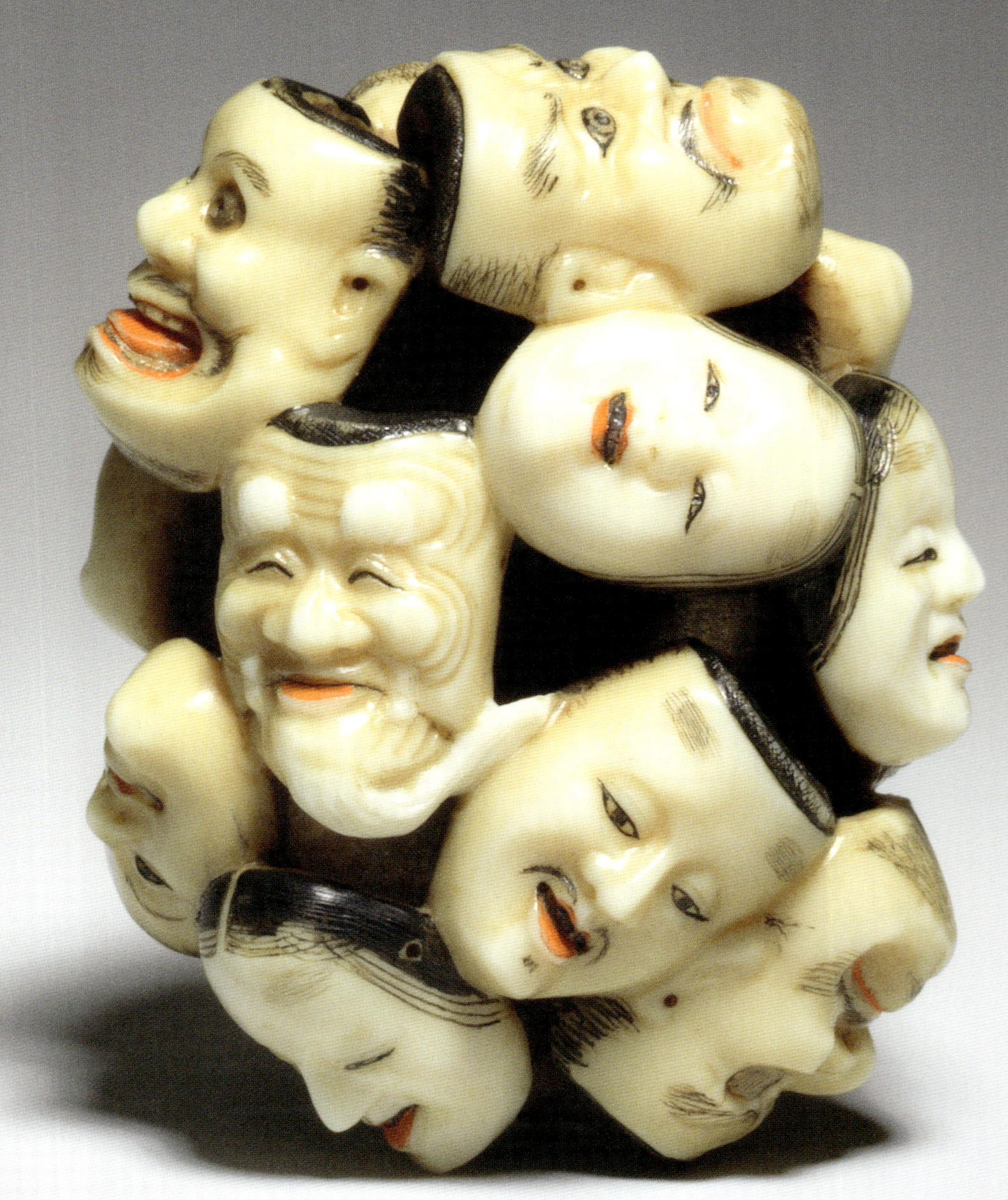

Noh masks

This intriguing netsuke is created out of a grouping of fifteen masks used during the performance of Noh plays. It was carved by a contemporary netsuke carver, Kishi Isshū. Noh, a form of Japanese classical drama with music, evolved in the thirteenth century out of earlier folk performances, both of which also employed masks to tell their stories. Noh transformed into a sophisticated dramatic art form in the fourteenth and fifteenth centuries under the two great actor-playwrights, Kan'ami Kiyotsugu (1333–1384) and his son Ze'ami Motokiyo (1363–1443). In the Edo period (1615–1868), Noh theatre became the authorized official ceremonial art of the Tokugawa shogunate, and as a result became more austere and solemn in character. Although rarely seen by commoners, Noh masks were quite popular as a netsuke motif. As a rule, Noh masks are neutral in expression. Great skill by the actor is needed to express varied emotions through the mask, by means of subtle changes in his physical attitude. There are over one hundred types of masks for the various set characters in the plays, including male, female, animal and supernatural beings. In this netsuke certain characters are recognizable, such as Okina (kindly old man), Ko-Omote (young woman) and Chūjō (young nobleman). Mask netsuke often feature groups of multiple masks, as seen in this example.

Kishi Isshū (his real name is Kishi Yoshio) started ivory carving after the Second World War in 1947, at the age of 30. He studied under his brother, who was an ivory sculptor and seven years his senior. Isshū started by making ornamental sculptures (*okimono*), but later became particularly fond of netsuke and specialized in traditional Japanese subjects. During the 1950s and 60s, when many U.S. troops were stationed in Japan, the brothers' works sold well, particularly coloured ivory objects and netsuke. Isshū carved netsuke for some 54 years until he retired in 2001.

A similar netsuke by the artist is in the Prince Takamado Collection, illustrated in Tokyo National Museum 2011, p. 24, pl. 34.

—

By Kishi Isshū (b. 1917)
Ivory, about 1975
H. 5.5 cm; w. 4.2 cm
British Museum 1981,1014.2

Animals

Animals have always been a popular source of inspiration for netsuke carvers. Netsuke of the twelve animals of the East Asian zodiac cycle or *jūnishi*, in particular, were linked either to the zodiac animal of the current year, or the birth year of the owner. The East Asian zodiac calendar, which derives from Chinese cosmology, is based on a twelve-year cycle, each year being represented by a different animal, starting with the rat, ox, tiger, hare, dragon, snake, horse, sheep (often represented in Japan as a goat), monkey, cockerel, dog and ending with the boar. According to legend, the Buddha once called all the animals to him in celebration, and these were the twelve animals that attended his call. They were arranged in the zodiac calendar in the same order that they arrived to greet the Buddha.

Twelve zodiac animals

Incredibly, this intricately carved netsuke represents all twelve animals of the zodiac cycle in a single work. The front is dominated by a rat, an ox, a dragon and a monkey with the other creatures skilfully intertwined around the edges and on the back. To carve all twelve animals together in a single netsuke requires all the carver's compositional and carving skills. The eyes of each animal are carefully inlaid with dark or red horn. Interestingly, the rat is carved riding on the ox's rump, which is based on yet another legend: when the animals were all called by Buddha to attend him the ox set out early, as it usually walks quite slowly. However, just before the ox reached the Buddha, the rat riding on the ox's back jumped off and pre-empted him to greet the deity. This last parable has significance in Buddhist doctrinal debates about whether to gain enlightenment through one's own efforts (J. *jiriki*), or to rely on others for help towards the goal of communal enlightenment (J. *tariki*).

—

Unsigned, in the style of Kaigyokusai Masatsugu (1813–1892)
Ivory, with eyes inlaid in different colours of horn, about 1880
H. 2.8 cm; w. 3.4 cm
British Museum F.1073
Given by Sir Augustus Wollaston Franks

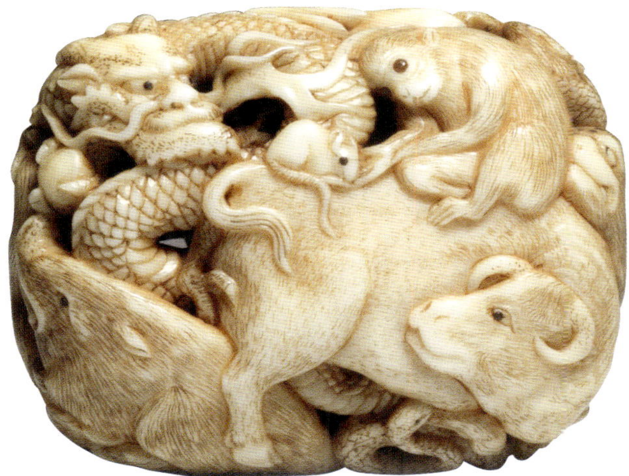

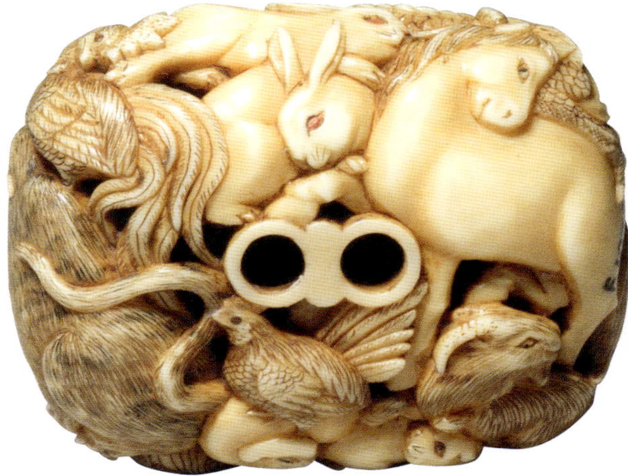

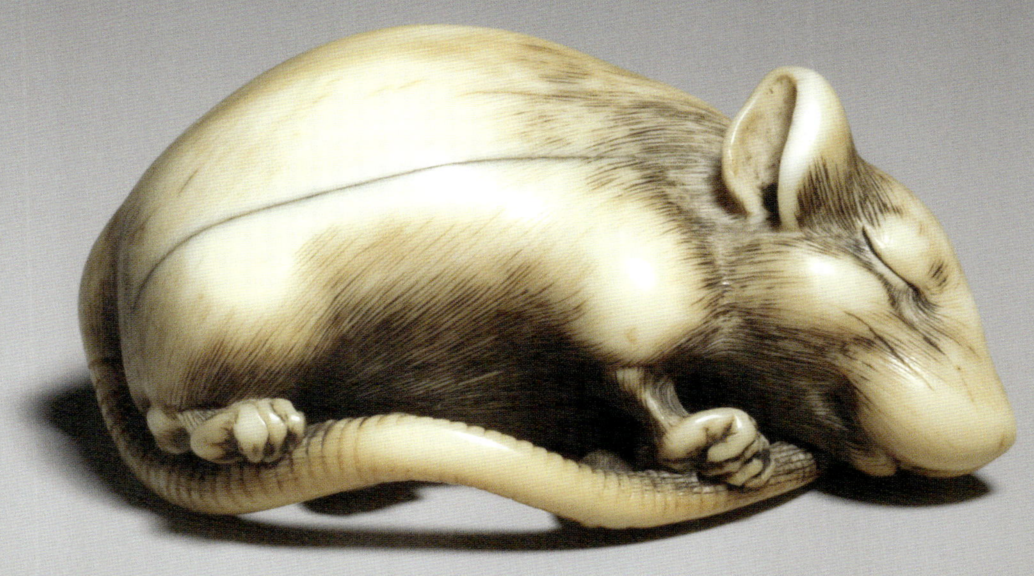

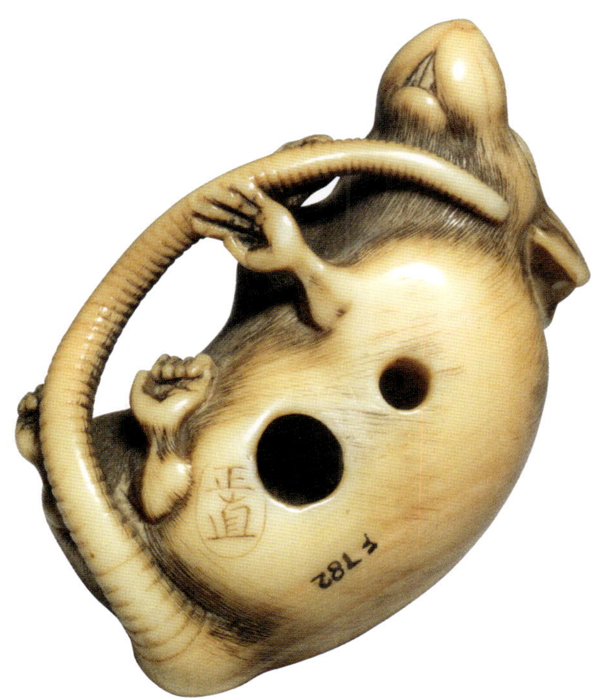

Sleeping rat

This ivory rat is sleeping contentedly with its paws clenched as if in the middle of a dream. The bulging body coated with fine fur accentuates the impression of sleekness. On the underside, the realistically ribbed tail coils around in front of the body adding to the compactness of the design. The carver, Masanao, was active in Kyoto during the second half of the eighteenth century. As the traditional capital city and centre of the arts in Japan, Kyoto was one of the important centres of netsuke production. During the late eighteenth century, the city emerged as the centre of classic animal netsuke. It was no coincidence that, in the field of painting, Maruyama Ōkyo (1733–1795) of Kyoto established the Maruyama-Shijō school at this time, which pursued realism by adopting elements of Western spatial techniques and sketching from life. This exerted a strong influence upon the creation of netsuke, in terms of keen observation and attention to detail, especially in the depiction of animals. This netsuke was probably worn by a man born in the year of the rat, or it may have served as a talisman for attracting prosperity, since rats are associated with Daikoku, one of the Seven Gods of Good Fortune (see pp. 68–69).

A similar example (ex-collection Mrs Anne Hull Grundy) is illustrated in Davies 1998, pp. 122–123. pl. 92.

This netsuke was previously published in Barker and Smith 1976, pp .42–43, fig. 43, and Lazarnick (ed.), MCI, vol. 1, 1986, p. 440.

—

By Masanao of Kyoto
Ivory, Kyoto, late 1700s
w. 5.7 cm
British Museum F.782
Given by Sir Augustus Wollaston Franks

Boy playing a flute on an ox

This ivory netsuke depicts a boy playing a flute while riding an ox on his homeward journey. The subject is a common one in the teachings of Zen Buddhism, and represents the sixth out of ten stages needed to reach enlightenment. It is also depicted in a series of paintings of *Ten Ox Herding Pictures* (J. *Jūgyū zu*), which illustrates the ten stages of enlightenment in terms of the relationship between the boy and the ox: the boy is the practitioner and the ox represents enlightenment (see right). Here and in the netsuke shown opposite, the boy is gracefully playing his flute on the ox and the reins are no longer needed. It indicates a harmonious relationship between the subject and the object, and a new state of enlightenment.

The work was created by the accomplished netsuke carver Otoman, who was based in Hakata in Kyushu. He was born into a family of hairpin and ornament makers. He travelled to Edo (present-day Tokyo) as well as working in Kyoto and Osaka, before taking over the Hakata family business. Hakata was close to the trading port of Nagasaki, and a collection of Otoman's works is known to have been taken to Holland by the German physician and botanist, Philipp Franz von Siebold (1796–1866), who resided in Nagasaki from 1823–1829. Formerly housed in the National Museum of Ethnology, Leiden, Netherlands, they were apparently lost during the Second World War.

This netsuke was previously published in Barker and Smith 1976, p. 115, fig. 219.

—

By Matsushita Otoman
Ivory, with eyes inlaid in dark horn, Hakata, early 1800s
H. 3.5 cm; w. 3.8 cm
British Museum F.663
Given by Sir Augustus Wollaston Franks

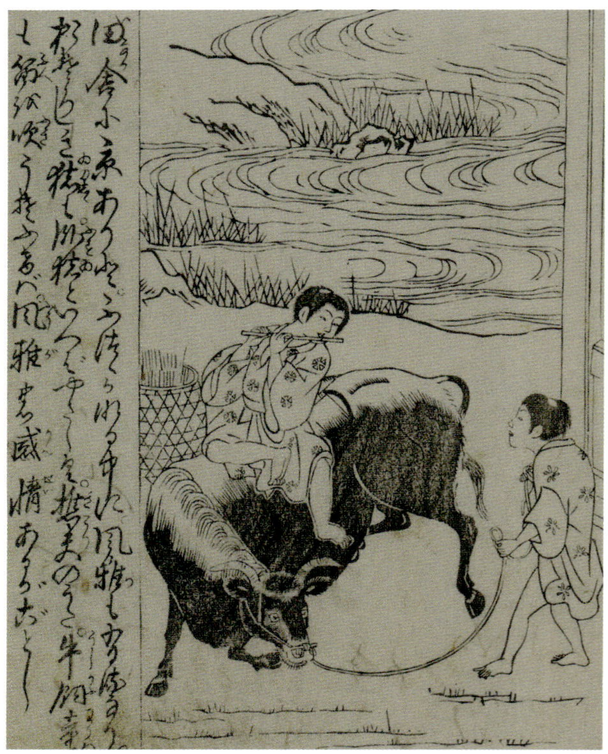

Boy playing a flute on an ox (detail), from Ishikawa Toyonobu (1711–1785), *Ehon kotowaza-gusa* (*Picture Book: Collected Popular Sayings*). Woodblock-illustrated book, 1752. 22. 5 x 16 cm (covers). British Museum 1921,0511,0.4-5.

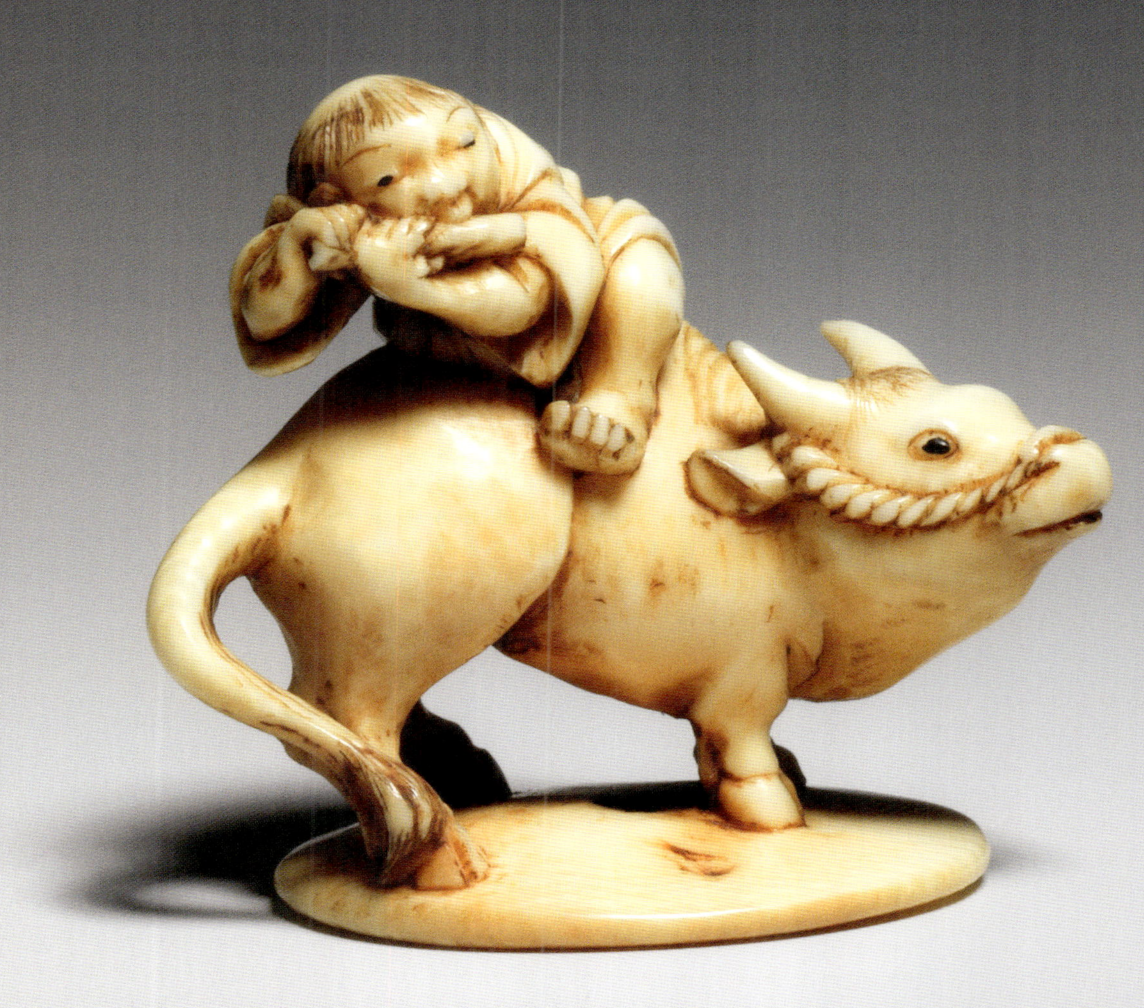

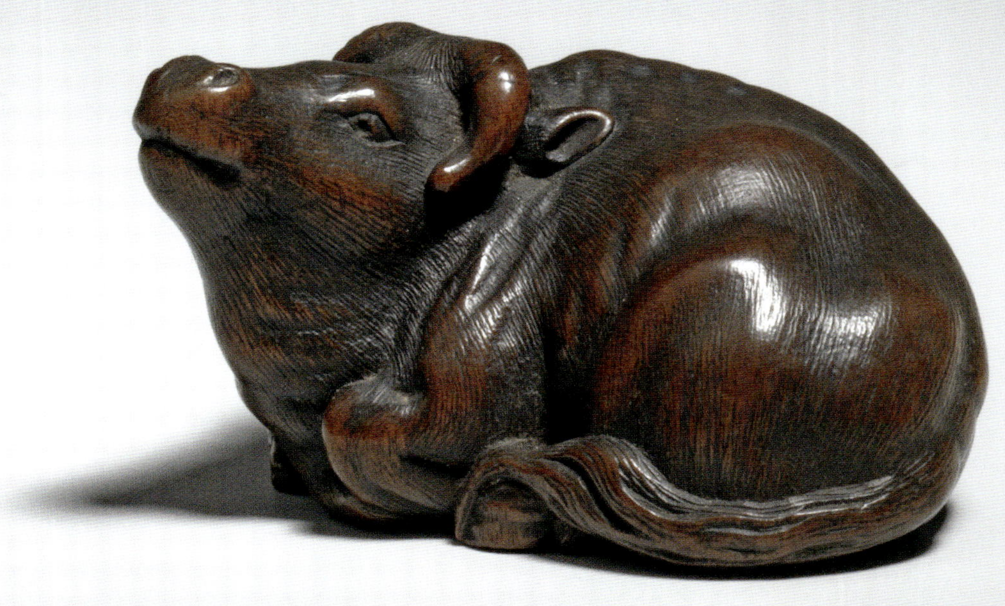

Reclining ox

This recumbent ox raises its head in characteristic pose.
Its front legs are tucked under its body and the tail is pulled
compactly around its rump. The spine is well defined against
the voluminous body and the hair of the coat is rendered
with long strokes. The carver, Ikkan, is said to have been
a priest at a temple in Nagoya. He always worked in wood
and chiefly made animals and figures. In this example,
his careful attention to anatomical detail can be admired,
for example, in the folds of flesh around the neck of the ox.
The netsuke has a relatively simple composition but attracts
the viewer with its natural charm.

—

By Ikkan
Wood, Nagoya, mid to late 1800s
w. 4.5 cm
British Museum 1981,0808.107
Bequeathed by Captain Collingwood Ingram

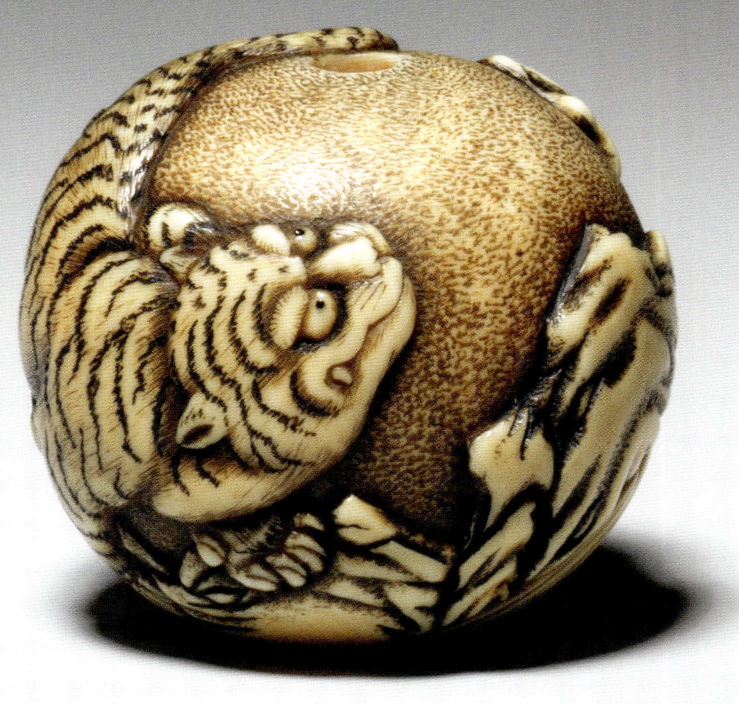

Sphere with tiger and bamboo

This spherical ivory netsuke is carved with a stalking tiger striding between rocks and bamboo by a stream. Tigers and bamboo have often been depicted together in Japanese art, symbolizing complementary aspects of strength. The tiger has aggressive strength, while the gentle but firm bamboo will bend but not break. Since the tiger is not native to Japan, artists had to rely on Chinese paintings or imported skins to depict them. This explains why the tigers depicted in Japanese art sometimes appear like an enlarged cat rather than the fiercer animal.

Here the carver, Mitsuhiro, shows off his mastery of various techniques through the details covering this small sphere (see also pp. 44–45, 160–161 and 168–169). Each motif is carved in high relief against a roughened surface that was created using the 'roughening up' (*arashi*) technique, employing the smallest and most delicate tools. He also skilfully used stippling and ink-staining to create the tiger's fur. Mitsuhiro's style of depicting tigers resonates with ink paintings of the Kano school. Kano school artists were professional painters patronized by the shoguns and samurai lords from the late Muromachi period (1333–1568) onwards, and they often executed decorative screens and wall paintings which synthesized Chinese ink painting with Japanese-style painting. The netsuke is signed Mitsuhiro, with seal Ōhara.

This netsuke was previously published in Harris 1987, p. 117, fig. 593.

—

By Ōhara Mitsuhiro (1810–1875)
Ivory, with eyes inlaid in dark horn, Osaka, mid 1800s
DIAM. 3.3 cm
British Museum HG.549
Given by Professor John and Mrs Anne Hull Grundy

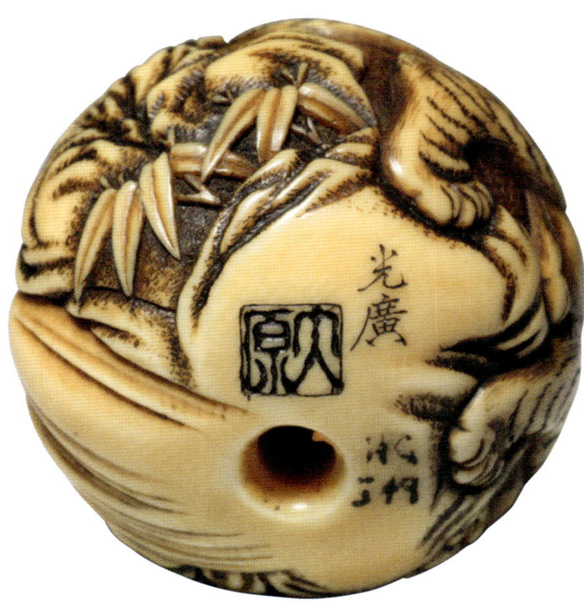

Snarling tiger

Although this ivory tiger is unsigned, it exemplifies the
special characteristics of the artist Otoman, who often did
not sign his works (see also pp. 110–111 and 146–147).
Tigers were a speciality of the carver and are highly prized
by collectors. Standing on rounded paws with a hunched
back, this ivory tiger is snarling with its mouth wide open.
The carver added a red stain to the inside of the mouth –
although most of this added colour has faded – and the
teeth are sharply defined. The tiger's long tail is drawn
tensely toward his body, which makes for an overall
compact composition, an important feature for a successful
netsuke. The most dramatic aspect of the representation
is the tiger's fur. The markings are cleverly rendered in
negative, with white unstained ivory representing dark
stripes, emphasizing the contours of the form of the animal.

This netsuke was previously published in Harris 1987,
p. 49, fig. 169, and as the cover illustration.

—

Unsigned, attributed to Matsushita Otoman
Ivory, with eyes inlaid in horn, early 1800s
H. 4.4 cm
British Museum HG.700
Given by Professor John and Mrs Anne Hull Grundy

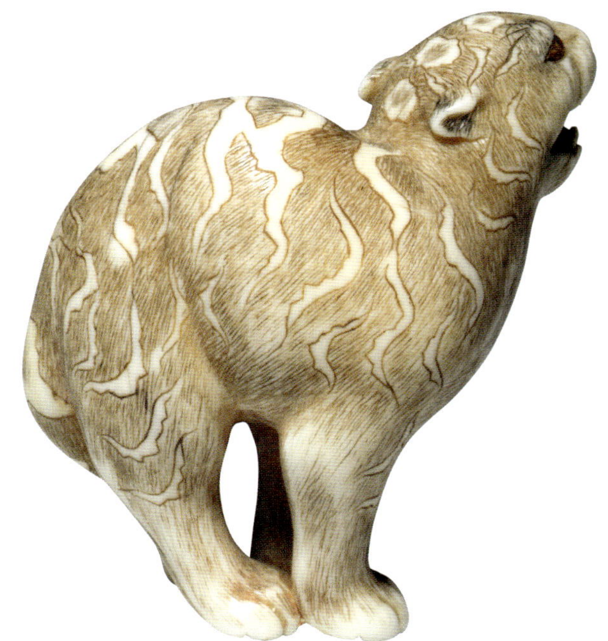

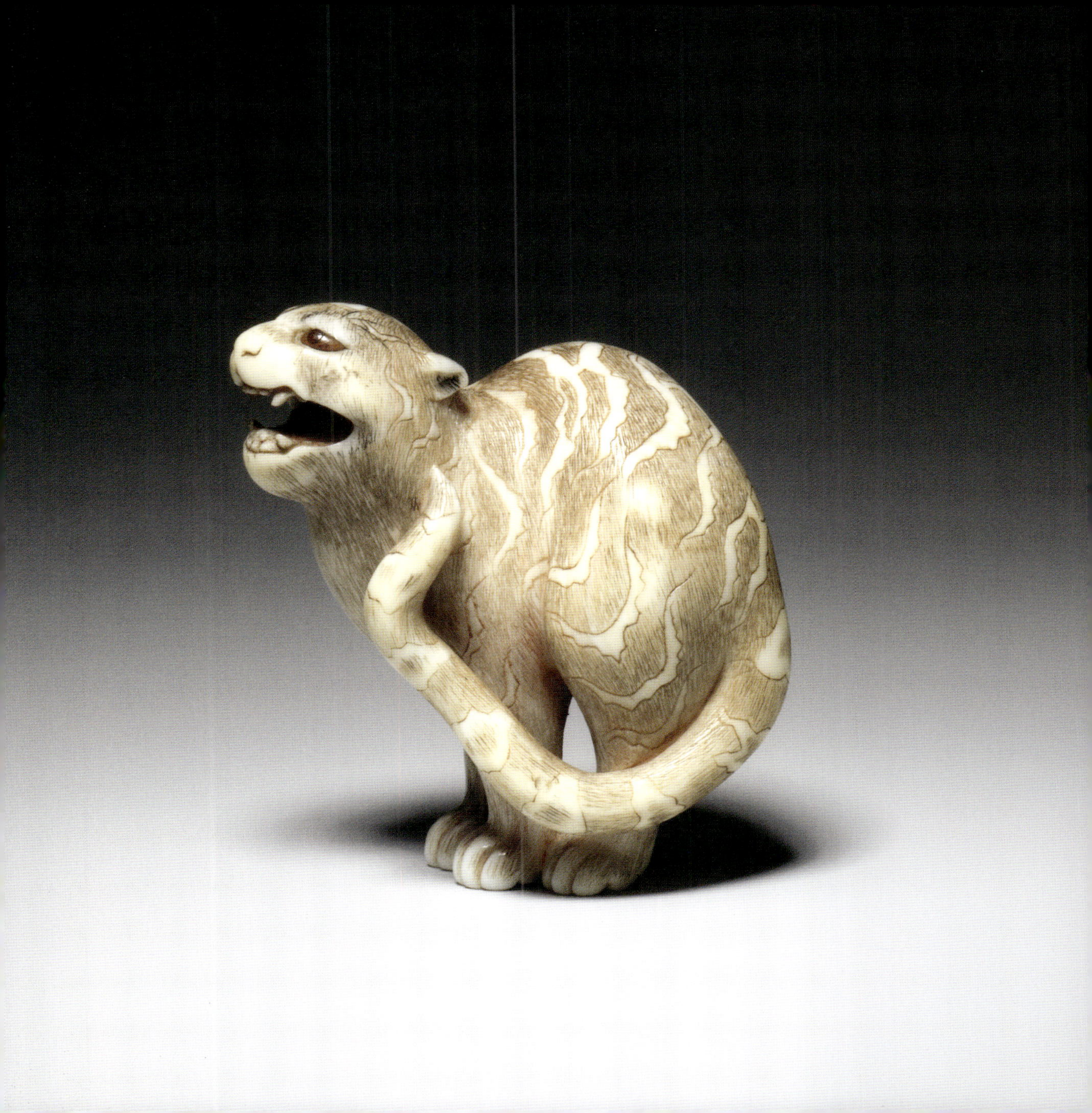

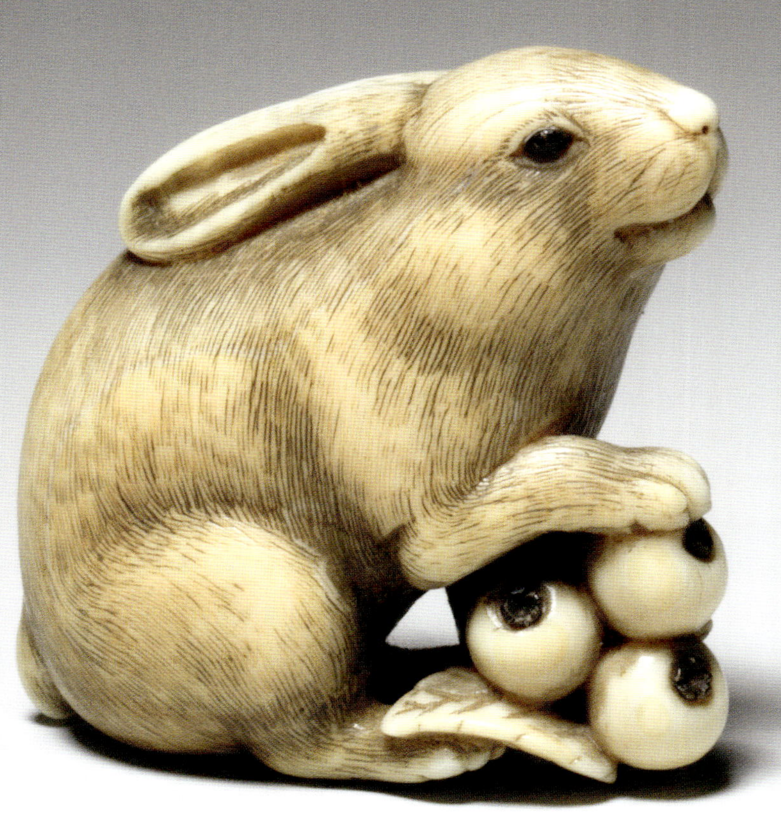

Hare with loquats

Ever present in Japanese folklore, and one of the twelve animals of the zodiac cycle, it comes as no surprise that hares are a common theme in Japanese paintings and decorative arts. The hare in this netsuke squats on its hind legs, with its right forepaw resting on a branch of loquats. The hare slightly raises its head and its long ears are flat, resting against its body. Okatomo, who is mentioned in *Sōken kishō* (*Strange and Wonderful Sword Fittings*), first published in 1781, was one of the outstanding animal carvers of Kyoto in the late eighteenth century. He is believed to have studied under another netsuke master who specialized in animals, Tomotada, and adopted the 'tomo' character from his master's name. Okatomo mainly created birds and animals in ivory, demonstrating a comprehensive understanding of the anatomy of his subjects. The hare's face and body are treated with great delicacy, and the depiction of fur has a silky quality executed with great finesse, incised with long straight strokes which have been darkened by intentional staining.

   This netsuke was previously published in Harris 1987, p. 52, fig. 190.

—

By Yamaguchi Okatomo
Ivory, with details inlaid in dark horn, Kyoto, late 1700s
H. 3.5 cm; W. 4 cm
British Museum HG.440
Given by Professor John and Mrs Anne Hull Grundy

Hare on a lotus leaf

Tortoiseshell is a rare material to be employed in the creation of an entire netsuke. It is more often used sparingly as an inlay for eyes. In the Edo period (1615–1868), tortoiseshell was generally imported from the Ryūkyū Islands (present-day Okinawa prefecture), or Luzon in the Philippines. Because it is relatively easy to carve basic shapes from, the material was used in the manufacture of a wide variety of flat items such as combs (*kushi*), hairpins, sash band decoration (*obidome*) and eyeglass frames. The netsuke here depicts a hare with long ears seated on a lotus leaf, and is carved out of a single section of tortoiseshell. The hare looks upwards to the moon with its right forepaw raised, while holding a long-stemmed flower in its mouth. Although it is said to be quite challenging to create detailed carving on tortoiseshell, this netsuke nonetheless boasts a delicate treatment. The edge of the leaf is elegantly turned inward, and its veins are finely carved in high relief. The carving is enhanced by the beautiful mottled and streaked appearance of the translucent brown of the shell, an appealing natural characteristic of the material. The hole for the cord is fashioned from the natural separation between the tortoise's upper and lower shell.

This netsuke was previously published in Harris 1987, p. 53, fig. 195.

—

Unsigned
Tortoiseshell, early 1800s
H. 5.2 cm
British Museum HG.257
Given by Professor John and Mrs Anne Hull Grundy

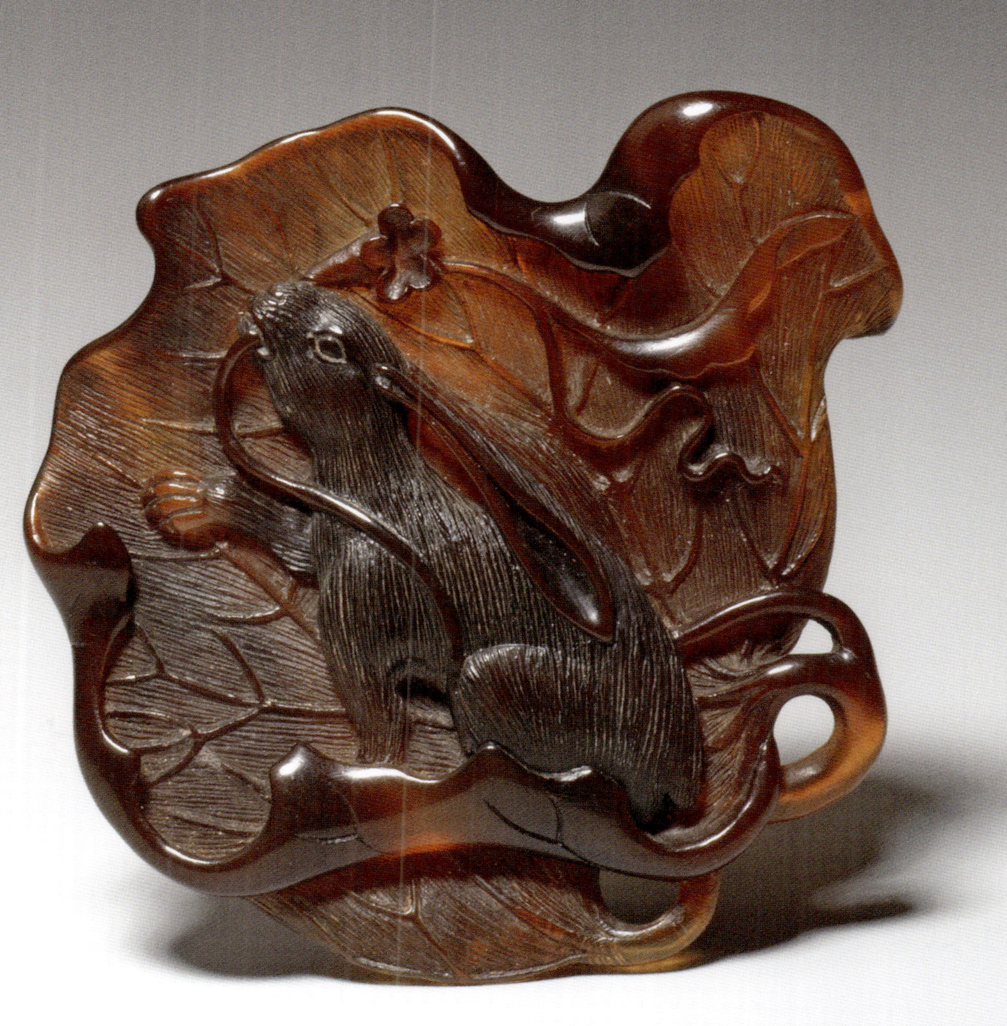

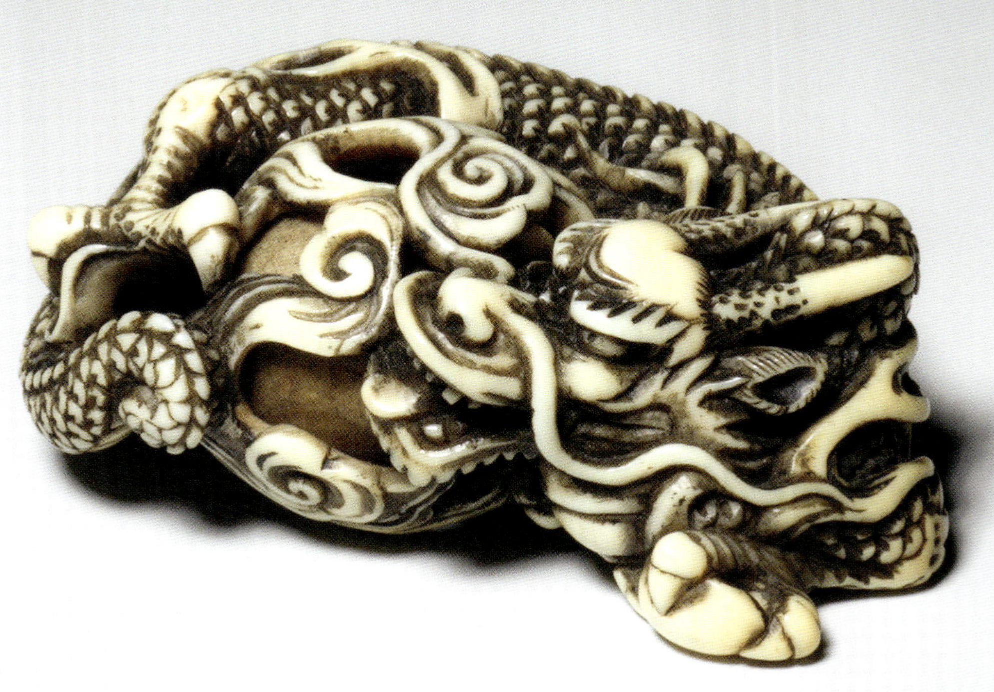

Dragon and ball

The dragon is the only supernatural animal among the twelve animals of the zodiac cycle, and perhaps the most commonly represented mythical creature in Japanese art. Unlike the western fire-breathing dragons, the dragons of Japan are regarded as water deities which control rainfall. They are typically depicted as large, serpentine creatures with two horns, long whiskers and clawed feet. Here the dragon's sinuous body is coiled around a cloud-shaped sphere, inside which a loose ball moves. Its mouth is opened in a fierce snarl and it holds a small wish-fulfilling jewel, *hōju*, in its three-clawed left talon. The snakelike body is covered with intricately carved scales and ridged spines, the details enhanced with dark stain. Cloud energy (*ki*) swirls around its body, contributing an element of drama.

You may wish to compare this netsuke with a dragon netsuke signed Tomotada in the Baur Collection, illustrated in Coullery and Newstead 1977, pp. 126–127, pl. C267.

—

Unsigned, in the style of Izumiya Tomotada
Ivory, late 1700s
w. 4.5 cm
British Museum F.1098
Given by Sir Augustus Wollaston Franks

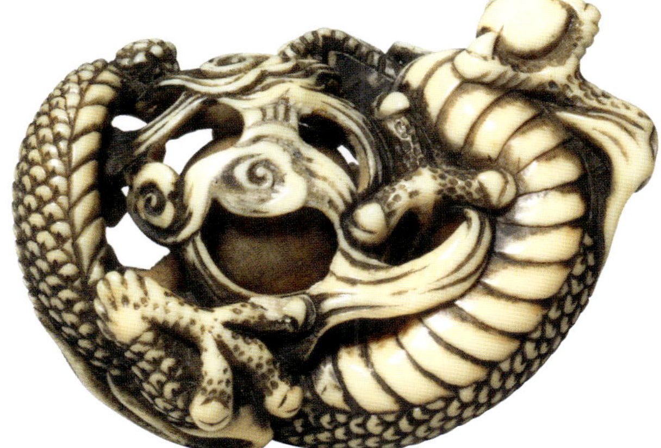

Coiled snake

Although feared as a dangerous and ominous creature
in many cultures, snakes have been worshiped as divine
messengers and appear in many myths and legends in
Japan. Because a snake sheds its skin, it has been
associated with fertility and regeneration. Here a snake
coils up forming a complex and strong composition, with
its head resting on the top of its own body. A long narrow
tongue reaches out as if the snake is trying to touch the tip
of its own tail. The scales on the back are carefully rendered
in an intricate reducing diamond pattern, a geometric feat in
itself, and the scales of the underside follow the movement
of the snake's body. Its coiled form provides a compact
design, which is perfect for use as a netsuke. As far as the
author is aware, this is a unique representation of a snake
in Okatomo's works.

This netsuke was previously published in Barker and
Smith 1976, p. 47, fig. 53, and Lazarnick (ed.), MCI, vol. 2,
1986, p. 621.

—

By Yamaguchi Okatomo
Ivory, with eyes inlaid in dark horn, Kyoto, late 1700s
w. 4.1 cm
British Museum 1945,1017.603
Bequeathed by Oscar Charles Raphael

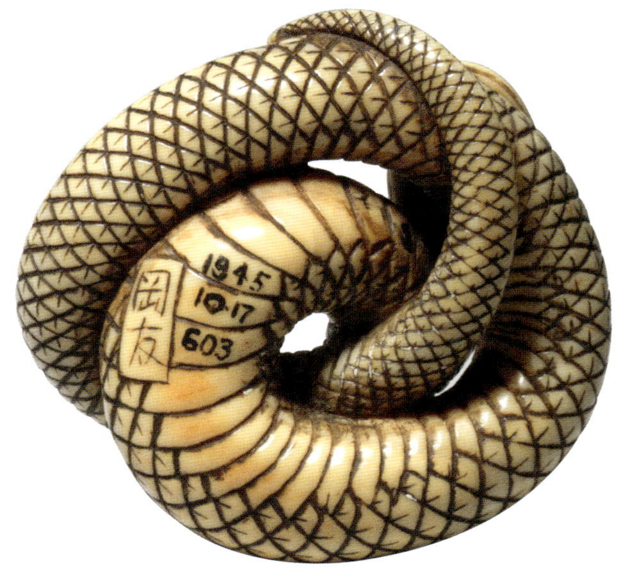

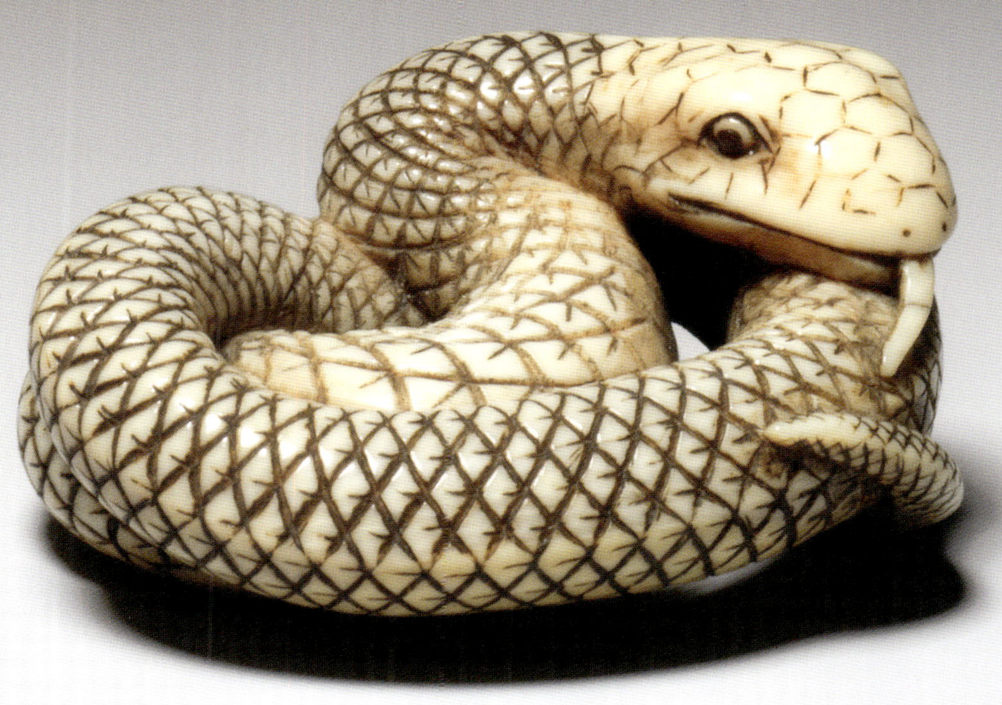

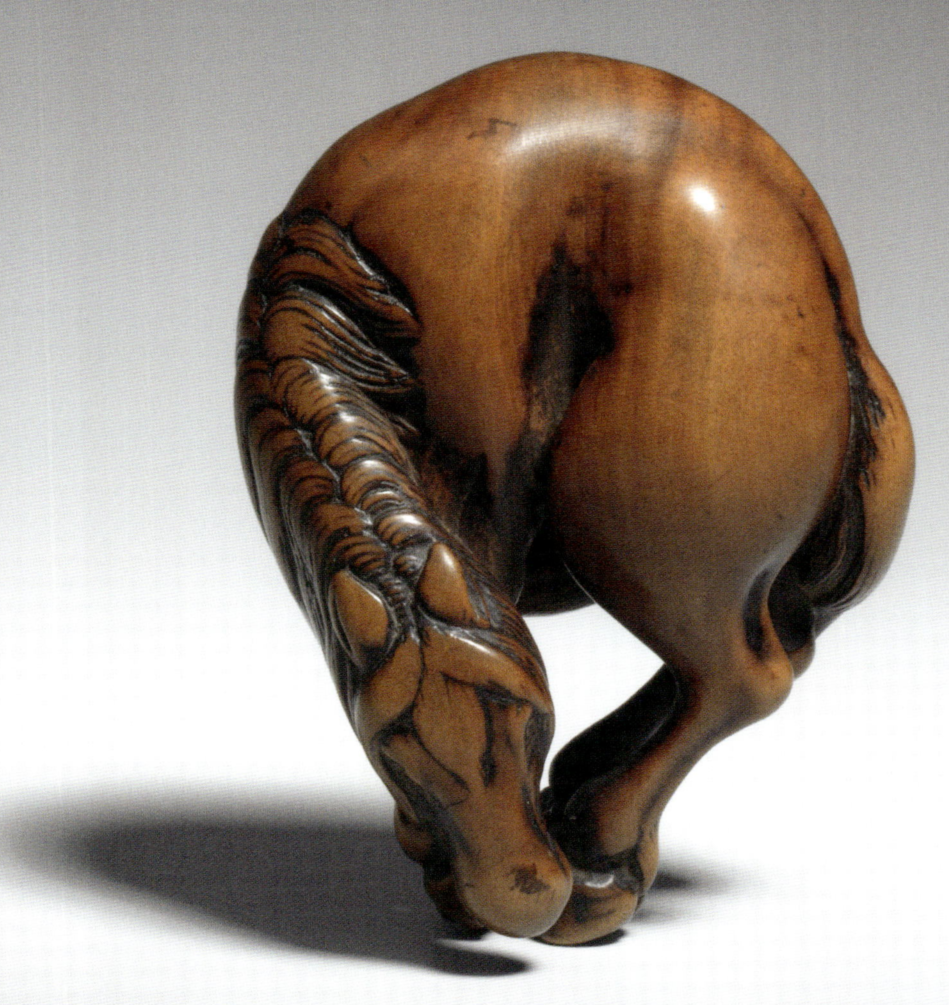

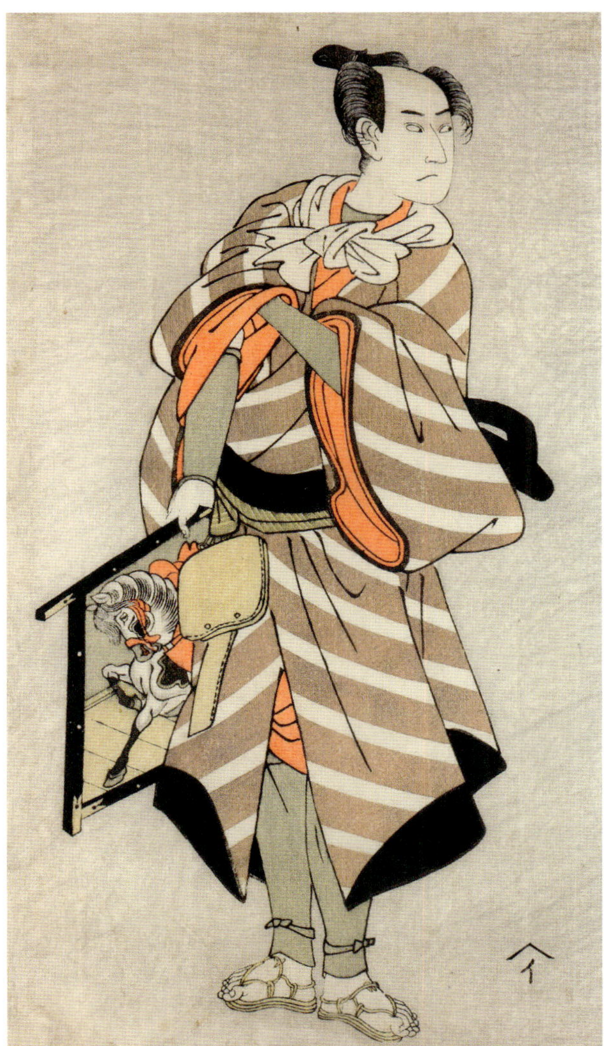

Kabuki actor Sawamura Sōjurō III holding a votive painting of a horse, with a tobacco pouch and pipe case hanging from his sash. Utagawa Toyokuni I (1769–1825), 1797. Colour woodblock print. 37.1 x 23.5 cm. British Museum 1909,0406,0.33.

Horse

As in many other cultures, the horse has long been admired in Japan, used as a steed for warriors and considered an object of worship also. In ancient times, people used to donate horses to shrines to gain the favour of the deities. Over time this custom has been replaced by the donation of painted wooden tablets known as *ema*, often depicting horses, on which the worshippers write their prayers and wishes (see left). This netsuke depicts a grazing horse, a favourite design. The horse's head is bent down, and its long tail swishes around to the back of the rump. The head and neck curve round via the arched body towards the hind legs, forming an elegant oval that is polished and smooth, contrasting with the flowing tresses of mane in high relief. The artist has rendered his subject in classic form, with gentle beauty.

—

Unsigned
Wood, late 1700s
H. 6.5 cm
British Museum 1981,0808.112
Bequeathed by Captain Collingwood Ingram

Reclining goat

The eighth animal in the zodiac cycle is the sheep. But as this animal was not indigenous to Japan, it has generally been depicted as a goat, as here. The reclining goat was carved by Kaigyokusai Masatsugu, who is considered one of the greatest netsuke carvers of the Osaka region, together with his contemporary, Ōhara Mitsuhiro. Masatsugu carved different types of animal, especially those represented in the zodiac cycle. His favourite material was ivory, of which he used only the finest quality. It is said that he was self-taught and had no teacher to help him to learn the carving techniques. So it is all the more remarkable that his netsuke always reveal extreme care in creating even the smallest details, such as ears, nose, mouth and feet – to superb perfection. Here the goat's head is turned back to the right and its limbs are folded naturally under the body. The dense fur is exquisitely engraved with long flowing strokes that beautifully continue around the base of the work. Many of Masatsugu's finest pieces are not stained. Instead he often used ink to accent facial features and fur, as seen in this example.

During the eighty years of his long life, Masatsugu experienced the Meiji Restoration of 1868 and saw the introduction of Western dress, which led to a fall in domestic demand for netsuke. In response to the new demand for netsuke from Westerners, however, his works were frequently designed to sit solidly on a flat surface and be used for decorative purposes. Although this netsuke has a natural opening between the belly and one hind leg on the underside, this hole is too small for practical use.

By Kaigyokusai Masatsugu (1813–1892)
Ivory, with eyes inlaid in coral and dark horn pupils
Osaka, late 1800s
H. 2.9 cm; w. 3.7 cm
British Museum HG.559
Given by Professor John and Mrs Anne Hull Grundy

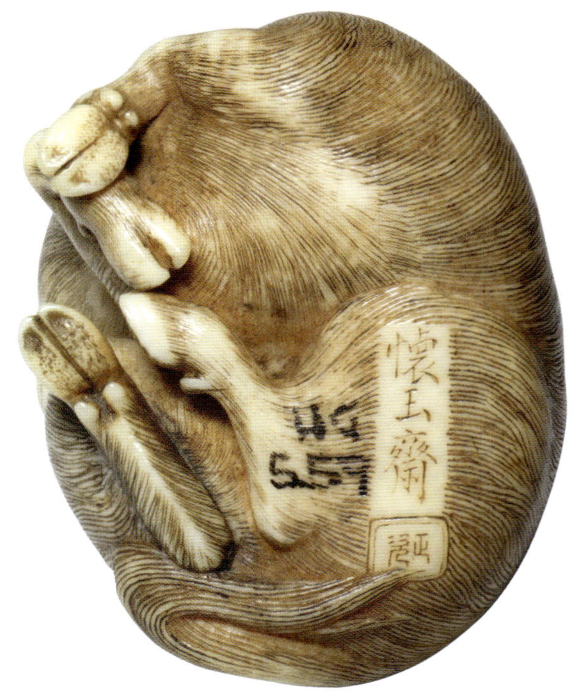

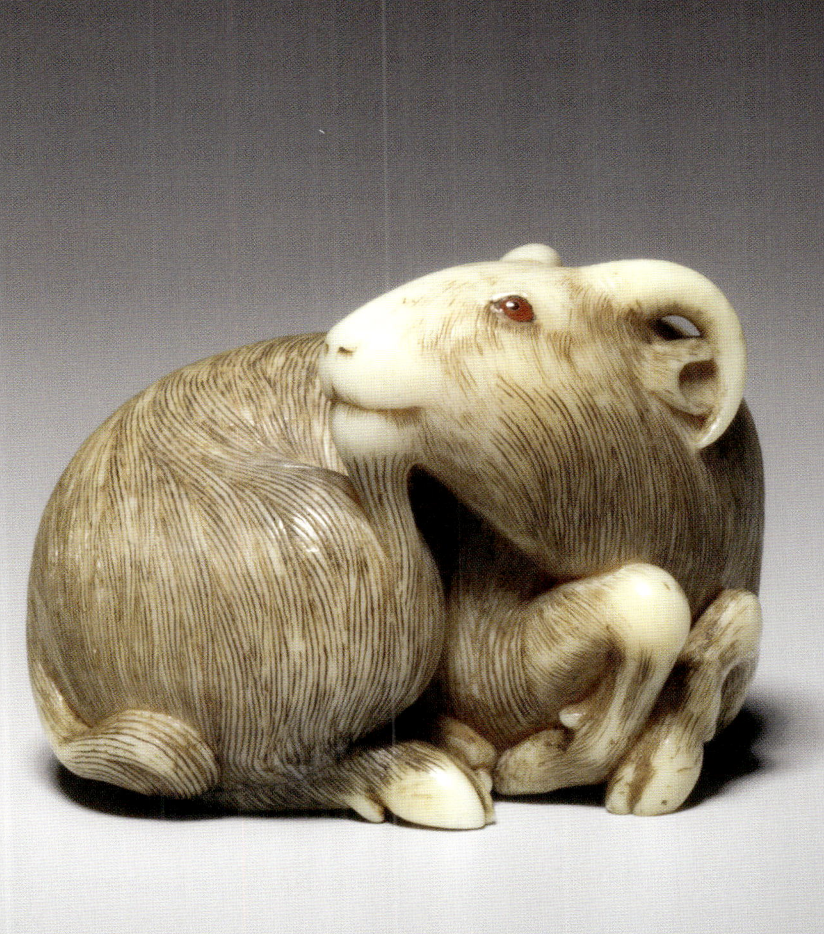

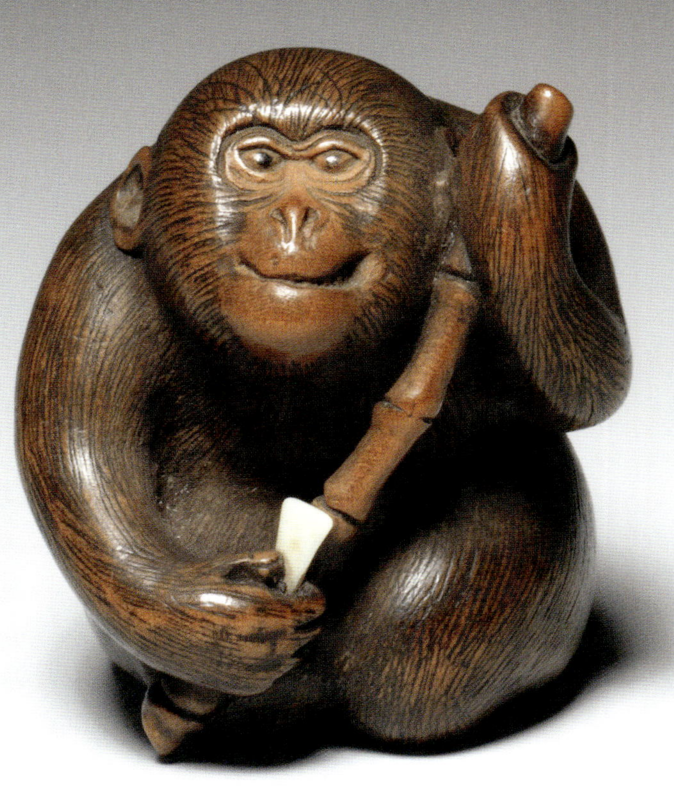

Seated ape

Apes are native to Japan and have traditionally played many roles in Japanese culture and religion. They may be depicted as divine messengers, protectors of horses in stables, or as the three wise apes, which embody the proverb 'see no evil, hear no evil, speak no evil'. In this netsuke, an ape sits on its heels with shoulders rounded, holding a length of bamboo and an ivory plectrum, as if playing a three-stringed banjo-like instrument, the *shamisen*. With the left corner of its mouth raised, half open, the ape appears as though it is about to sing. The pose of the animal appears quite natural and even emits a human-like aura. The history of anthropomorphic animals in Japanese art can be traced back to the famous set of four handscrolls, *Chōjū jinbutsu giga* (*Scrolls of Frolicking Animals*), painted in the twelfth and thirteenth centuries and preserved in the collection of Kōzanji temple, Kyoto. The first scroll, in particular, depicts lively anthropomorphized rabbits, apes and frogs engaging in many human activities, such as bathing, getting ready for a ceremony and wrestling. The much-loved artist Kawanabe Kyōsai (1831–1889) revived a similar theme half a millennium later, in the mid-nineteenth century (see below). For the Japanese people apes have always been an endearing and familiar animal, often depicted as being playful and having a sense of humour.

This netsuke was previously published in Barker and Smith 1976, p. 32, fig. 21.

—

By Tomochika
Wood and ivory, Osaka, early 1800s
H. 3.4 cm
British Museum F.679
Given by Sir Augustus Wollaston Franks

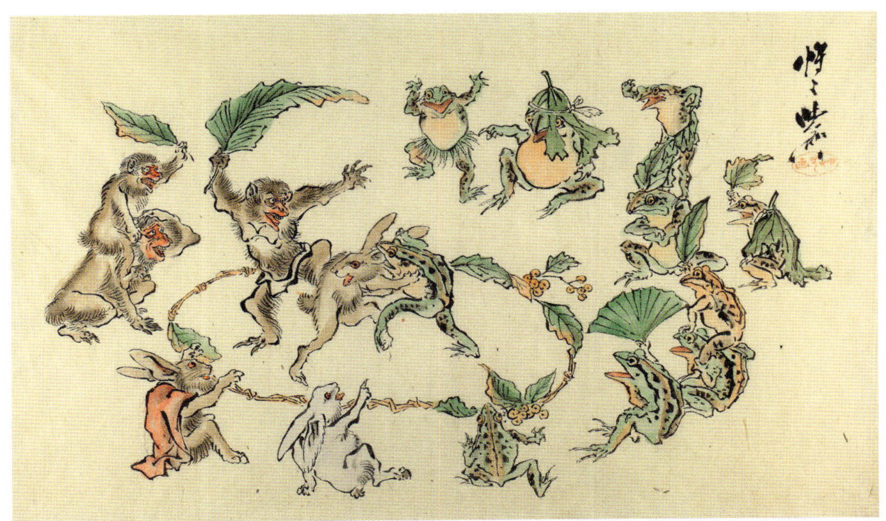

Frogs, rabbits and monkeys engaged in a sumō match. Kawanabe Kyōsai, ink and colour on paper, 1879. 38.1 x 53.3 cm. British Museum 1881,1210,0.1887.

Apes with persimmon

This is a good example of a netsuke exploiting the natural black colour of ebony, which acquires a smooth finish when polished. Here an ape, holding an amber persimmon with green-stained ivory leaves cradled between its arms, tries to protect this treasure from another, which climbs up to examine and possibly snatch the fruit. The faces of the apes are inlaid with coral and the carver shows extraordinary skill using different types of inlay in this single netsuke.

The motif of an ape with a persimmon is found in the Japanese folk tale, *Saru kani gassen* (*Monkey-Crab Battle*). In the story, a sly ape meets a crab holding a rice ball and persuades it to exchange the rice ball for a persimmon seed (see opposite). The crab plants the seed, which soon grows to supply abundant persimmons. The ape is then asked to climb the tree to pick some fruit for the crab. The ape, instead of doing as he was asked, eats the fruit by himself up in the tree. When the crab protests, the ape flings a fruit down at the crab and kills it. Punitive justice is the main theme of the story, with crab's offspring and their companions later getting their revenge on the monkey. In this netsuke, the ape is also depicted as a cunning and greedy animal.

—

By Hoichi (or Yasukazu)
Ebony, with details in coral, amber and stained ivory
Late 1800s
H. 2.9 cm
British Museum 1945,1017.642
Bequeathed by Oscar Charles Raphael

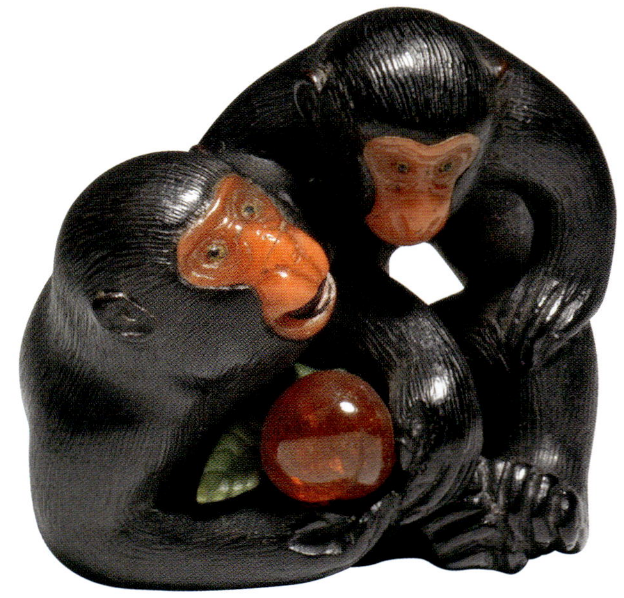

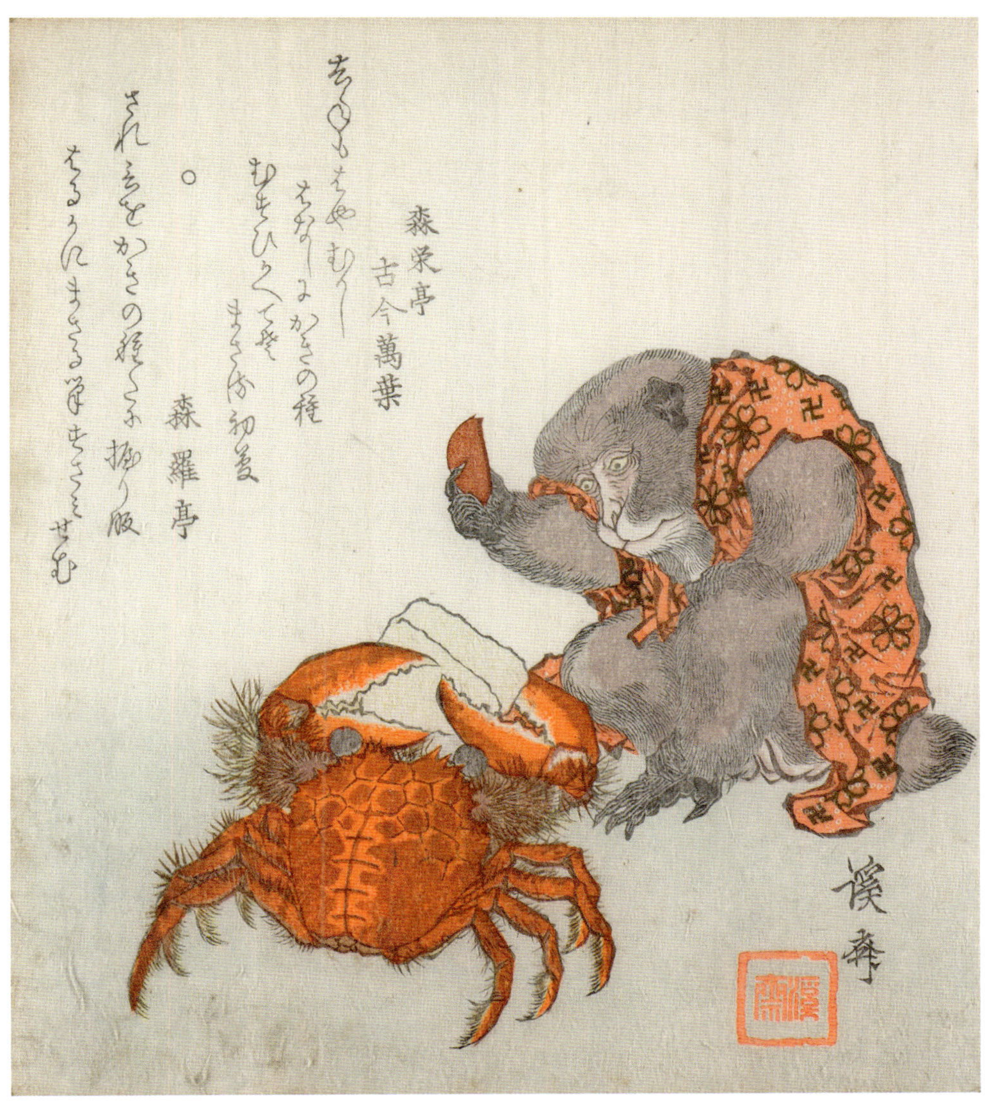

Monkey and crab with poem. Keisai Eisen (1790–1848), colour woodblock print (*surimono*), 1824.
20.4 x 17.9 cm. British Museum 1907,0531,0.448.

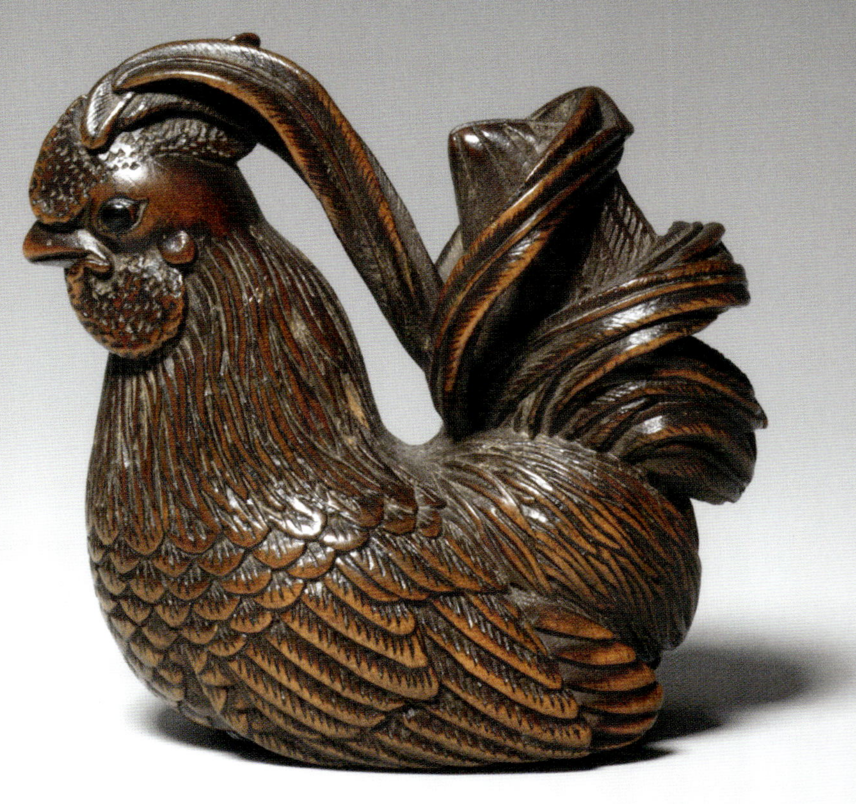

Cockerel

As the tenth sign of the Chinese zodiac and an auspicious
herald to welcome the sunrise, the cockerel has long been
a conspicuous motif in Japanese art. It is sometimes
depicted with a hen and chicks, and as a group they
become the symbol of a harmonious family. Prized
cockerels were also used in cockfights that were popular
throughout South East and East Asia and came to be seen
as symbols of virility, with individual birds garnering high
prices. Here a cockerel sits gracefully with its wings folded.
The carver has masterfully rendered various textures of the
feathers. While the comb and wattle are stippled, the long
sickles elegantly wind around the tail feathers. Yoshinaga
was mentioned in *Sōken kishō* (*Strange and Wonderful
Sword Fittings*), first published in 1781, and was one of
the principal masters working in Kyoto during the later
eighteenth century.

   This netsuke was also published in Harris 1987, p. 63,
fig. 265.

—

By Yoshinaga
Wood, with eyes inlaid in dark horn, Kyoto, late 1700s
H. 4.4 cm; W. 4.5 cm
British Museum HG.464
Given by Professor John and Mrs Anne Hull Grundy

Seated dog

As in many other countries, dogs are one of the most loved animals in Japan. They have appeared in a domestic role as man's faithful companion since the prehistoric Jōmon period (about 12,000–300 BC). In the Edo period (1615–1868), the fifth shogun Tokugawa Tsunayoshi (1646–1709) issued a proclamation protecting animals, especially dogs. It is said that his ruling derived partly from the fact that he was born in the year of the dog, and also because he was told by a Buddhist priest that the lack of the birth of a son to him might be due to his killing of dogs in a former life. In this work, the dog sits upright and alert with its head turning slightly to the left. Its large ears are pricked in readiness and its tongue hangs out, panting in anticipation. In Masanao's animals, distinctive characteristics tend to be slightly exaggerated, such as the large ears, thick neck and broad chest seen here. Depicting the animals in this way Masanao makes his subjects appear more lively, and his netsuke are uniquely memorable (see also pp. 108–109).

This netsuke was also published in Barker and Smith 1976, pp. 44–45, fig. 46.

—

By Masanao of Kyoto
Ivory with eyes inlaid in dark horn, Kyoto, late 1700s
w. 5 cm
British Museum F.772
Given by Sir Augustus Wollaston Franks

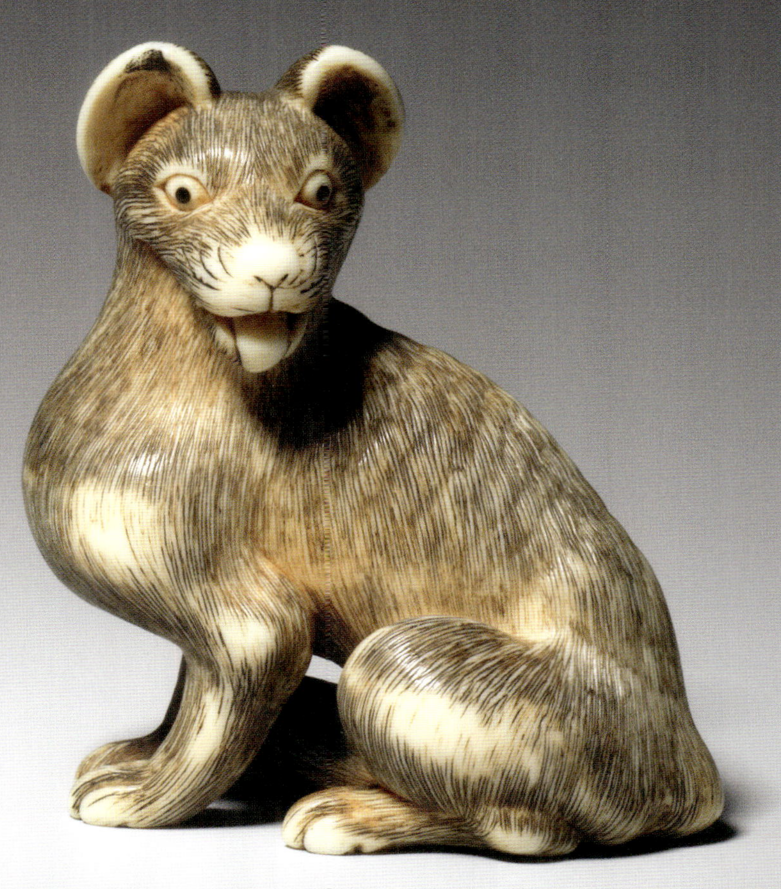

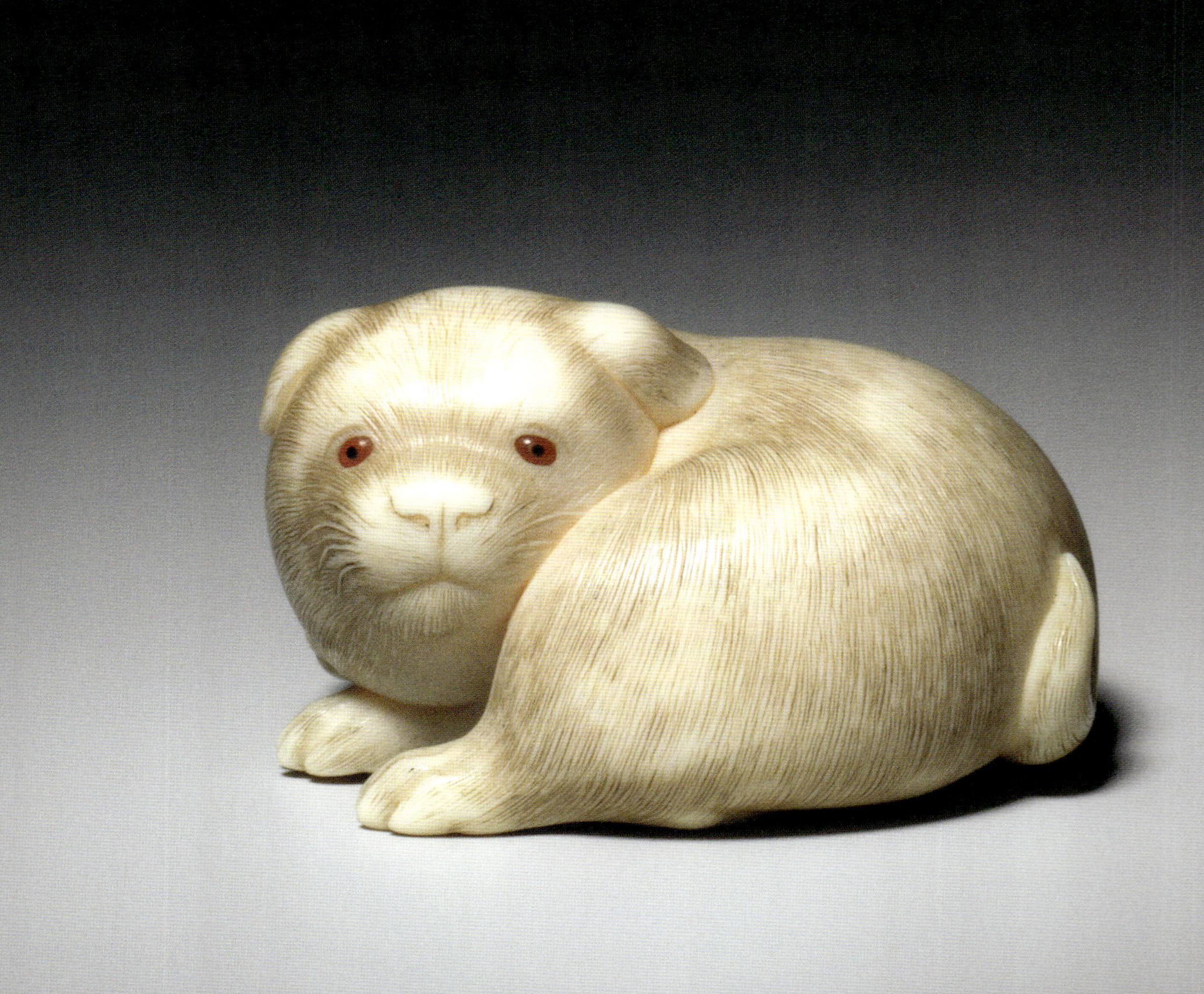

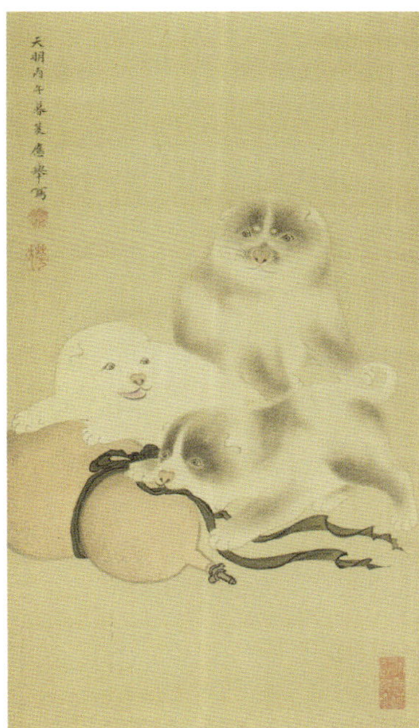

Three puppies with a gourd bottle (copy and detail), after Maruyama Ōkyo. Hanging scroll, ink and colours on silk, 1800s. 97.8 x 32.6 cm. British Museum 1881,1210,0.2255.

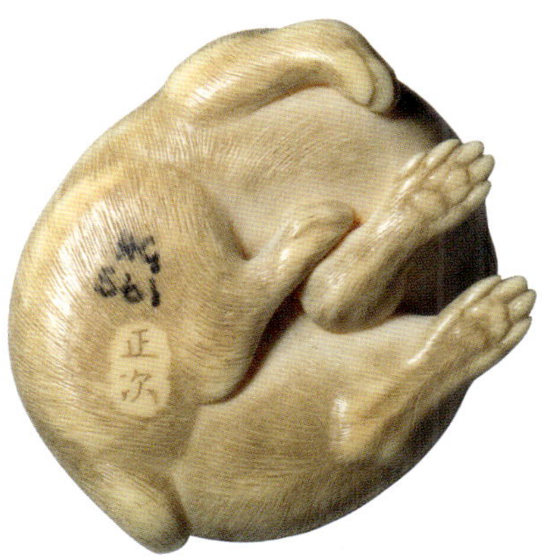

Puppy

This chubby and lovable puppy was carved by the famous netsuke maker of Osaka, Kaigyokusai Masatsugu. It is finely carved using high quality ivory, which Masatsugu always insisted on. As also seen on his goat (pp. 128–129), the fur on the sleek, plump body is engraved with long, delicate strokes. The puppy's whiskers are characteristically left in high relief, and its eyes are double-inlaid with coral and dark horn (as are the eyes of the goat). The face is endearing and all the innocent charm of a puppy is condensed into this single piece. This treatment is reminiscent of the chubby puppies typically done by the well-known painter Maruyama Ōkyo (1733–1795), who worked in Kyoto (see left). Ōkyo studied realism from imported paintings and his style emphasized the specific characteristics of his subjects after absorbing what he felt was their essence. He painted his puppies much plumper than is natural, for instance, appealing directly to our emotions. Kaigyokusai followed in the same strategy, as clearly seen in this alluring rotund puppy.

This netsuke was previously published in Harris 1987, p. 64, fig. 275.

—

By Kaigyokusai Masatsugu (1813-1892)
Ivory, with eyes inlaid in coral and dark horn pupils
Osaka, late 1800s
w. 4 cm
British Museum HG.561
Given by Professor John and Mrs Anne Hull Grundy

Boar and snake

In Japan the boar occupies the last position among the twelve animals of the zodiac cycle. In China the pig is traditionally assigned this last position, but as the pig is not a species native to Japan the indigenous boar took its place. The boar rushes headlong into attack, and is therefore regarded as a symbol of courage that is occasionally reckless. Here a recumbent boar, with upturned snout, struggles to escape from the snake that coils tightly around it. While its hind legs are flexed under its bulky body, the boar's forelegs rest on the curled snake's body. The snake's forked tongue licks at the ear of the boar. The snake is exactly six animals apart from the boar in the twelve-year animal cycle, and the two were therefore considered companions. Wearing a netsuke that featured paired zodiac animals was believed to combine the strengths of the animals and thereby enhance good luck.

This boar and snake netsuke was carved by Sukenaga, who lived in Hida province (present-day Gifu prefecture), which lies inland to the north of the city of Nagoya. Hida province is surrounded by mountains and forests and has a long-established tradition of wood carving. Born into a family of chopstick makers, Sukenaga is especially renowned for his acute skills of observation in the naturalistic representation of reptilian scales. This skill can be seen here in the luxurious rendition of the snake's scales, which are first dark stained then carved, after careful observation and planning, so as to feature the natural colour of the wood. Sukenaga is also admired as a master of the 'carving with a single knife' (*ittōbori*) technique, which became a hallmark of carving from Hida province.

This netsuke was previously published in Barker and Smith 1976, pp. 110–111, fig. 206.

By Matsuda Sukenaga (1800–1871)
Wood, with eyes inlaid in dark horn
Hida province, mid 1800s
w. 4.5 cm
British Museum F.676
Given by Sir Augustus Wollaston Franks

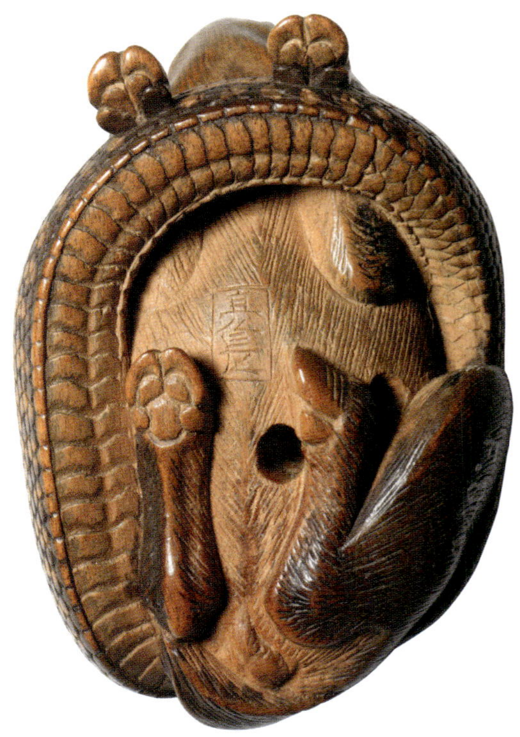

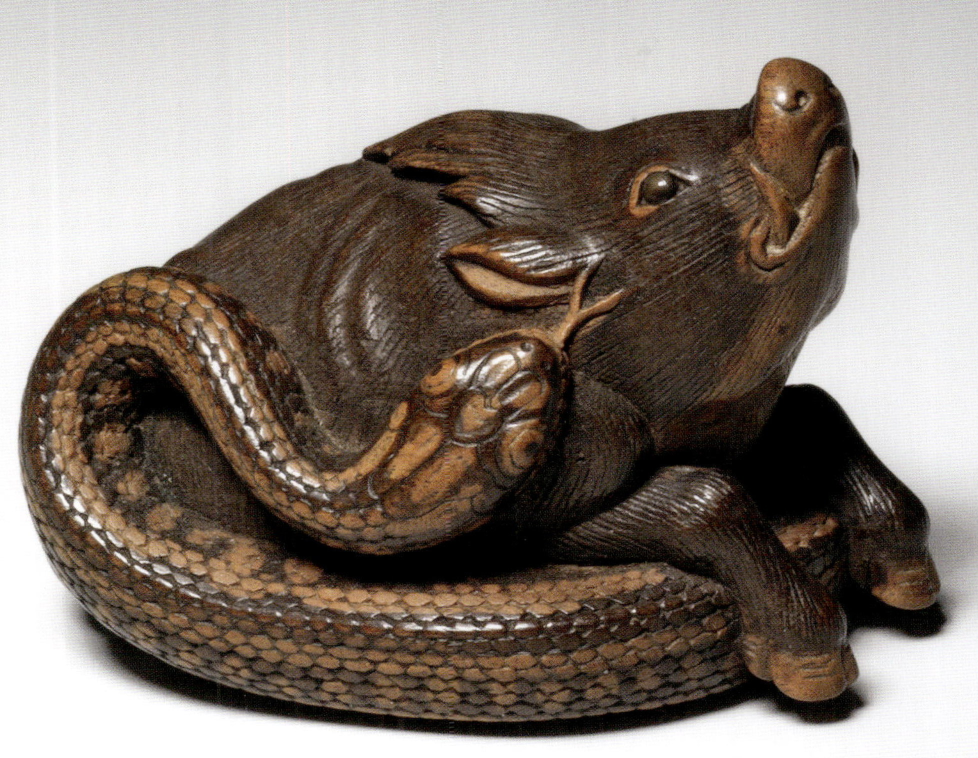

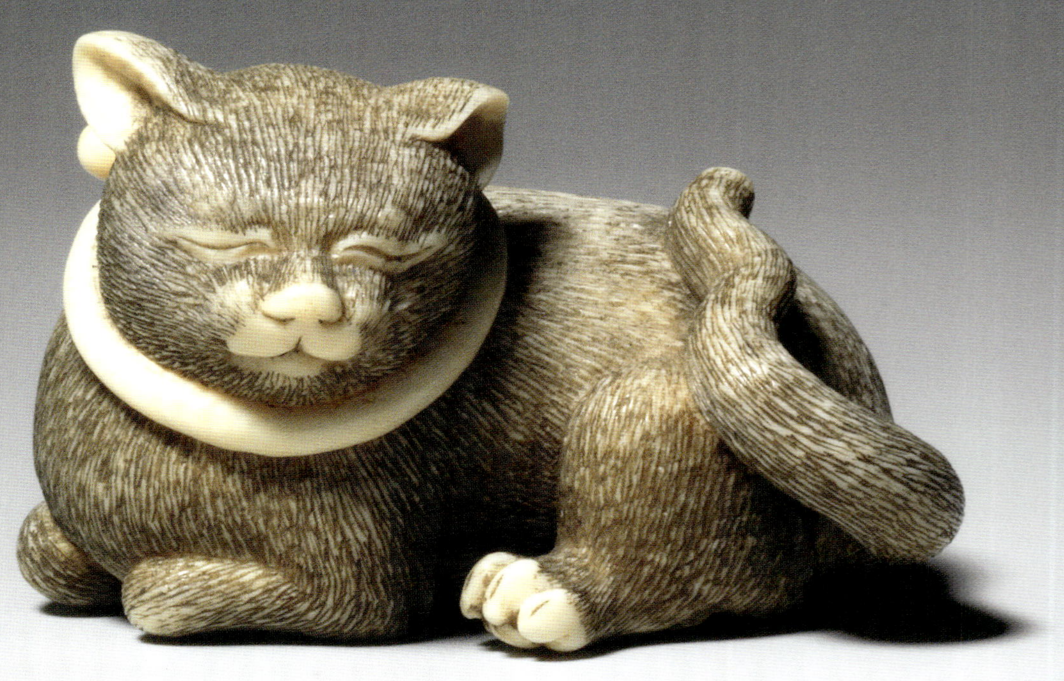

Sleeping cat

Through the ages, the cat has suffered from an undeserved reputation of being wily, sneaky and deceptive, probably due to its solitary nature and nocturnal habits. However, this netsuke of a sleeping cat catches the true loveable and endearing nature of the animal. Active at night, the cat usually sleeps most of the day. Here we see a domestic cat with a soft collar around its neck, dozing contentedly with its eyes closed. The head is rendered rather large, one of the ears perks up, and the thick tail is curled up against the body. The famous wood carving of a sleeping cat, the *nemuri neko*, is located at Tōshōgū shrine in Nikkō, which was dedicated posthumously to Tokugawa Ieyasu (1542–1616), the founder of the Tokugawa shogunate. The Nikkō cat sculpture is a symbol of peace, since the realm is so peaceful that even a cat can doze, and it had has long been of a source of inspiration for Japanese artists. It was not until the nineteenth century, however, that the true charming aspects of cats came to be depicted. Print artist Utagawa Kuniyoshi (1797–1861), who was known for his love of cats and kept many of them, observed closely their daily behaviour and expression (see p. 144). The carver of this netsuke must also have had the opportunity for close observation, as revealed here in details such as the well-padded paws underneath the body.

This netsuke was previously published in Barker and Smith 1976, p. 58, fig. 74.

—

Unsigned
Ivory, Osaka, about 1820–1840
w. 4.3 cm
British Museum F.778
Given by Sir Augustus Wollaston Franks

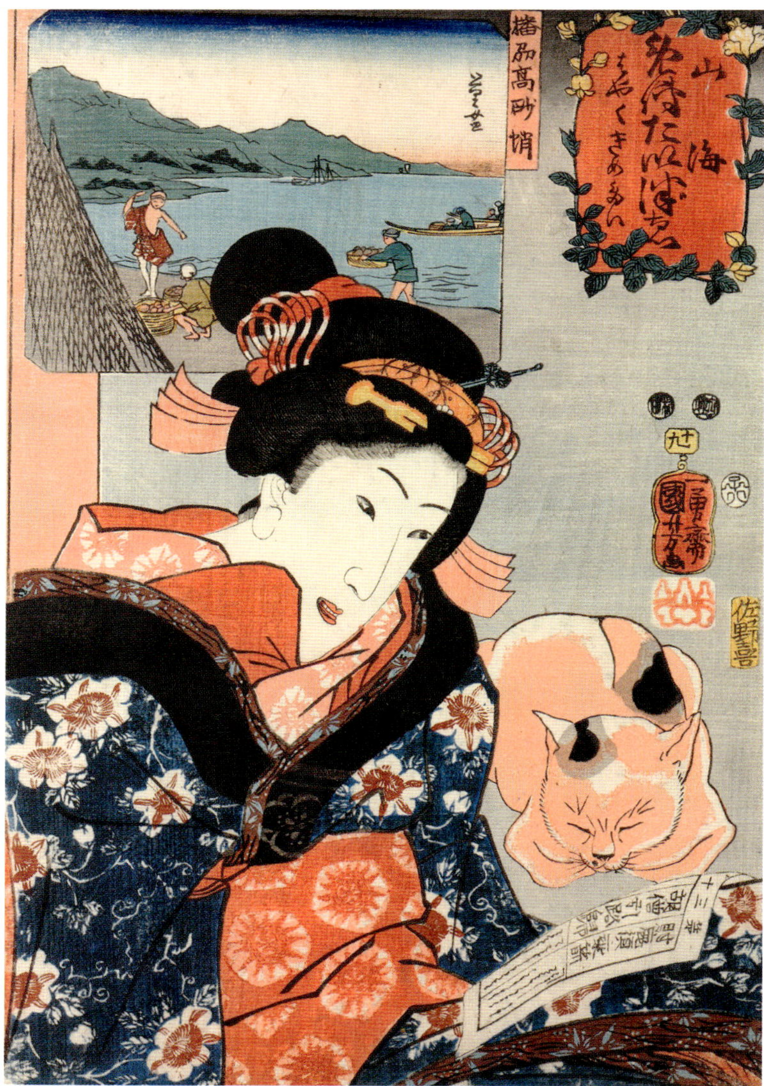

Woman reading a printed almanac with a sleeping cat beside her. Utagawa Kuniyoshi, colour woodblock print, 1852. 35.2 x 25.2 cm. British Museum 2008,3037.02115. Loaned by the American Friends of the British Museum (Prof. Arthur R. Miller collection).

Two dromedaries

This netsuke depicts two dromedaries snuggled closely together, with their long necks turned so as to look at each other in an affectionate pose. Their bodies are deliberately polished, rendering the netsuke extremely sleek, and their expressions are gentle, projecting an elegant mood. During the Edo period (1615–1868), Dutch traders occasionally brought large and exotic animals as gifts for the shogun. Drawing on their Indian Ocean trading networks, these exotic animals included tigers, parrots, ostriches, elephants and camels. A pair of dromedaries that was brought to Japan in 1821 gained great popularity.

As part of a menagerie, these dromedaries made the long trip from Nagasaki to Edo (present-day Tokyo) along the highways, causing enormous excitement and curiosity among the general populace. It was believed that to view rare animals which were not native to Japan – much as a prayer to Buddhist images – would drive away evil spirits or prevent disease. Artists quickly tried to record the likeness of these animals and many anonymous broadsheet prints, *kawara-ban*, and books were created rapidly to report every single piece of information known about the animals to the public. This netsuke might have been carved in response to the boom around the importation of these two dromedaries.

A similar, unsigned netsuke is illustrated in Meinertzhagen 1956, no. 128.

This netsuke was previously published in Barker and Smith 1976, p. 144, fig. 314.

—

Unsigned
Wood, with eyes inlaid in dark horn, early 1800s
H. 3.4 cm; w. 4.3 cm
British Museum 1945,1017.533
Bequeathed by Oscar Charles Raphael

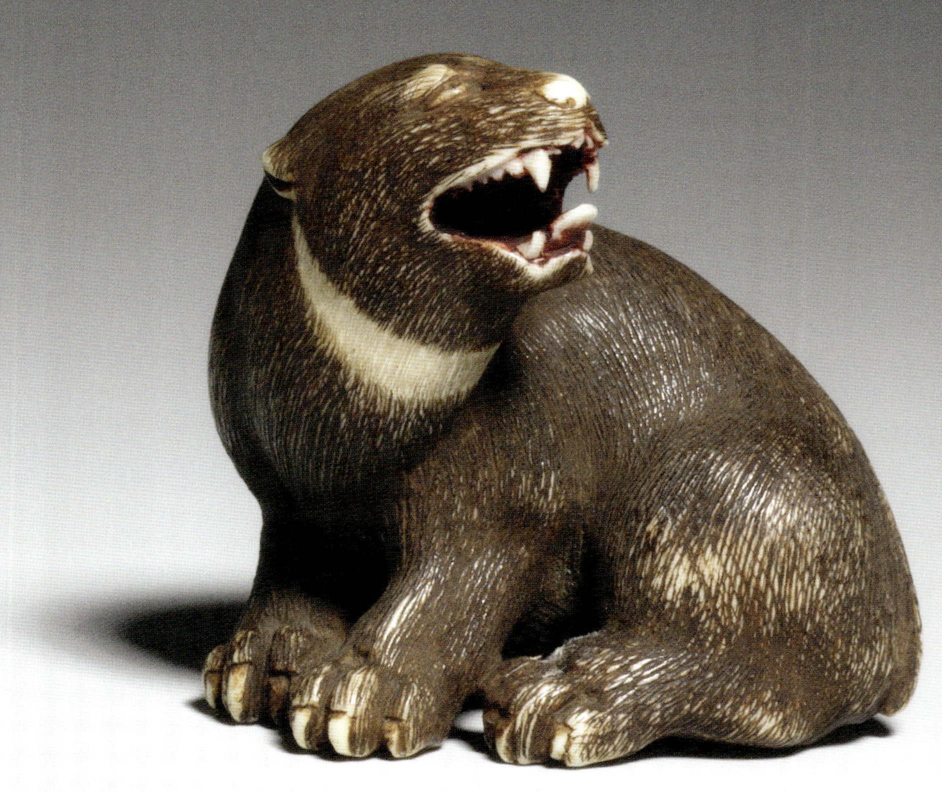

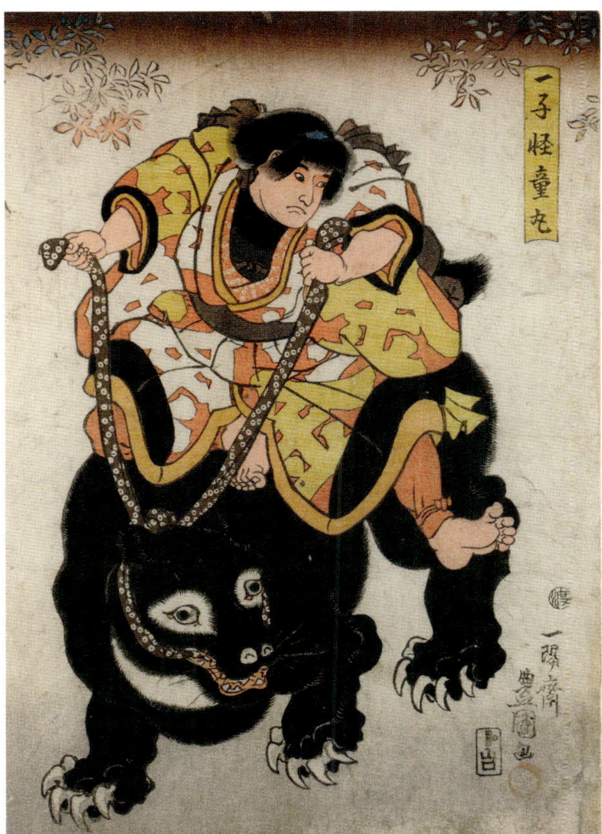

Kintarō riding a black bear. Utagawa Kunisada (1786–1864), colour woodblock print, mid 1840s. 36 x 25.5 cm. British Museum 1902,0212,0.332.

Black bear

Bears have long been hunted in Japan and also appear frequently in Japanese folk tales. The most famous is probably the story of Kintarō, a child with superhuman strength. He is said to have been raised by a mountain hag, Yamauba, who lived on Mount Ashigara. His friends were the animals of the mountain, including a bear, and he grew up wrestling with them. Kintarō is typically depicted as a plump and ruddy boy, wearing only a bib, and holding an enormous axe, or sometimes riding a bear (see left).

This netsuke of a black bear, with a crescent-shaped white mark on its neck, turns its head to the left and snarls with gaping mouth. Although unsigned, its characteristics suggest the hand of the great carver Matsushita Otoman, who worked in Hakata. As with the snarling tiger also attributed to Otoman (see pp. 116–117), the carver added a red stain to the inside of the mouth, and created sharp teeth that are finely realized. The protruding tongue is another feature typical of Otoman, seen in both his figural and animal subjects. The entire body of the bear was stained in black ink, but the maker skilfully left the natural white ivory colour for the facial features, neck mark and claws.

—

Unsigned, attributed to Matsushita Otoman
Ivory, early 1800s
H. 3.5 cm; w. 3.7 cm
British Museum F.673
Given by Sir Augustus Wollaston Franks

Elephant and man in the form of a seal

Elephants, like dromedaries (see p. 145), are not native to Japan, but were brought to Japan as gifts for the shogun on several occasions during the Edo period (1615–1868). The elephants surely impressed Edo-period Japanese people with their enormous forms.

This netsuke depicts a kneeling elephant, with its trunk slung to the left and a chain wrapped around its body. A man, wearing only a loincloth, is trying to mount the beast by grasping the elephant's ear and placing his foot on its kneeling foreleg. The man's posture is like a puppet, with only simple facial features depicted. On the other hand, the elephant looks well trained and obedient, with its appealing round inlaid eyes. This is one of the oldest netsuke in the British Museum, and as a result of its age and handling, it has garnered a beautiful golden patina.

The netsuke takes the form of a seal, although the underside is plain without any inscribed characters. During the late Ming period (1368–1644), a large quantity of Chinese seals made of various materials such as wood, ivory, bronze or semi-precious stone were imported into Japan (see p. 13). A sculptural carving was often attached to the top of these seals, which might have served as a design source for netsuke carvers. This example was probably carved to imitate a seal rather than for use as an actual seal. The seal netsuke, whether for use or not, became a standard netsuke format and designs of this type were illustrated in an Edo-period printed book *Chōkō hinagata* (*Models for Carving*), published in 1827.

—

Unsigned
Ivory, with eyes inlaid in dark horn, about 1700
H. 5.5 cm; w. 5.2 cm
British Museum 1945,1017.636
Bequeathed by Oscar Charles Raphael

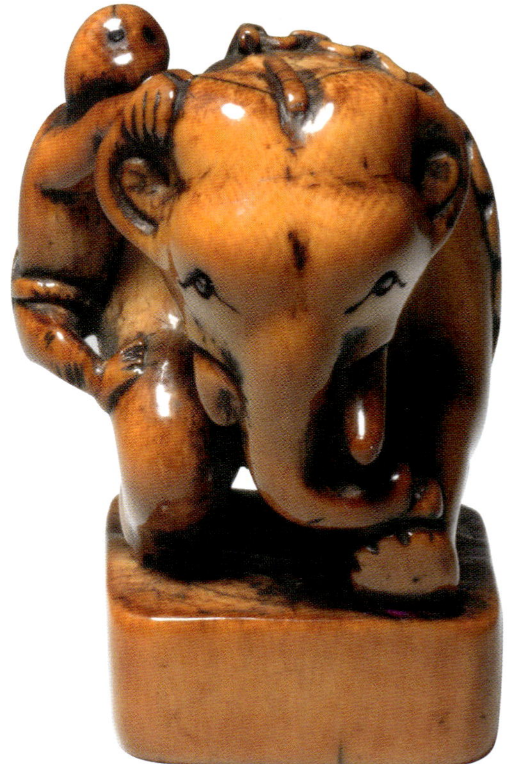

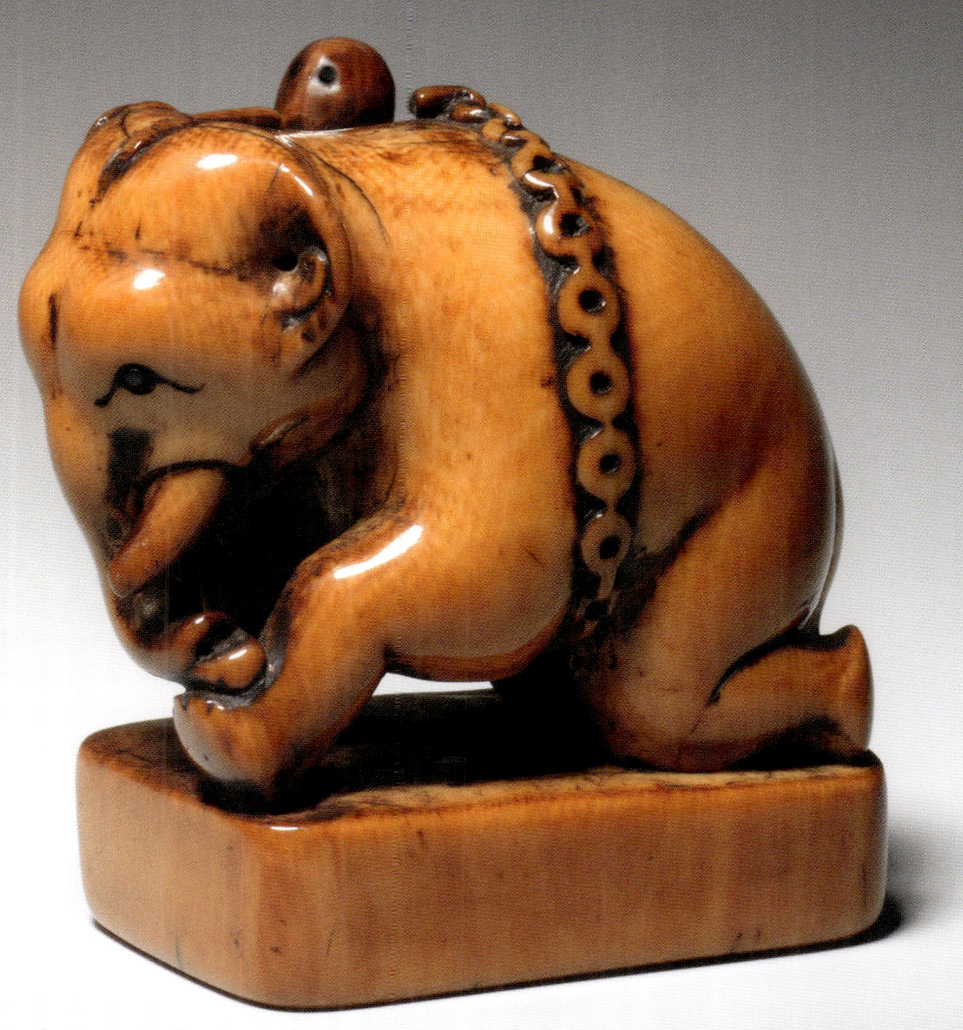

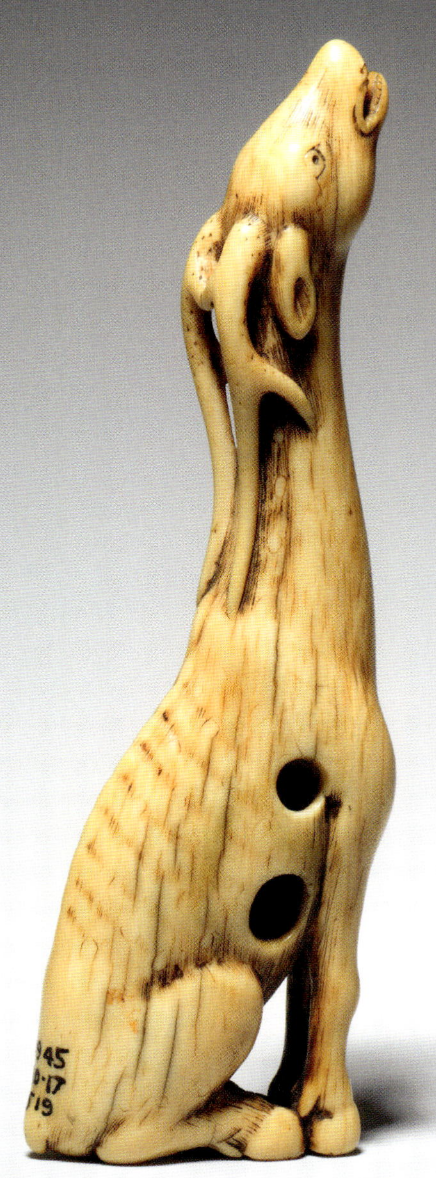

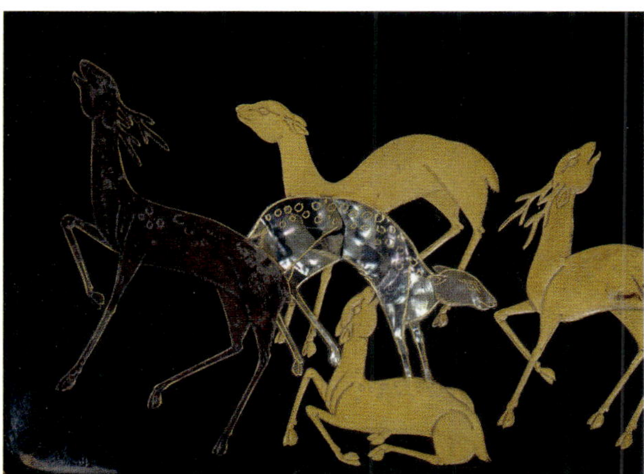

Detail of the lid of a lacquer writing-box, seventeenth century. w. 23.5 cm; D. 21 cm; H. 9.5 cm (with lid). British Museum 1974,0513.8.a-b.

Crying deer

The deer is a symbol of autumn in Japan. A deer calling to seek its mate in the mountains has often been used to evoke a melancholy mood. Deer often appear in classical poems, *waka*, from ancient times referring by inference to the desolate feelings of poets who long for their partners when far away from them. In paintings deer are sometimes depicted with maple trees, and a beautiful vignette of deer crying in autumn is depicted in lacquer and mother-of-pearl on the interior of the lid of a seventeenth-century writing box in the British Museum (see left). This graceful, seated deer netsuke with upturned head cries towards the moon. The animal's slender body is enhanced by its extended neck and the treatment of its antlers which lie flat against the back of its neck. The simplicity of the composition contrasts with the attention to such details as the spotted markings of the deer's coat, the prominent ribs and the stippled surface of the antlers.

This netsuke was previously published in Barker and Smith 1976, pp. 50–51, fig. 59. Further information about its provenance can be found in W. L. Behrens, illustrated in Joly 1912, reprinted 1966, no. 1542A, pl. XXVI.

—

Unsigned, in the style of Izumiya Tomotada
Ivory, late 1700s
H. 9.5 cm
British Museum 1945,1017.519
Bequeathed by Oscar Charles Raphael

Elephant

The miracle of this stag antler netsuke lies in the carver's ability to capture an enormous motif and convert it into an extremely tiny object. An elephant crouches on a round base. Its body is smoothly rendered using the challenging, uneven material of stag antler that varies from smooth areas to more spongy areas. The trunk and tail touch and curl softly in opposite directions, and the tusks and claws are carved with a delicate sharpness. However, the most unusual aspects of the elephant are its caterpillar-like eyebrows and the smiling slits of its eyes. These were distinctive characteristics of the style of Ishikawa Rensai, who worked in the Asakusa district in Tokyo.

An elephant with smiling eyes also reminds us of the beasts depicted by Itō Jakuchū (1716–1800), the famous eccentric painter of the mid-Edo period (1615–1868) who was active in Kyoto (see below). Jakuchū painted white elephants in profile to show their oddly shaped, smiling eyes on panels and folding screens in ink, and occasionally in colour. Rensai's designs, which are similarly full of originality, may have been influenced by the example of this earlier painter. Underneath, there are two large holes for the cord (*himotōshi*). Notwithstanding its small size, this netsuke has a strong and powerful aura.

This netsuke was previously published in Barker and Smith 1976, p. 92, fig. 158.

—

Unsigned, attributed to Ishikawa Rensai
Stag antler, Tokyo, 1870s
w. 2.6 cm
British Museum OA+.226

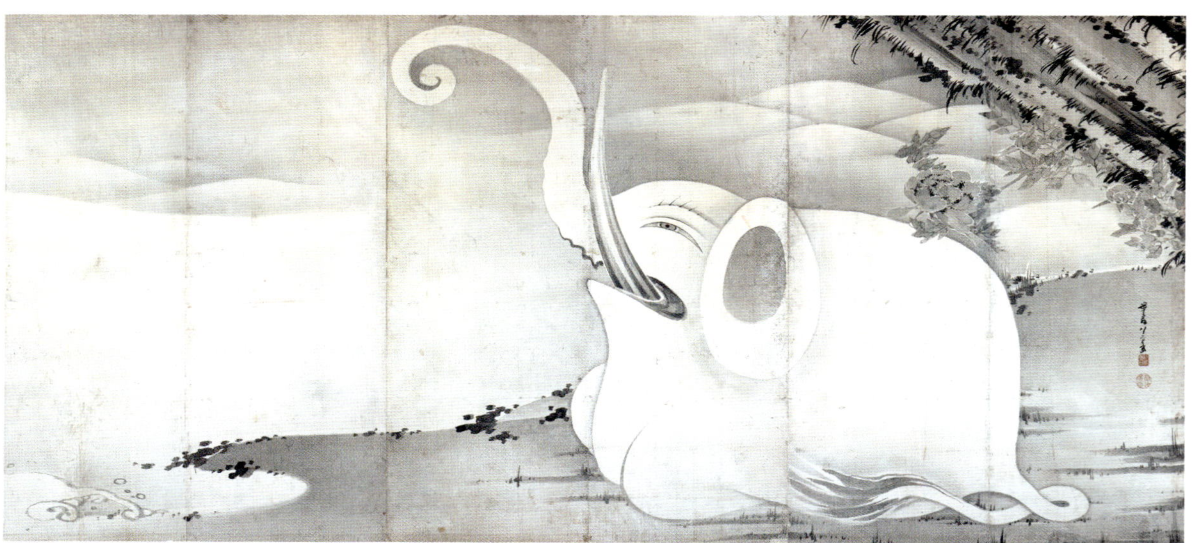

Black whale and white elephant (right screen), from a pair of six folding screens. Itō Jakuchū, ink on paper, 1795. 159.4 x 354 cm. Miho Museum, Shiga prefecture.

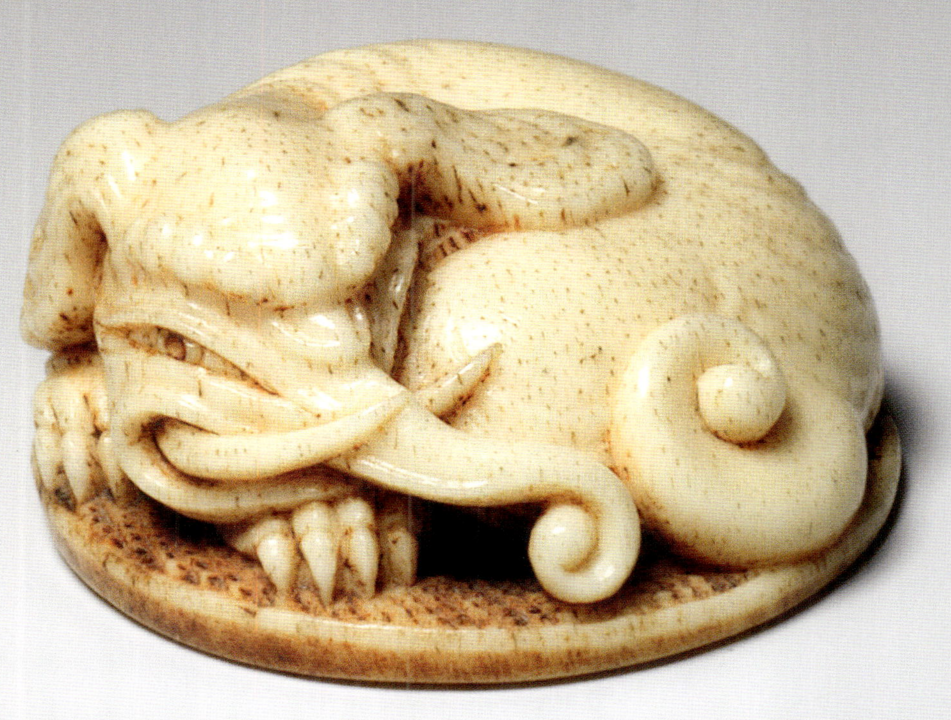

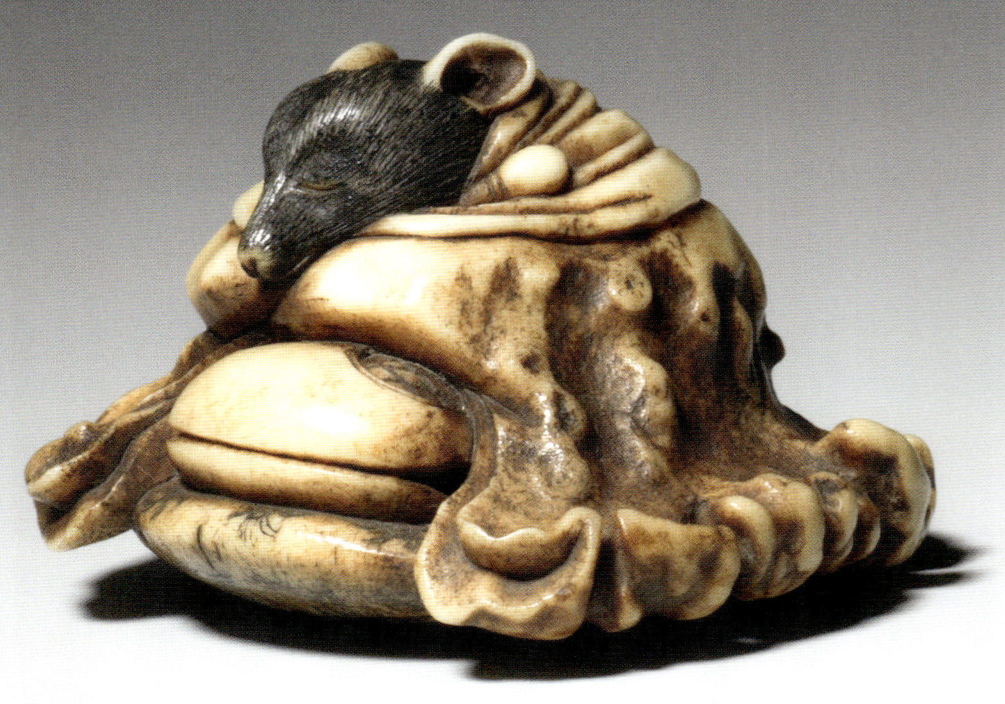

Racoon dog dressed as a priest

The racoon dog or *tanuki* appears in various Japanese folklores as one of the most mischievous animals. With its ability to shape shift, the *tanuki* often transforms itself into human form or inanimate objects in order to play tricks on people. It is also depicted as having a distended stomach or enlarged scrotum, which they are even known to beat like a drum. Here a *tanuki*, wearing a priest's robe, dozes while holding a Buddhist wooden gong (J. *mokugyo*) under its clothing, with the stick clutched to its breast.

Hōshunsai Masayuki was one of the most talented carvers from the Asakusa district of Tokyo. He worked at about the same time as Kokusai (see p. 102–103) and Rensai (see p. 152–153), and all three were partial to the use of stag antler. Here he has inventively adapted his design to the shapes and varied textures of the material. The robe's folds were formed, for example, from the wrinkled, broken edges of the crown. When we examine the underside, we recognize a crying face, with the two cord holes forming a nose and open mouth. Moreover, the forehead is simultaneously the distended scrotum of the *tanuki*, replete with engorged blood vessels. As seen in this example, Masayuki's carvings are full of originality, with a sense of humour to the design, making them uniquely attractive.

This netsuke was previously published in Barker and Smith 1976, pp. 92–93, fig. 157.

—

By Hōshunsai Masayuki
Stag antler, Tokyo, 1870s
w. 4 cm
British Museum F.809
Given by Sir Augustus Wollaston Franks

Hawk's claw

This rare subject was no doubt inspired by netsuke made from such things as bear and monkey paws, and the feet of raptors and other birds, which were not uncommon in themselves. These trophies were made into netsuke by attaching a metal mount with a ring to the severed animal part. Wearing such netsuke that incorporates a part of an animal's body was believed to protect the wearer from any evil spirits from the natural world. The hawk (J. *taka*) in particular was viewed as a symbol of courage, power and masculinity. Hunting with hawks was a popular sport among the samurai class during the Edo period (1615–1868). Hawks used in this sport were so highly regarded that the owners spent large sums of money to obtain a beautiful specimen and train them. A sharp bill and talons, as well as their beautiful quills, were considered the most important parts of the bird and they were pared, polished and preened by professional hawk trainers, *takajō*. The possession of fine hawks was a great source of pride for their owners and they were often portrayed in various art forms (see right).

The netsuke shown here is realistically carved with a scaly leg, sharp talons and foot with wrinkled skin, revealing the carver's mastery in depicting different textures. Masanao, considered by many to be one of the greatest netsuke carvers of all time, goes all out to give us a lifelike rendering of this subject.

This netsuke was previously published in Barker and Smith 1976, p. 42, fig. 42, and Lazarnick (ed.), MCI, vol.1, 1986, p. 444.

—

By Masanao of Kyoto
Ivory, Kyoto, late 1700s
w. 5.9 cm
British Museum 1945,1017.628
Bequeathed by Oscar Charles Raphael

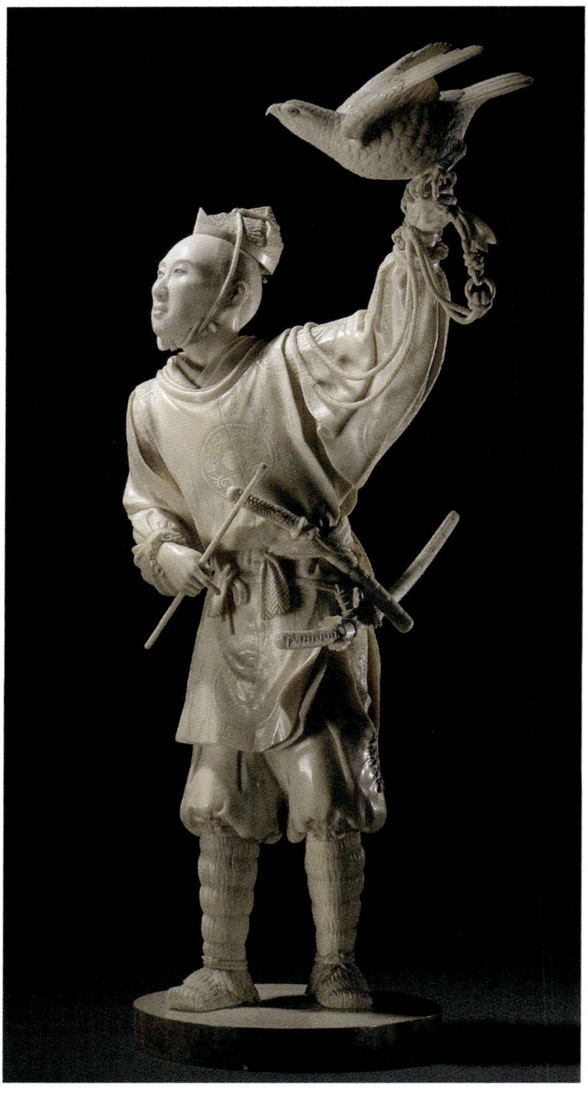

Ivory ornament (*okimono*) of a falconer, about 1900. H. 43.5 cm. British Museum 1979,0702.3.

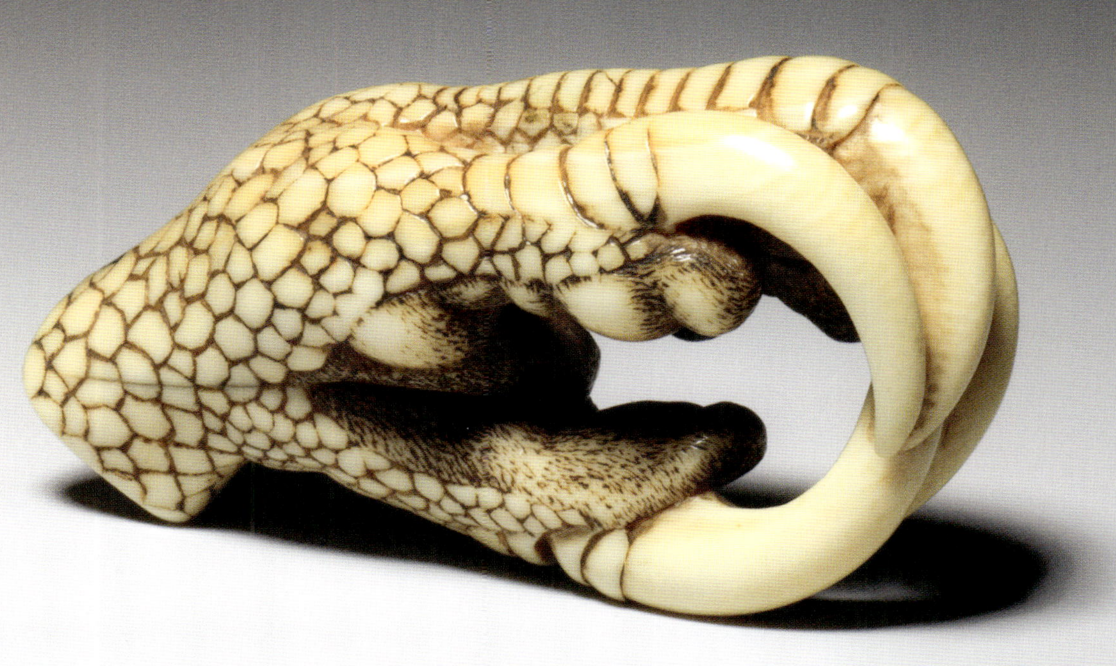

Frog on a curled lotus leaf

In this elegantly slender netsuke, a frog with protruding eyes clings on top of an unopened lotus leaf. The frog in netsuke form is quite often carved atop other things, such as a broken roof-tile, bucket, straw sandal or a branch. However, the most picturesque combination is with aquatic plants. On account of its cleanliness and innocence, the frog is often depicted with the sacred flower of Buddhism, the lotus, or with the lotus leaf. The ridged body of the frog with its long-toed, webbed feet makes a pleasing contrast to the smoothly polished surface of the leaf. The textured skin of the amphibian is rendered using the technique called *ukibori*, literally, 'raised carving', one of the characteristic skills of the Iwami school of carvers. The *ukibori* technique is usually employed for features in relief such as scales and warts on fish and amphibians, and the Iwami school carvers skilfully used the technique on ivory as well.

Iwami province (present-day Shimane prefecture) produced some of the most distinctive netsuke outside of the main urban centres of Edo (present-day Tokyo) and Kyoto. It was geographically isolated with wild natural scenery and so carvers there tended to choose their subjects from among local plants and animals, occasionally reptiles, amphibians and insects. Although it is unsigned, this netsuke is attributed to Seiyōdō Tomiharu (d. 1811), the leading master of the Iwami school and its most prolific artist. Based on careful study from life, he carved with great sensitivity, working chiefly in ebony, black persimmon and boar tusk.

A netsuke of the same subject signed Tomiharu is in the Victoria and Albert Museum, A.982-1910.

This netsuke was previously published in Barker and Smith 1976, p. 114, fig. 216.

—

Unsigned, Iwami school, in the style of Seiyōdō Tomiharu
Dark stained wood, Iwami province, late 1700s
w. 8.2 cm
British Museum F.801
Given by Sir Augustus Wollaston Franks

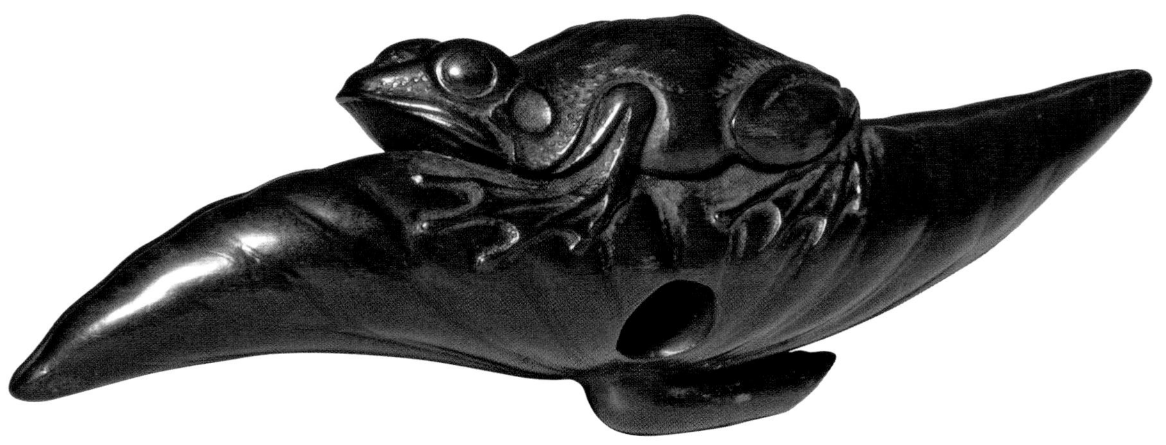

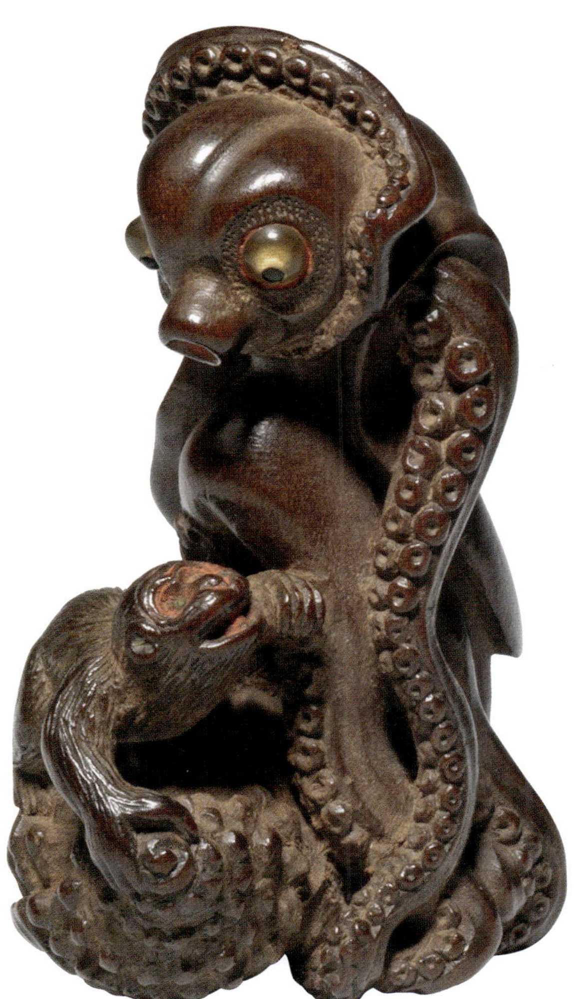

Octopus and monkey

In this comical netsuke, a large octopus wearing a coat towers over a terrified small monkey, which grips onto a conch shell. This combination of octopus and monkey, a favourite of the carver's, alludes to an episode from the popular legend of the Dragon King of the Sea, who was believed to live in an underwater palace. One day the Dragon King became dangerously unwell and the octopus, his doctor, prescribed the liver of a live monkey as the cure for the illness. The octopus was sent to the earth to find a monkey, but failed in his mission. Here the octopus, with paunchy stomach, stands on its own tentacles like a human, playfully raising one of the legs to its head. Meanwhile, the poor monkey gazes up in awe at its nemesis, its mouth agape. There are highlights in red pigment round the eyes and mouth of the octopus, and on the face of the monkey.

The carver, Minkō, was active in Tsu, the principal town of Ise province (present-day Mie prefecture). As a rule his carving style is generally good-naturedly rustic and somewhat crude; here, however, the details of the suckers and the monkey's fur are well rendered, exploiting the texture of the material to the full.

—

By Tanaka Minkō (1735-1816)
Wood, with eyes inlaid in pale and dark horn
Tsu, early 1800s
H. 4.7 cm
British Museum F.289
Given by Sir Augustus Wollaston Franks

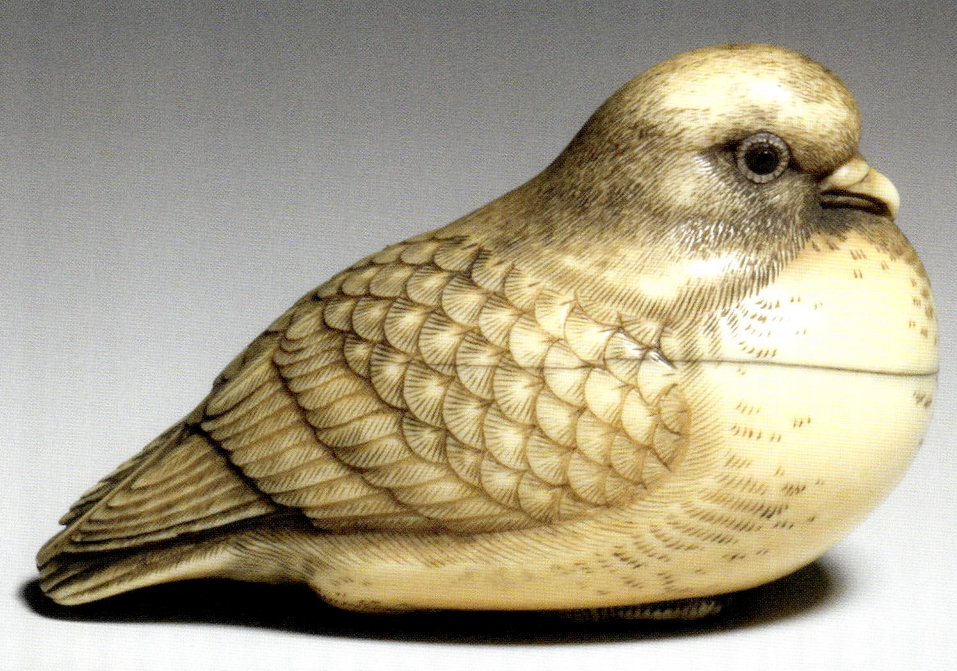

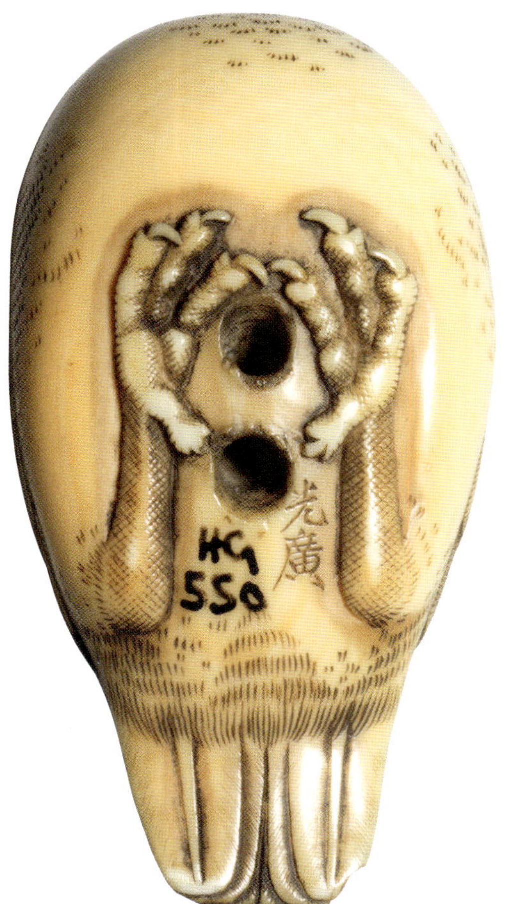

Pigeon

The pigeon, or *hato*, was a familiar bird in Japan, and it is known that carrier pigeons were used for commercial purposes in the Edo period (1615–1868). This beautiful ivory pigeon is a closely-observed depiction, carved by Ōhara Mitsuhiro from Osaka (see also pp. 114–115 and 168–169). The pigeon rests on the ground with its bulging body and broad chest, and has an overall rounded shape. The carver masterfully employs his characteristic techniques to represent different textures, from the finely stippled head to the varied feathers of body, wings and tail, all of which are stained with ink. The eyes have received special attention, with pupils inlaid in dark horn within light horn, surrounded by finely cut segments of mother-of-pearl. The legs with sharp claws are carved in high relief on the underside.

This netsuke was previously published in Harris 1987, p. 81, fig. 389

—

By Ōhara Mitsuhiro (1810–1875)
Ivory, with inlaid horn and mother-of-pearl eyes
Osaka, mid 1800s
w. 4.5 cm
British Museum HG.550
Given by Professor John and Mrs Anne Hull Grundy

Flying crane

The crane (J. *tsuru*) has long fascinated people with its majestic appearance. In East Asia it is regarded as an auspicious bird that brings long life and good luck. It was believed to live for a thousand years and thus became a symbol of longevity. In paintings, sometimes as a celestial companion of the immortals, the crane has been depicted mostly in combination with the pine tree, to represent evergreen, ageless existence, and with the sun, to symbolize everlasting life (see right).

This elegant crane netsuke is carved in flight with its left wing stretched out and its long neck lying flat against its body. The composition is concerned less with realism than with achieving a compact design, with no protruding elements which might easily break. The layered effect of the feathers is carved with great delicacy. On the underside, one can see the crane's left wing is folded back and the legs are extended to fit neatly beneath the wing.

This netsuke was previously published in Harris 1987, p. 82, fig. 397.

—

Illegible signature (possibly Masakazu or Shōichi)
Wood, with eyes inlaid in metal, mid 1800s
w. 6.7 cm
British Museum HG.612
Given by Professor John and Mrs Anne Hull Grundy

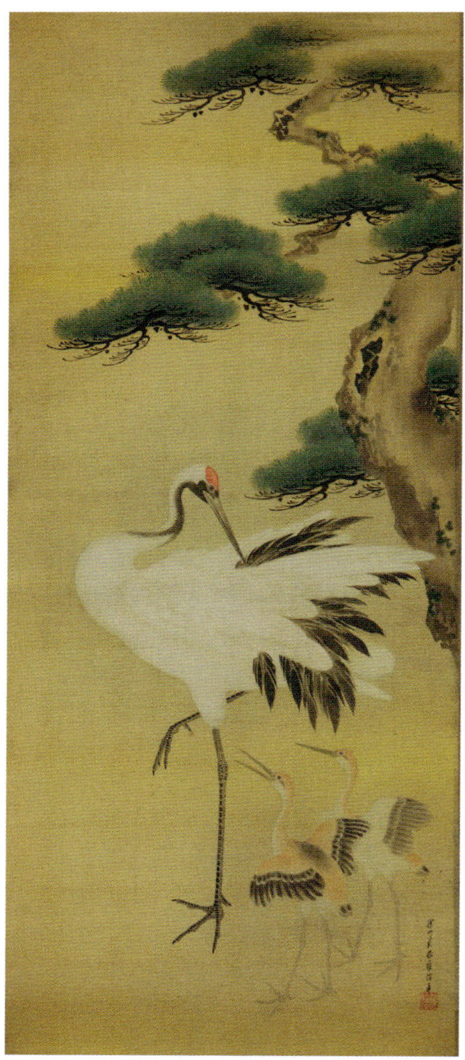

Cranes and pine tree. Kano Shōsen'in Masanobu, pair of hanging scrolls (detail), ink and colour on silk, about 1840–1880. 101. 7 x 38.9 cm. British Museum 1913,0501,0.188-189. Given by Sir W. Gwynne-Evans.

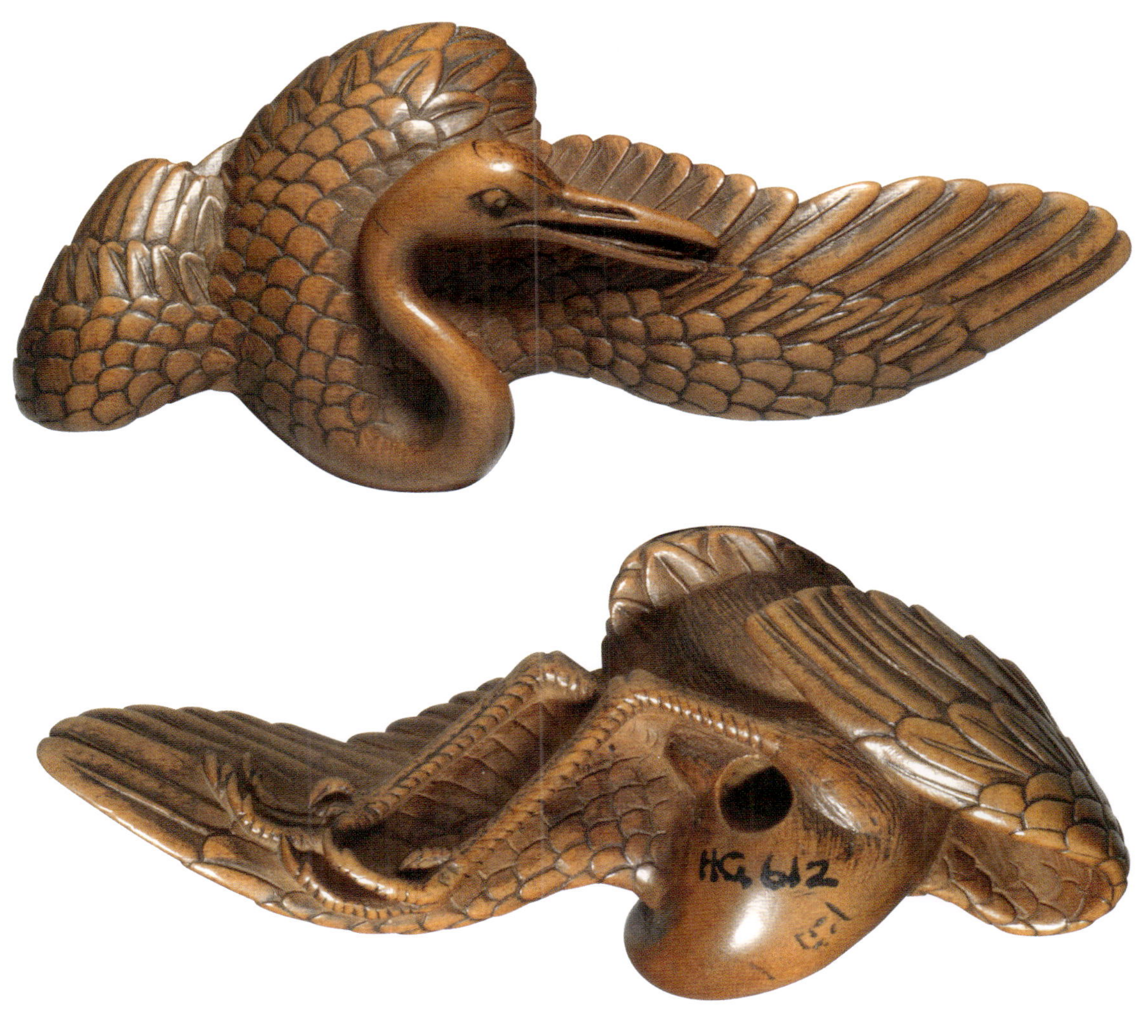

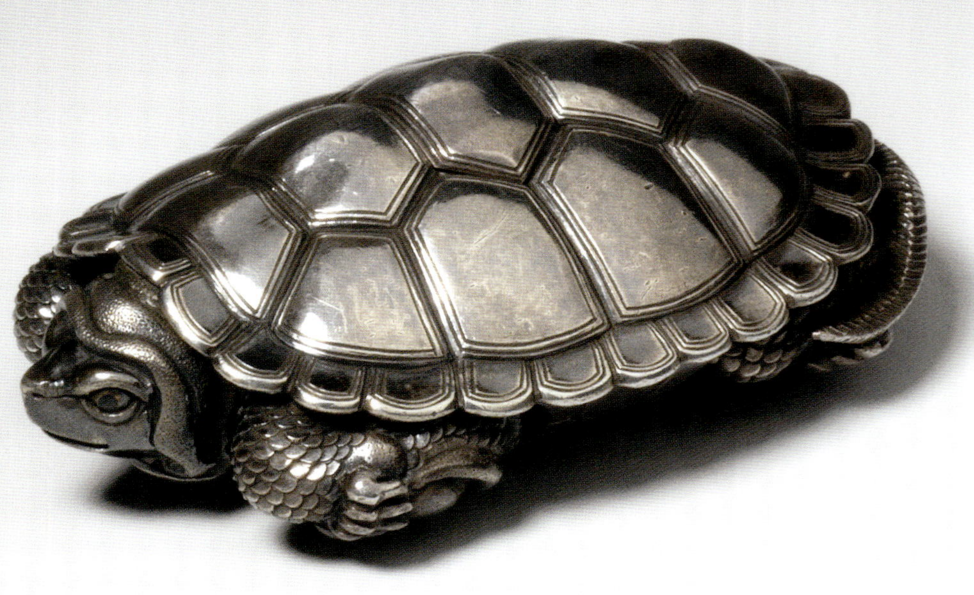

Turtle

Netsuke made of metal were generally created by metalworkers, who did not specialize in netsuke. Especially in the latter part of the Edo period (1615–1868), at the peak of netsuke production, various artists working in metals made netsuke using special techniques to accommodate an increasing demand for innovative netsuke, and to supplement their main output. The Kikugawa were a family who specialized in metalwork in Edo (present-day Tokyo). This silver model of a turtle, which has substantial weight, demonstrates the artist's considered and subtle craftsmanship. The detailing throughout is finely engraved, and the turtle's half protruding head, carapace, legs and tail stand out in strong relief, with orderly arranged plates and scalloped edges making up the shell. The eyes are inlaid in gold, with *shakudō* (an alloy of copper and gold) used for the pupils. A ring is attached to the inside of the removable central scute of the carapace, permitting a cord to be tied through a hole in the centre of the turtle's belly. Together with the crane (see pp. 162–163), the turtle is seen in Japan as an emblem of happiness and longevity, and it was believed that it had a lifespan of ten thousand years.

—

By Kikugawa
Silver, late 1800s
w. 5.4 cm
British Museum HG.291
Given by Professor John and Mrs Anne Hull Grundy

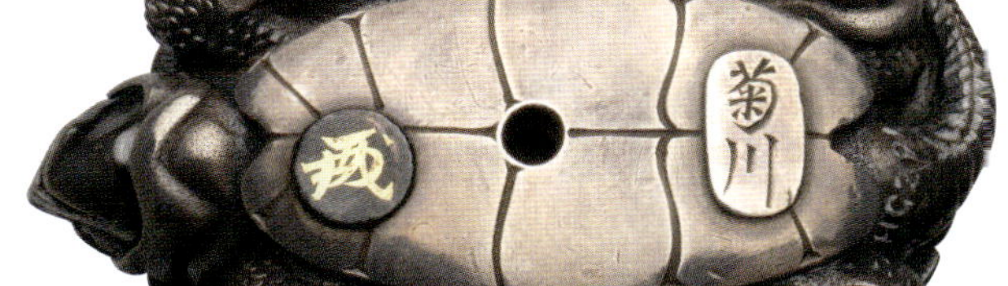

Beetles

This dynamic netsuke was carved by the contemporary
netsuke maker Kawahara Meishū (b. 1934). Born in Tokyo,
he started to carve netsuke in 1958. Meishū uses various
materials and his favourite subjects include human figures
and animals. A large Japanese rhinoceros beetle or *kabuto-
mushi* (literally 'warrior's helmet insect') is fighting with a
stag beetle or *kuwagata-mushi* (literally 'hoe-shaped insect')
over part of a branch from a tree. The rhinoceros beetle,
regarded as the king of insects in Japan, hooks its T-shaped
horn into the branch and tries to entangle its legs between
the big mandibles of its opponent, to wrestle the branch
away. The smaller stag beetle hiding behind the branch
seems somewhat frightened, but still has curiosity and
spirit. The elytron (the hardened forewings) of each beetle
is covered with glossy dark brown tortoiseshell (or horn)
to represent the reflective surface of metallic appearance.

Insect fighting has always been a popular pastime among
children. Usually two different male beetles are placed on
a log. They battle each other, trying to push their opponent
off the log, and the one that manages to stay on the log,
or knock over its rival, is considered the winner. In the
summer in particular, insect fights are sometimes held at
local shrine festivals. This netsuke is accompanied by an
original wooden storage box, inscribed with the title and
signature of the artist.

—

By Kawahara Meishū (b. 1934)
'Intertwining' (*Karami-ai*)
Wood and tortoiseshell or horn, with eyes inlaid in dark
horn, late 1900s
H: 4.2 cm, w: 3.7 cm
British Museum 1981,1014.4

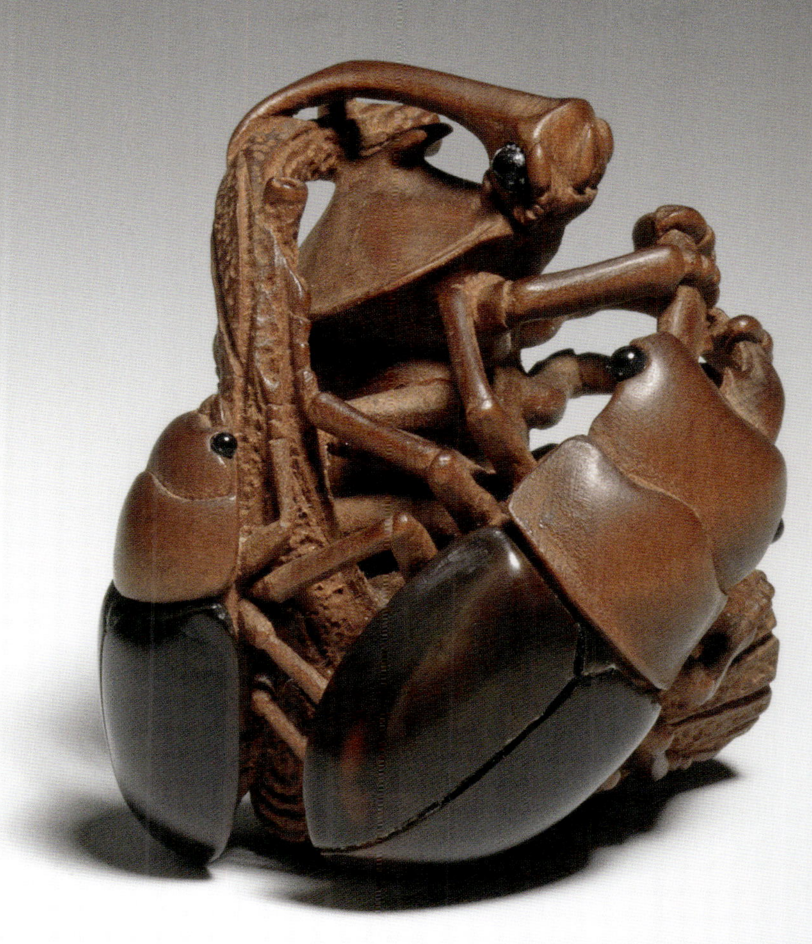

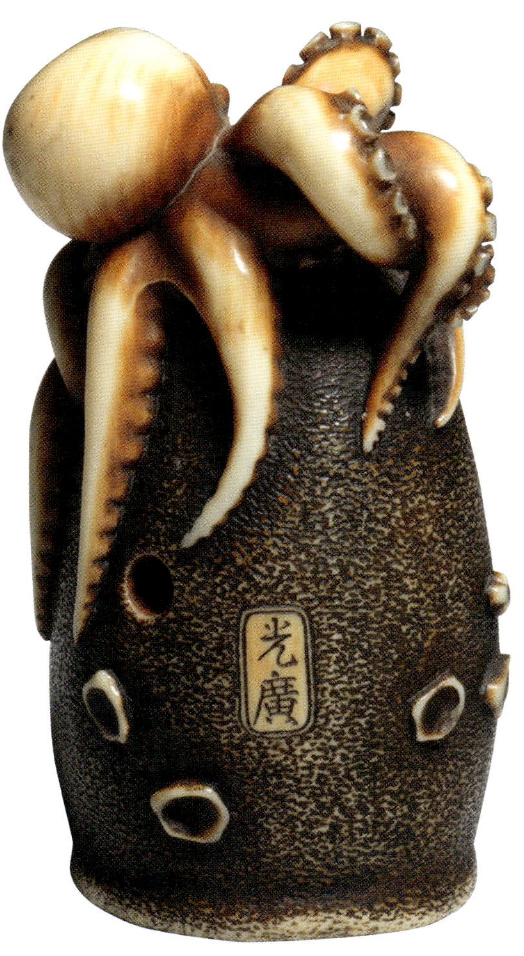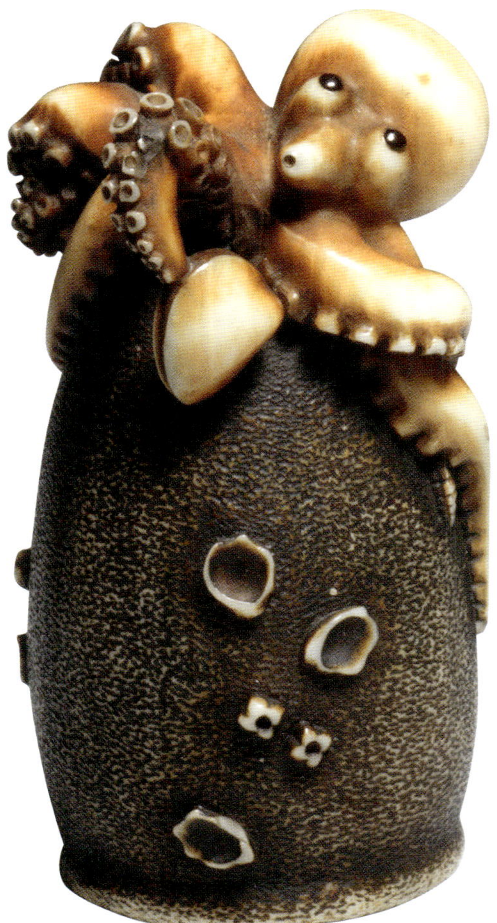

Octopus and pot

An octopus clings to the top of an upturned octopus pot, which is partially covered in barnacles. With one of its tentacles caught in a clam shell, the octopus' face comically expresses pain, its mouth in an elongated funnel shape and bulging eyes rolling upwards. The realism of the twisted tentacles is heightened by the accurately depicted suckers, which are stained to a mellow shade of brown. The slippery slickness of the octopus makes for a strong textural contrast with the roughened surface of the pot, which is minutely stippled and ink-stained to simulate earthenware. This technique is a hallmark of the great carver Ōhara Mitsuhiro of Osaka (see also pp. 44–45, 114–115 and 160–161).

Usually octopus traps are left on the sea bed for days, and the octopuses enter and remain inside, using the pot as both shelter and protection. When the pot is raised, the creature will not normally attempt to escape. This netsuke may have been created to evoke a poem by Matsuo Bashō (1644–1694), the most famous *haiku* poet of the Edo period (1615–1868):

Octopus pots
fleeting dreams
under the summer moon

Takotsubo ya
hakanaki yume o
natsu no tsuki

On the sea bed on a moonlit summer's night, an octopus in the pot is having a fleeting dream. It cannot know that it will be caught the next day and eaten. How ephemeral life is! Infact, the British Museum also has a netsuke (F.288) on the same subject, which is inscribed with this very poem.

This netsuke was previously published in Harris 1987, p. 87, fig. 423.

—

By Ōhara Mitsuhiro (1810–1875)
Ivory, with eyes inlaid in dark horn, Osaka, mid 1800s
H. 4.2 cm
British Museum HG.542
Given by Professor John and Mrs Anne Hull Grundy

Sea horse

This strange creature looks at first glance like a sea horse, but when one takes a closer look the features are in fact imaginary. The creature bends its head down in a contemplative pose and its slender curving body ends in a reverse curl. It has a long horse-like face with pricked ears, curled up side whiskers and a sacred jewel made of coral embedded in its forehead as a kind of 'third-eye', or *urna*. A single horn lies flat against the top of the head, from under which a mane of long hair flows over the back. The body is partly enveloped in a leaf-like mantle and the ridged scales are carved in a twisting diagonal arrangement.

This elongated shape is called a *sashi* netsuke. *Sashi* comes from the verb '*sasu*', meaning 'insert'. It is simply hung from the sash, hooking the bended head over the fabric. The cord is then attached through the space at the end of the curled tail. Great attention has been lavished on the netsuke's design, even though while being worn the body of this imaginary creature would largely be unseen under the sash.

This netsuke was previously published in Barker and Smith 1976, p. 94, fig. 161.

—

Unsigned
Bone and coral, with eyes inlaid in dark horn, mid 1800s
H. 7.5 cm
British Museum F.810
Given by Sir Augustus Wollaston Franks

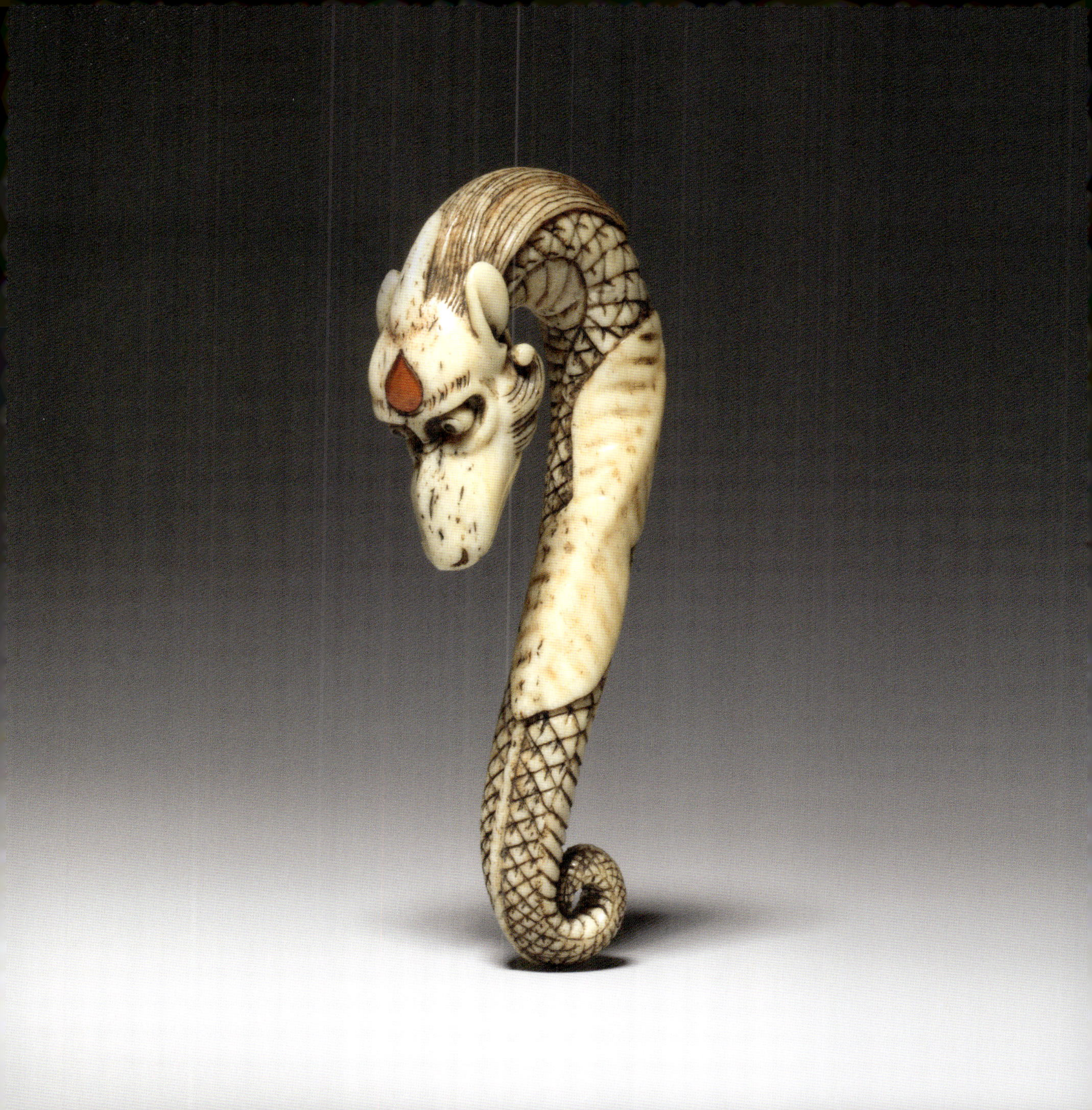

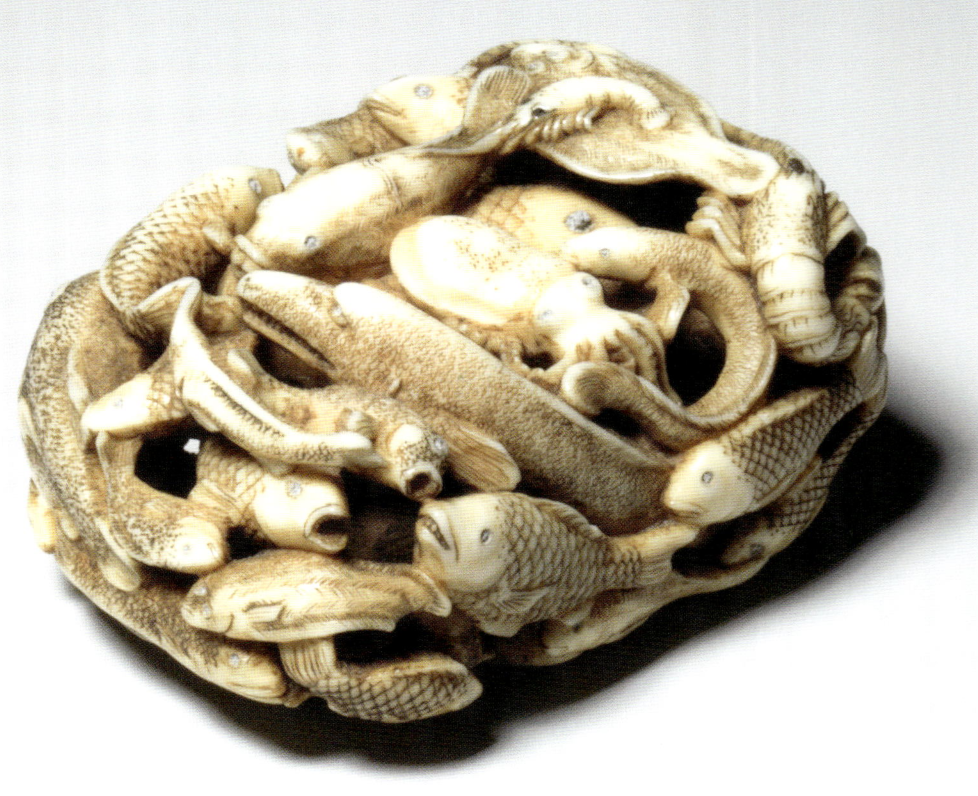

Group of sea creatures

While rice has long been a major component of the Japanese diet, fish has also played an important part, one that continues to the present day. In Edo (present-day Tokyo), fresh fish was sold at the fish market in Nihonbashi in the centre of the city, predecessor of today's famous Tsukiji fish market. The first fish market in Edo was established by the first shogun, Tokugawa Ieyasu (1542–1616), to provide supplies for Edo castle. The remainder not purchased by the castle was then sold at a market near Nihonbashi bridge. The fish was so fresh that it could be eaten raw as sashimi or soaked in vinegar, grilled or boiled in broth.

The carver of this netsuke, Tōun, was also from Edo, and must have enjoyed the richness of the seafood available in the markets. He chiefly carved netsuke with elaborate designs. In this intricate group of assembled sea creatures, we can easily identify the many varieties: sea bream, octopus, blowfish, carp, shrimp, flatfish and ark shell. Each creature is carved with careful detailing; some have their mouths open. The most astonishing tribute to the maker's skill is that each eye is inlaid with metal.

This netsuke was previously published in Barker and Smith 1976, p. 80, fig. 127.

—

By Tōun
Ivory, with eyes inlaid in pewter, Edo, mid 1800s
H. 2.6 cm; w. 4.5 cm
British Museum 1945,1017.523
Bequeathed by Oscar Charles Raphael

Dried salmon

This uncommon netsuke subject realistically represents a dried salmon by using actual fish skin for the surface. Details such as the fin, tail and rope are highlighted with gold lacquer and the cut portion is covered with a thin strip of mother-of-pearl over a red painted ground so as to reveal the dried flesh transparently. The back is lacquered with a design of randomly scattered Latin letters, which appeared as a curiosity to the Japanese.

Dried salmon has long been prized as a local product of Ezo (present-day Hokkaido), home of the indigenous Ainu people. The Ainu have a very different language and way of life, fishing for salmon and worshipping the bear. In the 1600s, the samurai government established the Matsumae domain in Ezo to conduct trade relations. The Japanese traded items for daily use against Ainu marine products and furs. Because salt was still highly valuable, until the mid Edo period (1615–1868) salmon were exported after simple gutting and drying, rather than being salted for preservation. When eaten, they were thinly sliced and soaked in Japanese *sake*, or reconstituted in water then cooked. There are other examples of the same subject with different designs on the back, and some of them bear the signature or seal of Ogawa Haritsu (1663–1747). Haritsu is one of the earliest craftsmen known to have signed his netsuke. He encouraged the use of new materials, such as ceramic, coral, stone and tortoiseshell for the inlay work, and new colours of lacquer. Although unsigned, this netsuke is one of the finest examples of its kind, with exquisitely executed inlay, and it is possible to attribute the piece with confidence to Haritsu (also known as Ritsuō).

This netsuke was previously published in Barker and Smith 1976, p. 165, fig. 380. Similar netsuke are illustrated in Joly 1912, reprinted 1966, no. 1772, pl. XXX, and Moss 1982, pp. 36–37, no. 30.

—

Unsigned, attributed to Ogawa Haritsu (1663–1747)
Lacquered wood, with fish skin and mother-of-pearl
Early 1700s
w. 11 cm
British Museum F.1078
Given by Sir Augustus Wollaston Franks

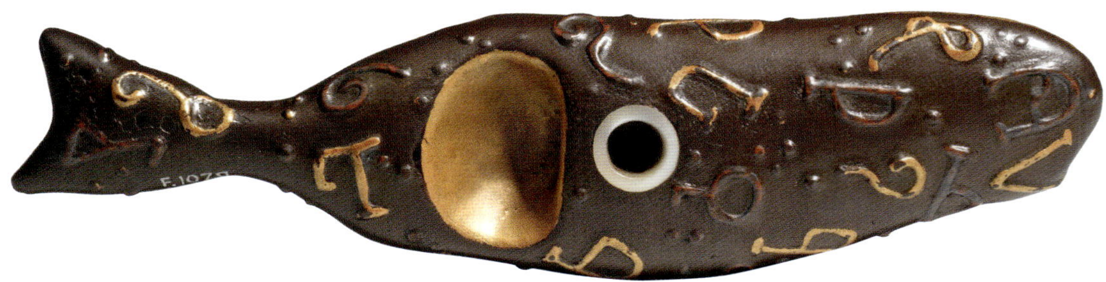

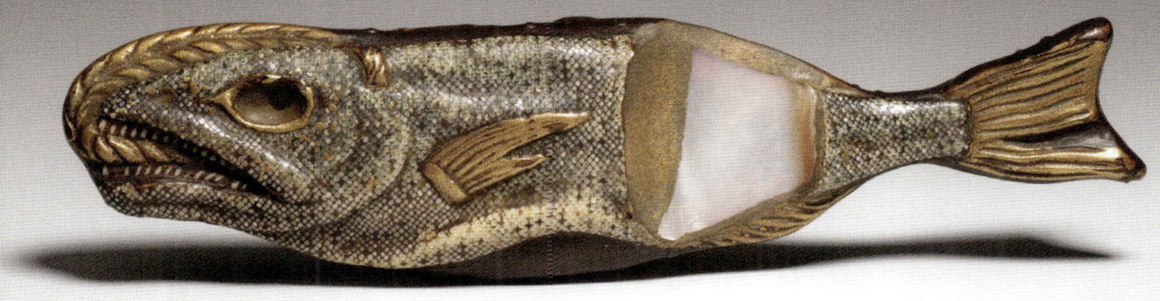

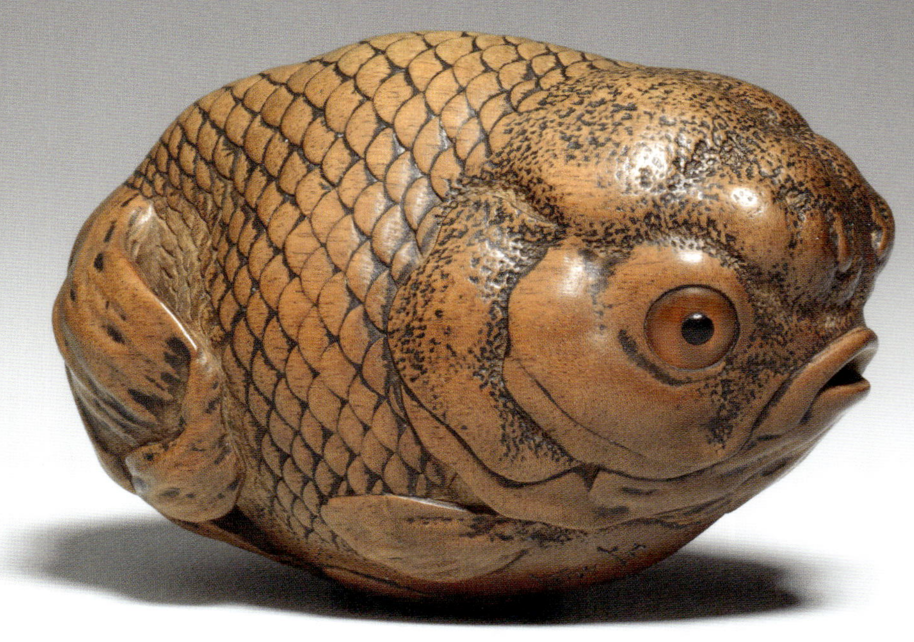

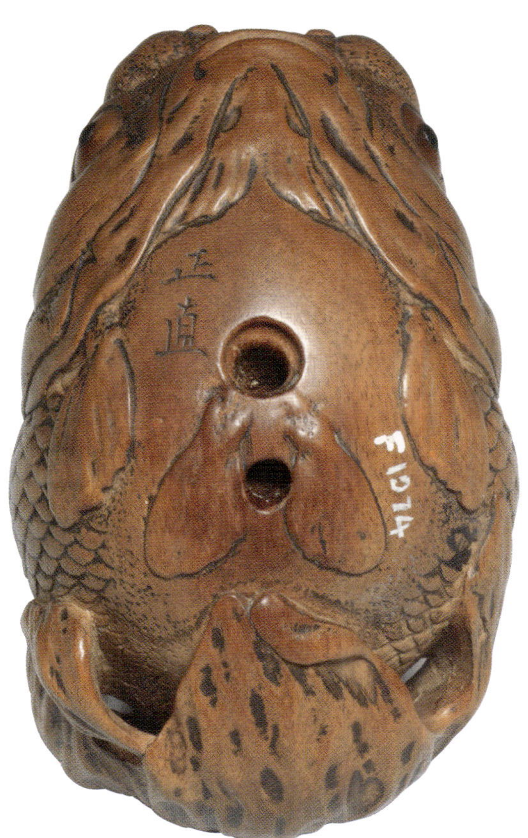

Goldfish

This ugly – yet adorable – goldfish is called the 'lion-head goldfish' or *ranchū*, and has been highly regarded and specially bred in Japan. It has an egg-shaped body without a dorsal fin, and its most distinctive feature is the bulbous head with broad forehead. Keeping goldfish (*kingyo*) as pets became popular among the general population from the later Edo period (1615–1868). By the beginning of the nineteenth century, a goldfish industry had been well established, and they became reasonably affordable. People would buy them from goldfish peddlers or in a goldfish-scooping game on the street or during festivals. In Utagawa Kuniyoshi's (1797–1861) memorable print, a tub of goldfish is featured with turtles suspended above it, while alongside a baby boy on his mother's shoulders reaches out towards them (see p. 178). At that time, a glass bowl would have been a luxury and quite expensive, so goldfish were usually kept in a wooden basin or a ceramic bowl. Therefore, goldfish were viewed from above, and not from the side as they usually are today. Because the fish were viewed in this way, the most appreciated goldfish were *ranchū*, and they were referred to as the 'king of goldfish' mostly because they cut a fine figure when viewed from above.

This *ranchū* netsuke was carved by Masanao I of Yamada in Ise province (present-day Mie prefecture). He was the founder of a distinctive regional group of netsuke carvers who mainly specialized in creating animal subjects in boxwood.

This netsuke was previously published in Barker and Smith 1976, p. 103, fig. 186, and Lazarnick (ed.), MCI, vol. 1, 1986, p. 450.

—

By Masanao I of Ise (1815–1890)
Boxwood, with eyes inlaid in light and dark horn, Ise, 1800s
w. 5.5 cm
British Museum F.1074
Given by Sir Augustus Wollaston Franks

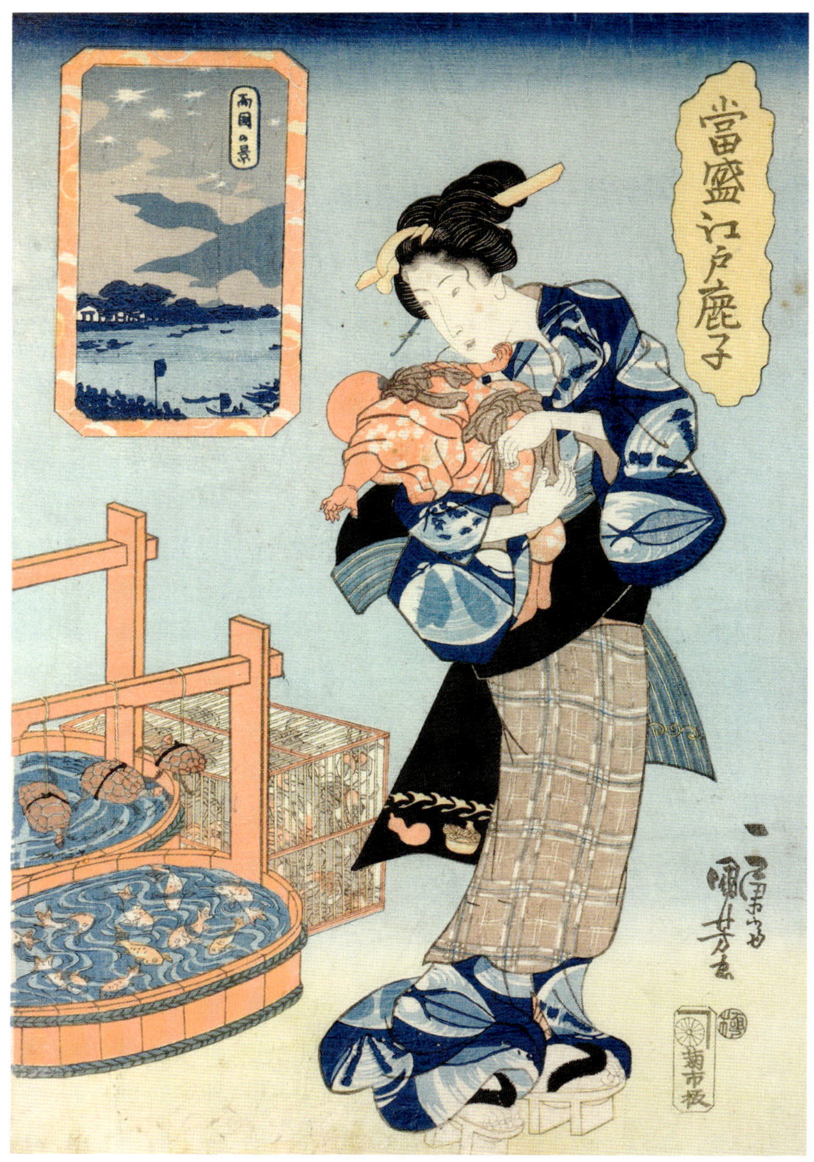

Ryōgoku no kei (A View of Ryōgoku), from the series *Tōsei Edo kanoko* (*Modern Tie-dyed Fabrics of Edo*). Utagawa Kuniyoshi, colour woodblock print, about 1834. 138.3 x 26.3 cm. British Museum 2008,3037.09102. Loaned by the American Friends of the British Museum (Prof. Arthur R. Miller collection).

Manjū and other objects

Manjū refers to a round type of netsuke, named after a sweet cake of flattish round shape filled with bean paste. Their flatter surfaces were well-suited to reproducing pictorial scenes. In the late nineteenth century, the subjects of *manjū* netsuke were often derived from the contemporary ukiyo-e ('floating world') prints, which depicted myths, legends and bloody battle scenes.

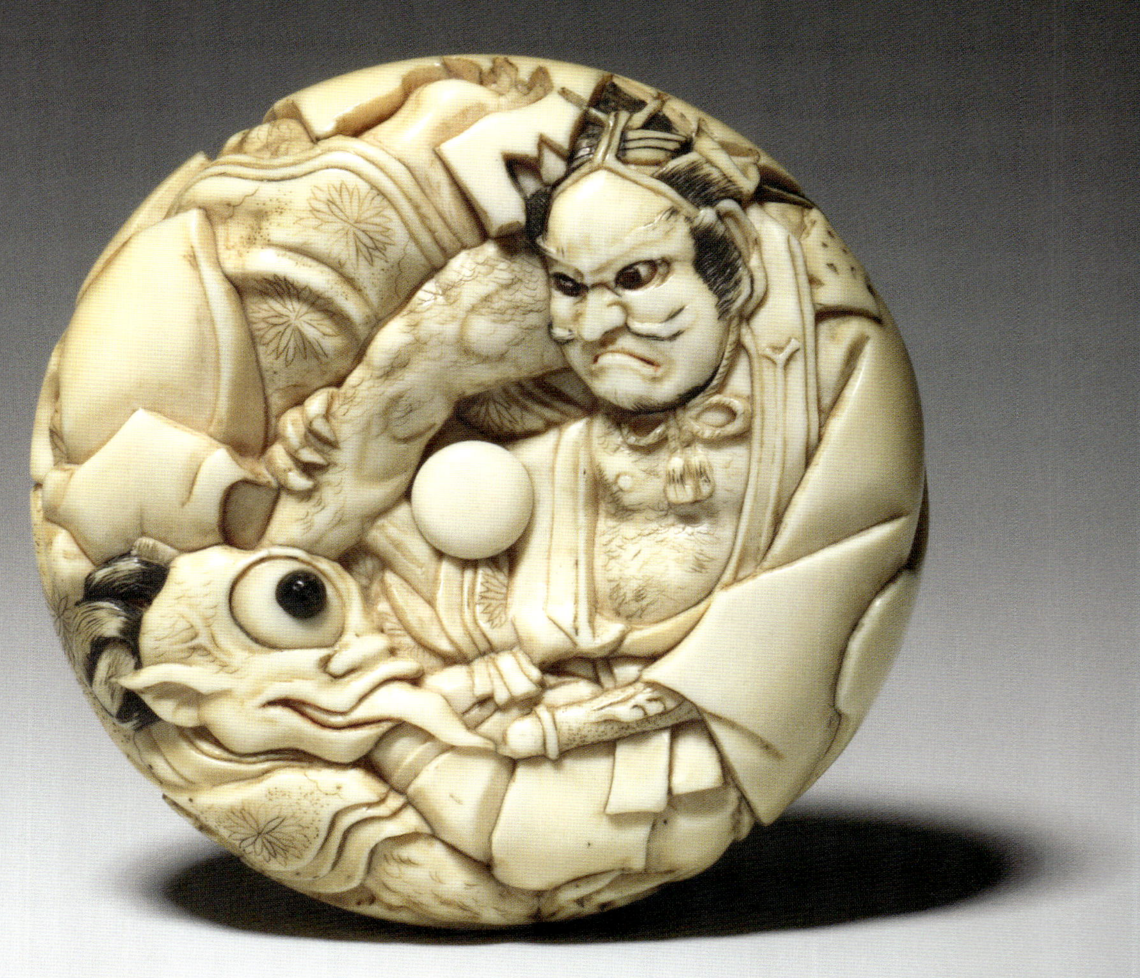

Kintoki and the single-eyed demon

This *manjū* netsuke dynamically depicts the legend of
Sakata Kintoki, one of the four retainers of the famous
warrior leader Minamoto no Yorimitsu (948–1021). One
day Kintoki and his colleague Usui Sadamitsu were on
night-watch at Yorimitsu's mansion. They were passing
time by playing the board game of *Go*, which originated
in China, when various goblins appeared one after another
to kill Yorimitsu. The two warriors realized that the goblins
were merely conjured up by the evil Earth Spider and
succeeded in despatching them, thereby protecting their
lord. The story became popular and fictionalized as a Kabuki
play and was also illustrated in ukiyo-e prints (see below).

The netsuke pictured here captures the instant when
Kintoki grabs the arm of the single-eyed demon, and s

about to draw his sword to kill it. His voluminous left sleeve
bears the first 'kin' character of the name Kintoki, carved
on the reverse of the piece. The details of this netsuke are
finely carved in both high and low relief, which succeeds in
reproducing the printed scene in ivory to dynamic effect.

This netsuke was previously published in Barker and
Smith 1976, pp. 134–135, fig. 280, and Lazarnick (ed.),
MCI, vol. 1, 1986, p. 94 (without image).

—

By Gyokuhōsai
Ivory, with eyes inlaid in dark horn, late 1800s
DIAM. 5.5 cm
British Museum F.393
Given by Sir Augustus Wollaston Franks

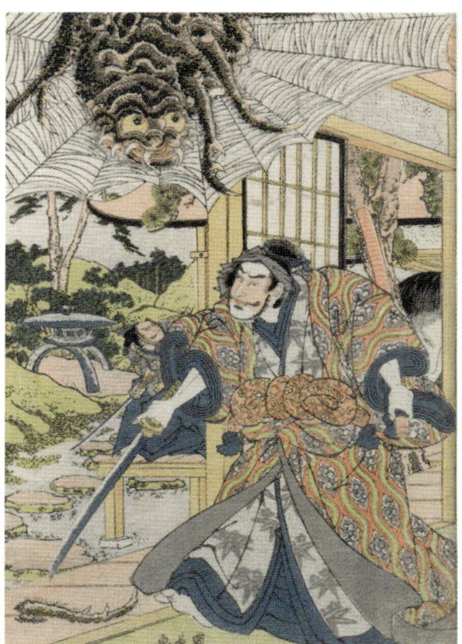
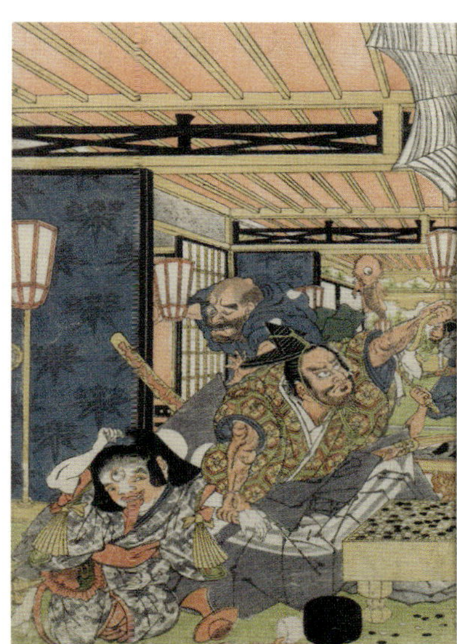
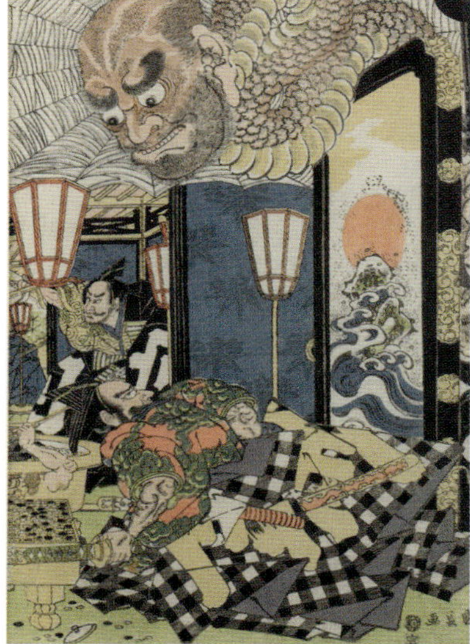

Yorimitsu and his retainers battle against the Earth Spider and its demons. Utagawa Kuninaga (worked
1820s), colour woodblock print (triptych), about 1829. Each sheet about 37.1 x 25.5 cm. British Museum
1907,0531,0.524.1-3.

Gibbon and hibiscus

The *ryūsa*-style netsuke is a distinctive variety of *manjū* in which the ground is extensively cut away leaving the motifs clearly visible. This type is named after a craftsman from Edo (present-day Tokyo) named Ryūsa who is credited with the innovation in the late eighteenth century. This walrus tusk netsuke is delicately carved with a gibbon among hibiscus flowers. With a round face sporting a comical expression, the gibbon holds onto the stem of the flowers with its long tail curling upwards. The white polished body stands out against the intricately carved floral design.

Although gibbons were not native to Japan, Chinese paintings depicting them were imported from the end of the Kamakura period (1185–1333) and exerted considerable influence on the development of Japanese ink painting. Hibiscus was also not native to the Japanese archipelago, and according to the written records, it was first presented to the shogun Tokugawa Ieyasu (1542–1616) by the lord of Satsuma province (present-day Kagoshima prefecture) in 1609. This is the year that samurai of the Satsuma domain invaded and essentially annexed the Ryūkyū Islands (present-day Okinawa prefecture), a chain of islands extending south-west from Kyūshū. Specified local produce, including hibiscus, was sent as tribute to the shogun on a regular basis from 1609 onwards. Since then, the hibiscus has become popular in Japanese art as a tropical flower with bright colours (see right).

In the netsuke here, the flowers are prized for their novelty and are shown at different angles, from both the front and back; one is still cupped in a bud. The carver, Ishikawa Rensai, worked in downtown Asakusa in Tokyo and his most typical works are beautifully designed *ryūsa*-style netsuke of animals among foliage, as seen here. The reverse is carved with a stylized arabesque design.

By Ishikawa Rensai
Walrus ivory, Tokyo, 1870s
w. 4.5 cm
British Museum F.433
Given by Sir Augustus Wollaston Franks

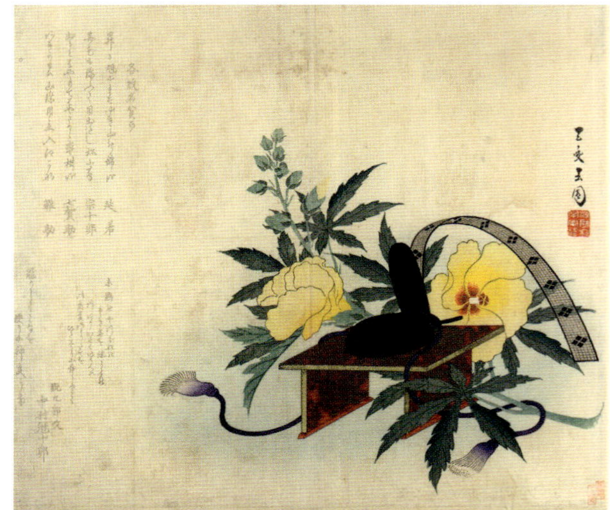

Courtier's hat on lacquered stand with hibiscus (detail). Gyokuen, colour woodblock print, (*surimono*), mid 1800s. 35.7 x 39 cm. British Museum 1902,0212,0.411.

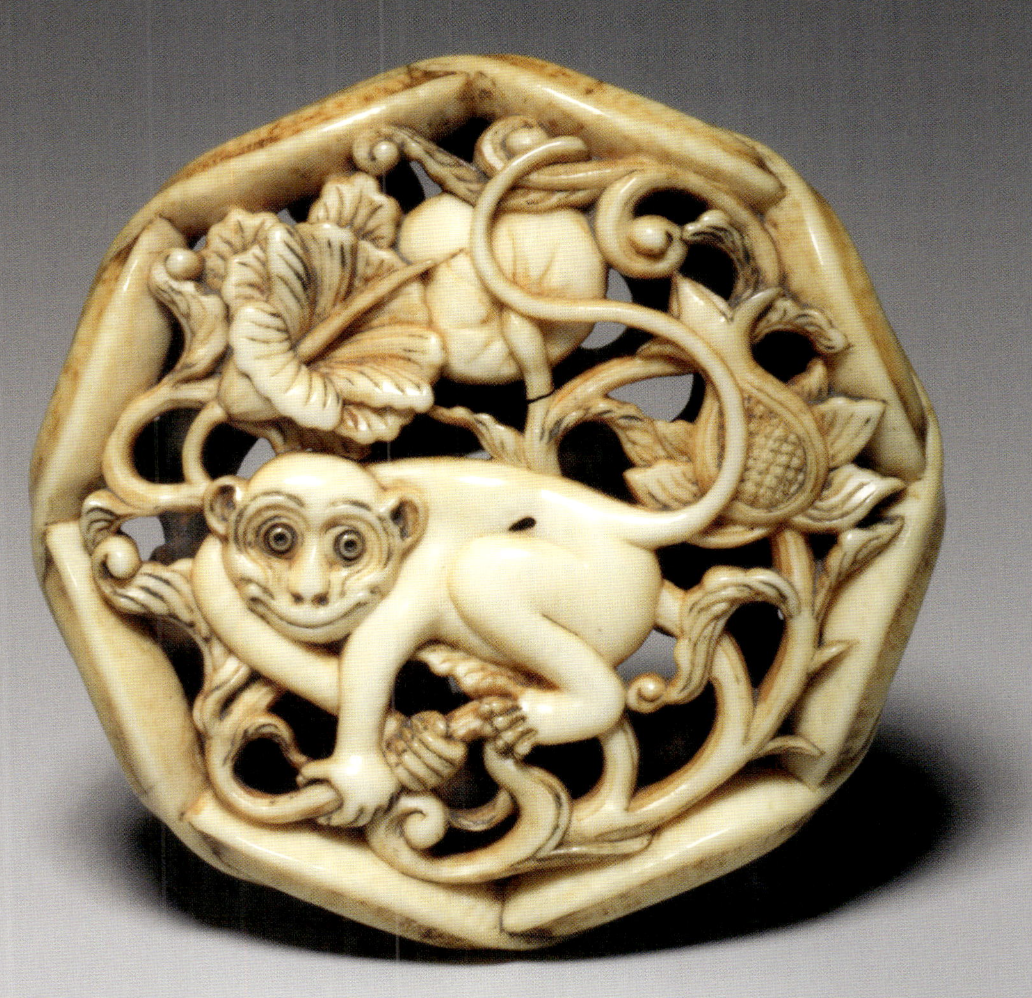

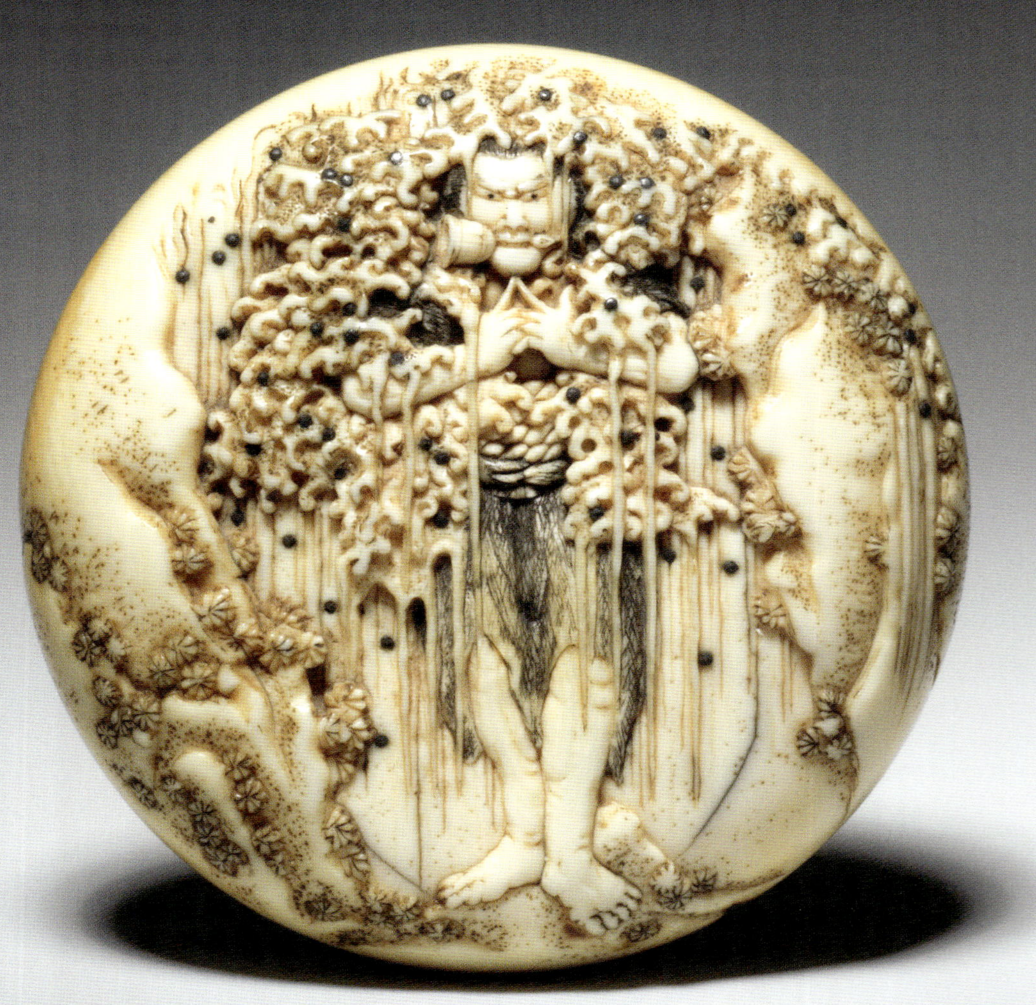

By Yamada Chōgetsu (1826–1892)
Ivory with metal studs, late 1800s
DIAM. 5.3 cm
British Museum 1945,1017.638
Bequeathed by Oscar Charles Raphael

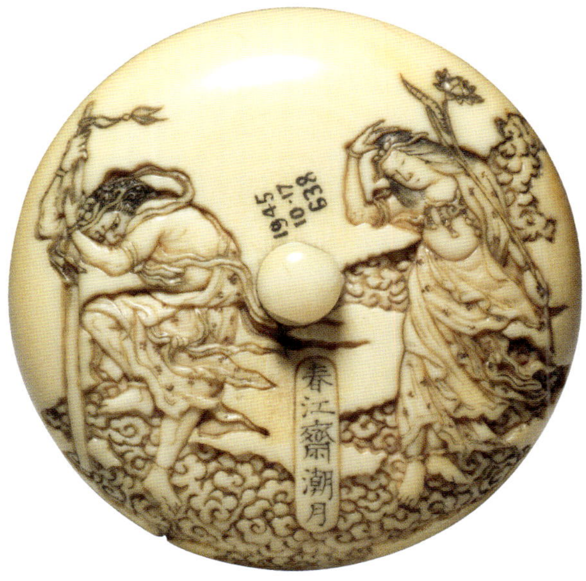

Mongaku Shōnin beneath a waterfall

This outstandingly well-carved *manjū* netsuke depicts the monk Mongaku Shōnin in repentance beneath a waterfall, and on the reverse two Buddhist figures looking down at the event from a cloudbank. The design is based on the legend of Endō Moritō (1139–1203), the secular name of Mongaku, who was originally a samurai guard of the imperial family in Kyoto. In his late teenage years, he fell in love with Kesa, the beautiful wife of his samurai colleague Watanabe Wataru. She rejected his persistent entreaties until one night she agreed to receive him in her house at night, where she said he would find her husband asleep in a room and could kill him. However, too late, Moritō realized that the person he killed was actually the lady herself, who had put herself in her husband's place to save her honour. Moritō repented his evil ways and became a monk using the new name of Mongaku. As a harsh penance, he prayed under the waterfall of Nachi in Kumano (present-day Mie and Wakayama prefectures) in the freezing winter for twenty-one days, reciting incantations to the deity Fudō Myōō (Sanskrit *Acala*). It is said that at the point of death, Mongaku was rescued by the two attendants of Fudō Myōō, Kongara (Sanskrit *Kimkara*) and Seitaka (Sanskrit *Cetaka*), so that he could complete the full three weeks of austerities.

The design is taken from an illustration by Katsushika Hokusai (1760–1849) in *Ehon sakigake* (*Picture-book of Warrior Heroes*) published in 1836. The motif is carved in *shishiai-bori* technique, a high relief which does not project above the surface of the object. The spray of the foaming waterfall on the priest's body stands out in undercutting, enlivened with scattered metal studs.

This netsuke was previously published in Barker and Smith 1976, p. 84, fig. 135.

Forty-seven loyal retainers

This large *manjū* netsuke is intricately carved with a scene from the final episode of the famous tale 'Treasury of the Loyal Retainers' or *Chūshingura*. The story is based on an actual historical event which took place in the beginning of the eighteenth century. In 1701, Asano Naganori (1667–1701), the lord of Akō (in present-day Hyōgo prefecture), was provoked by the arrogant treatment he received from the protocol official Kira Yoshinaka (1641–1702), and drew his sword in an attempt to kill Kira, within the precincts of Edo Castle. For this, Asano was sentenced to commit suicide, while Kira escaped without punishment. Asano's domain was confiscated and the retainers who had served him were dismissed and became masterless samurai, or *rōnin*. For nearly two years, they bided their time while plotting revenge. Finally, on the fourteenth day of the twelfth month, 1702, the band of forty-seven *rōnin* broke into Kira's mansion at night and killed him. Although they were regarded as heroes by many for their unswerving loyalty, they were all nevertheless ordered by the authorities to commit suicide on the same day in 1703. The story became extremely popular as a theme for plays and paintings.

This minutely carved *manjū* depicts one of the best-known scenes, the storming of the mansion of their dead master's enemy, detailing all forty-seven of the *rōnin* individually. While the fight goes on around a stone lantern in the garden on the front, Kira is discovered by the loyal retainers hiding in a woodshed on the reverse.

This netsuke was previously published by Barker and Smith 1976, p. 80, fig. 126, Lazarnick (ed.), MCI, vol. 1, 1986, p. 403, and Lazarnick, vol. 1, 1981, p. 688. Further information about its provenance can be found in W. L. Behrens, illustrated in Joly 1912, repr. 1966, no. 1120, pl. XXI.

By Kyōmin
Ivory with metal ring, late 1800s
DIAM. 7 cm
British Museum 1945,1017.602
Bequeathed by Oscar Charles Raphael

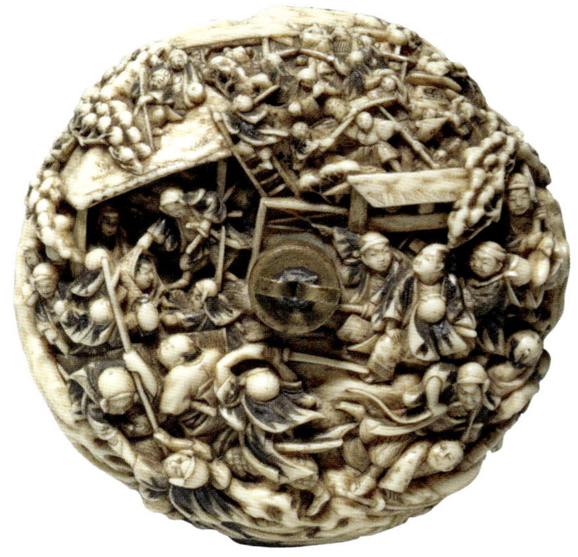

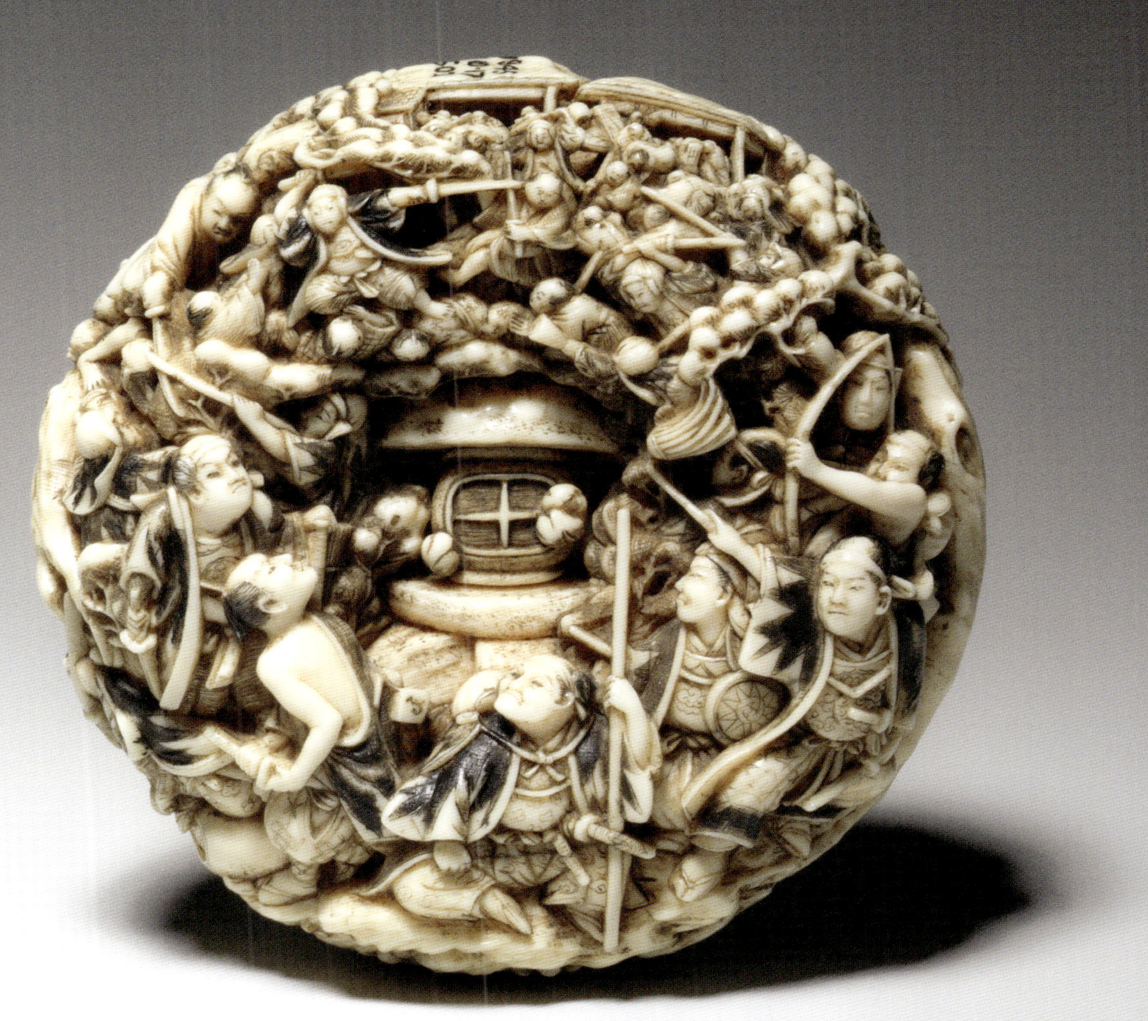

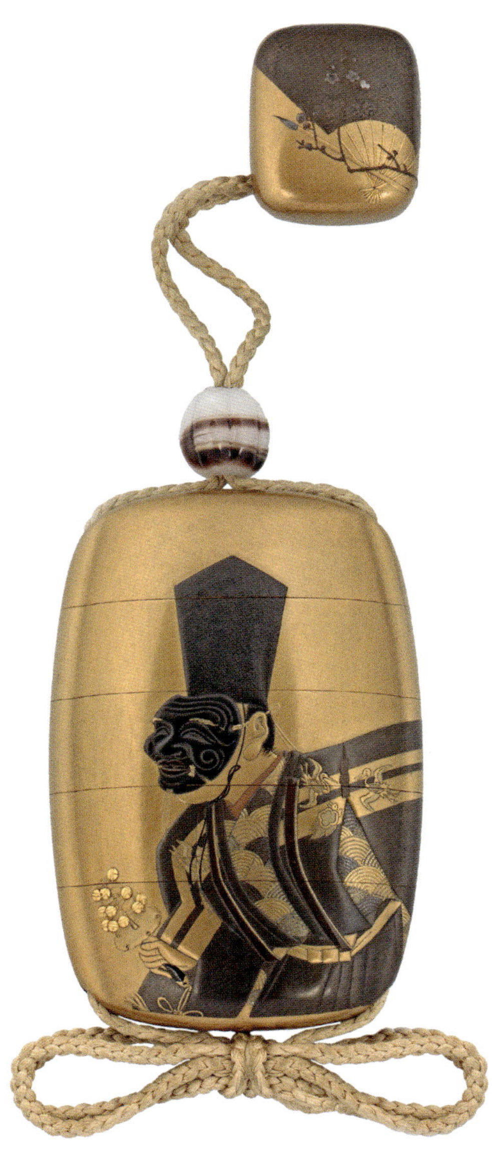
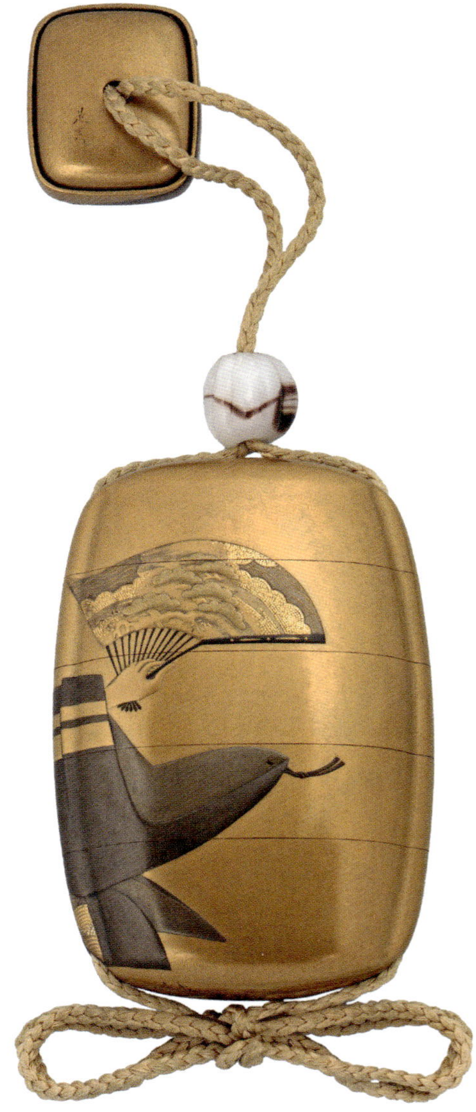

By Shibata Zeshin (1807–1891)
Lacquered wood, detailing in gold foil and mother-of-
pearl with opaque glass *ojime* (see p. 8), late 1800s
Inrō: H. 8.6 cm; w. 5.9 cm
Netsuke: H. 3.4 cm; w. 2.8 cm
British Museum 1945,1017.421.a-c
Bequeathed by Oscar Charles Raphael

Gold lacquer four-case *inrō* with netsuke

This *inrō* (see p. 8) and netsuke are a fine example of a
lacquered ensemble made by a single artist, Shibata Zeshin
(1807–1891). The oval *inrō* features a Noh actor wearing
the mask of an old man (*okina*), lacquered on a subdued
gold powder ground. The particular dance of the old man
wearing a black mask is called *Sanbasō* and it celebrates
the rice harvest. On the front, the dancer wears a black
pointed hat and holds a cluster of bells. The design
continues on to the reverse, where the man's outstretched
arm holds an opened fan which is decorated with pine
trees among clouds.

The box-shaped netsuke, or *hako* netsuke at the top of
the cord, depicts a plum branch and a writing brush lying on
an open fan. These motifs allude to Sugawara no Michizane
(AD 845–903), an outstanding cultural figure of the Heian
period (794–1185). Michizane was widely worshiped as
the patron of scholarship, and he is often portrayed holding
these items. His story was fictionalized in a Kabuki
play which became very popular during the Edo period
(1615–1868).

Because the designs of both *inrō* and netsuke are related
to drama, they may have been commissioned by a theatre
fan. The design is entirely in gold and black lacquer in the
hira-makie (literally 'flat sprinkled picture') technique. This
is one of the common techniques for lacquer decoration,
whereby pigment (often gold or silver powder), mixed with
charcoal dust and lacquer is applied in a thin layer.

Shibata Zeshin was a painter and a lacquer artist whose
career spanned either side of the Meiji Restoration of 1868.
He was a prolific artist, experimenting with new techniques,
such as painting in lacquer, which helped him to gain
great popularity around the world in several international
expositions.

Kagamibuta netsuke

This rare netsuke consists of a copper plate in the form of
a coin inserted into a wooden bowl. This type is called a
kagamibuta, literally 'mirror lid'. This derives from the fact
that in the East Asian countries, polished-metal mirrors,
mostly made of bronze, were used for centuries before the
development of glass mirrors. The material used for the
inserted disc varies: iron, gold, silver, brass, bronze, copper,
as well as various alloys. The plate was the focal point of
the decoration, while the base or bowl, usually made of
wood or ivory, takes a simple shape with only a cord hole
at the back. The carving of the metal disc was usually
carried out by a professional metalworker – metalworkers
were generally makers of sword-fittings, and all of the
engraving techniques typically used on sword guards, or
tsuba, can also be found on this type of netsuke.

Here, the copper plate is carved in relief with a long-
bearded sage holding a scroll and surmounted by a mock
inscription in Latin letters. A few netsuke of this kind are
recorded, and they are typically carved with half-length
portraits of European or Chinese legendary figures with
(generally) meaningless inscriptions. They may have been
copied from early European coins brought by Dutch
merchants to Japan in the Edo period (1615–1868).

Similar netsuke are illustrated in Bushell 1975, p. 107,
figs 97–99, and Joly 1912, reprinted 1966, no. 456, pl. X.

—

Unsigned
Wood and copper, early 1800s
DIAM. 4.6 cm
British Museum F.1306
Given by Sir Augustus Wollaston Franks

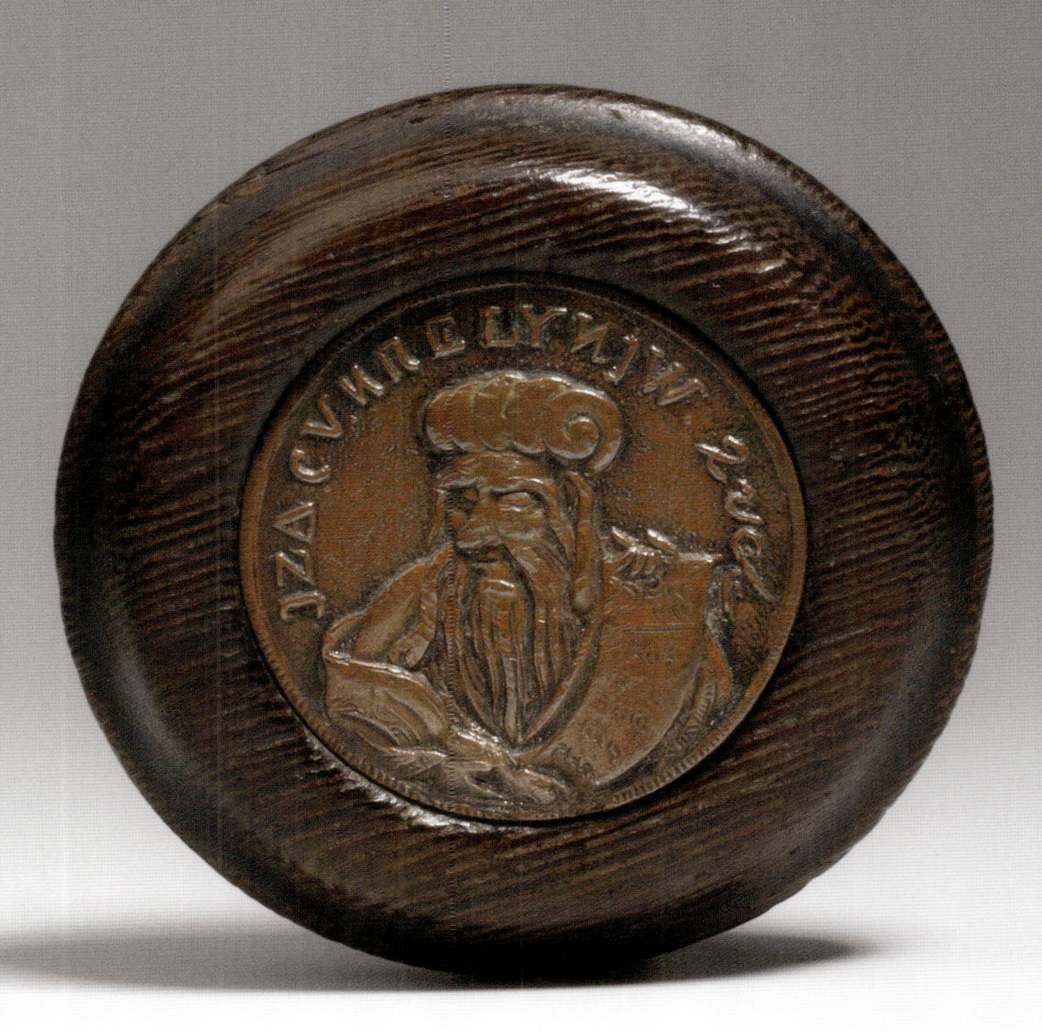

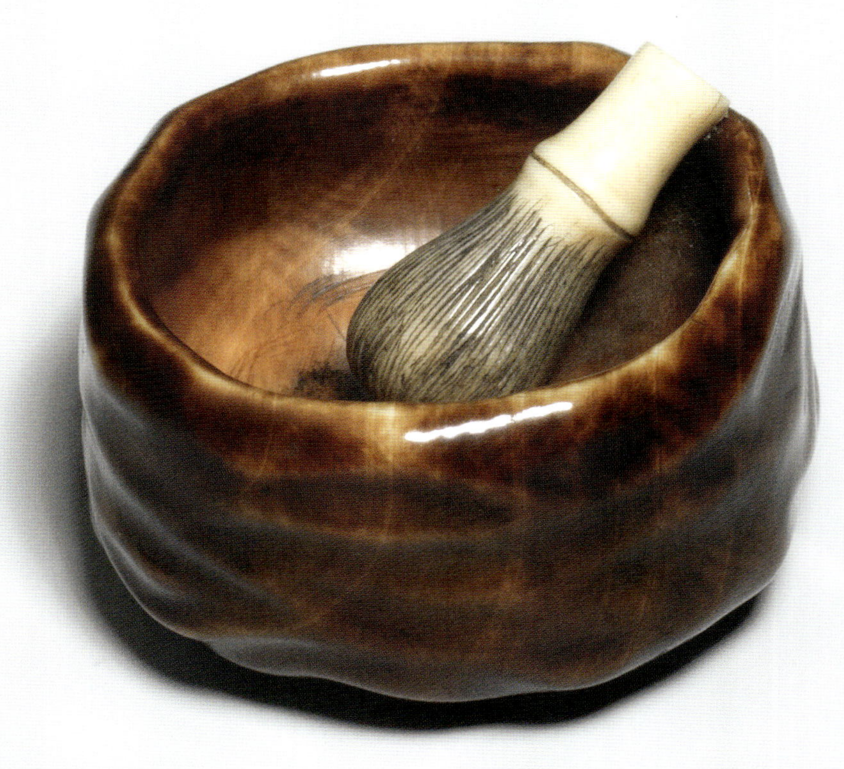

Teabowl and tea whisk

This ivory netsuke cleverly imitates an earthenware teabowl, with a bamboo tea whisk placed inside as if for a tea gathering, *chanoyu*. The teabowl netsuke is skilfully stained to simulate the thick brown glaze which covers and pools towards the base of a real teabowl. It realistically conveys the deliberate hand-formed appearance of Raku ceramics, along with the roughly stippled texture of the unglazed surface beneath. The tea whisk has a node of bamboo separating the handle, and the split tips are rendered with finely painted lines in ink. On the base, just off the footring, there is even a 'Raku' seal inside a circular cartouche, carved as though impressed in the clay, which follows the practice of the famous Raku family of potters.

In Kyoto, Raku wares were first made during the Momoyama period (1568–1615) by a tilemaker called Chōjirō. His work caught the eye of Sen no Rikyū (1522–1591), Japan's most renowned tea master, who asked him to create teabowls for his use out of the same material as the tiles. Rikyū's patron, the military leader, Toyotomi Hideyoshi (1536–1598) also appreciated Chōjirō's work and gave him the name 'Raku', meaning 'pleasure'. Since then Raku potters have continued to work throughout the Edo period (1615–1868) and up to the present day. Raku teabowls are especially prized for their earthiness and sturdiness, which makes them inviting to touch, and for their sombre colours, which contrast pleasingly with the fresh chartreuse green of whisked tea.

—

By Masayoshi
Stained ivory, late 1800s
H. 2.2 cm; W. 3.7 cm
British Museum F.1122
Given by Sir Augustus Wollaston Franks

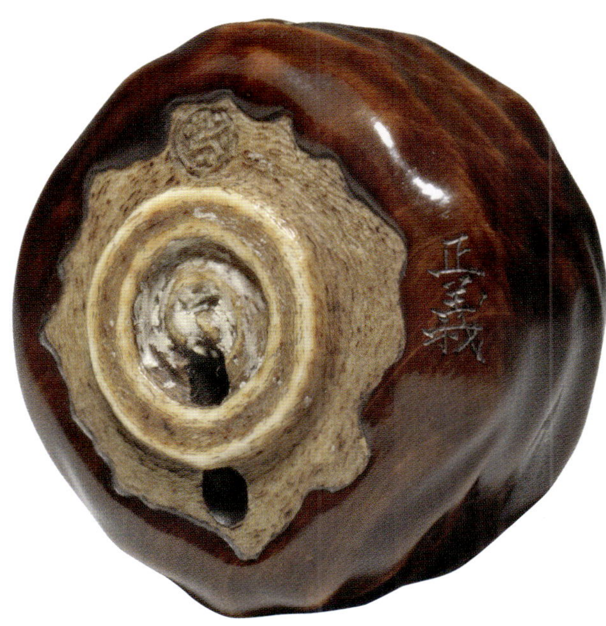

Tea gathering utensils

This finely woven rattan netsuke, comprising a tea kettle with loose ring handles, a teabowl and a mat, forms a compact composition. Due to its durability and lightness, rattan has been extensively used for making furniture, handcrafts and art objects in Japan. After cutting the rattan into sections, the inner core of the material is separated and worked into wicker. Before being woven, the strips are soaked in water to soften and, once they are dry, left to harden again. Rattan is not native to Japan. It is believed that the material was first brought back by a Japanese envoy to the Chinese court during the Tang period (AD 618–907). Since then rattan has been highly prized for use in items such as bows, hand-grips of hatchets (or axes) and the lacing of armour. During the Edo period (1615–1868), written records reveal that rattan was imported into Nagasaki in bundles by the thousand through Dutch merchants. By that time, rattan had become part of daily life and was used in its woven form for hats, basket palanquins, flower baskets and summer pillows. These traditional uses of rattan continue to the present day, often in combination with bamboo.

This netsuke was previously published in Harris 1987, p. 105, fig. 522.

—

Unsigned
Woven rattan, late 1800s
w. 4.9 cm
British Museum HG.229
Given by Professor John and Mrs Anne Hull Grundy

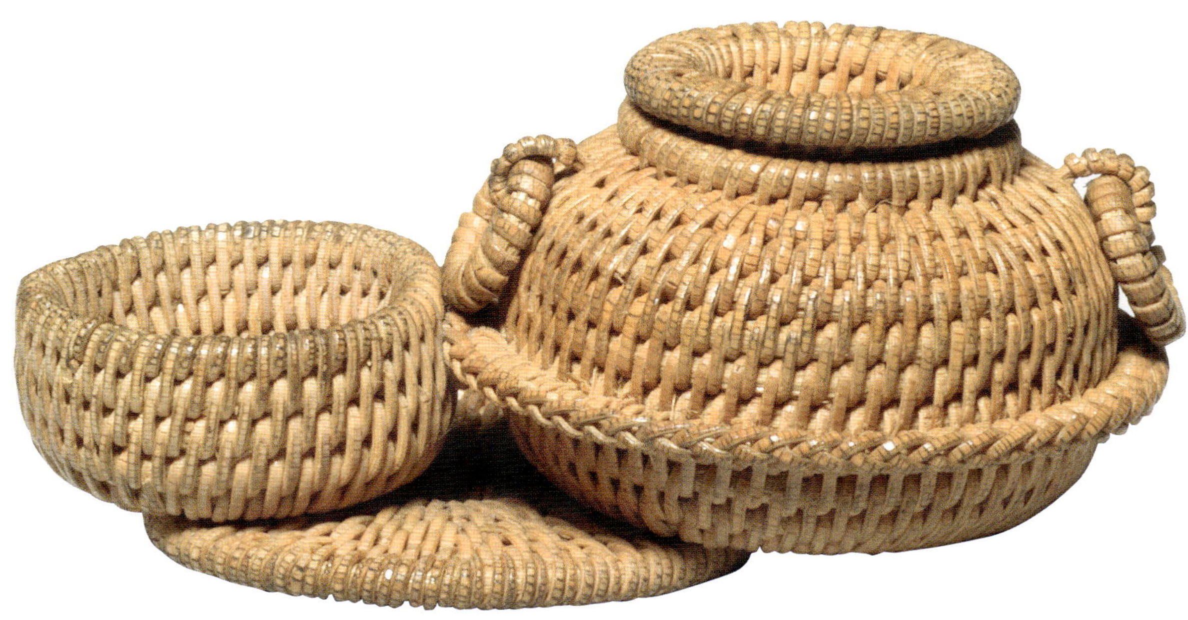

Japanese transverse harp (*koto*)

This ivory netsuke faithfully represents a traditional Japanese transverse harp called a *koto* (the more archaic name is *sō*). A *koto* is typically made of paulownia wood and has thirteen strings. It varies in length from around 160 to 200 centimetres, with a convex face and concave underside. The pitch is adjusted using moveable bridges placed under each string. The player uses picks worn on the fingers to pluck the strings, while the left hand presses down on the strings to vary the notes and create other musical effects. The instrument was originally imported from China during the Nara period (AD 710–784). It was performed as part of Japanese court music and became an important part of the cultivated lifestyles of the elite. It was only during the Edo period (1615–1868) that the instrument became popular among the general public. In China, mastery of the transverse harp was regarded as one of the 'Four Accomplishments', the four main arts required of Chinese scholars, together with Chinese chess, calligraphy and painting. In Japan, following Chinese practice, playing the *koto* was also seen as lofty and refined, and became one of the feminine arts – especially among daughters of elite samurai warriors. On the sides of the netsuke, Chinese characters are inscribed in gold lacquer, partly worn away and therefore illegible, but the text most likely alludes to a Chinese poem.

—

Unsigned
Ivory, mid 1800s
w. 9.1 cm
British Museum 1930,1217.105
Bequeathed by James Hilton

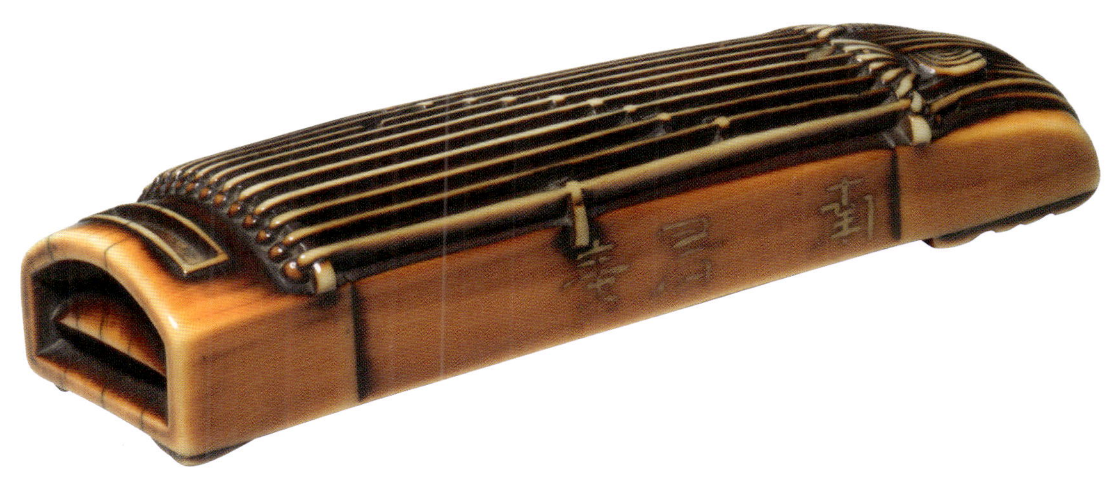

Broken-off bridge post

This is a very unusual subject for a netsuke. The bridge post is broken off raggedly at the bottom, and the top has an ornamental finial in the shape of an onion-bulb jewel, called a *giboshi*. Such finials are commonly found on old bridges or railings of temples and shrines in Japan. This netsuke most likely alludes to Gojō bridge in Kyoto, which is believed to have been one of the first bridges to have adopted this style (the present bridge is a later replacement). The bridge is famous for the legend of Ushiwakamaru, the childhood name of the famed warrior Minamoto no Yoshitsune (1159–1189). He is said to have fought the giant warrior-monk Benkei by moonlight on this bridge (see right). Defeated by the younger man, Benkei became his most faithful follower during many further adventures. The subject has been extremely popular and depicted repeatedly, and frequently the bridge post with the *giboshi* finial is referenced somewhere in the design. Although the netsuke probably does not represent the legend directly, people during the Edo period (1615–1868) would immediately have connected the broken post to this famous story.

This netsuke was previously published in Barker and Smith 1976, p. 128, fig. 258, and Lazarnick (ed.), MCI, vol. 2, 1986, p. 766.

—

By Shūgetsu
Dark wood with ivory, mid 1800s
H. 5.7 cm
British Museum F.1054
Given by Sir Augustus Wollaston Franks

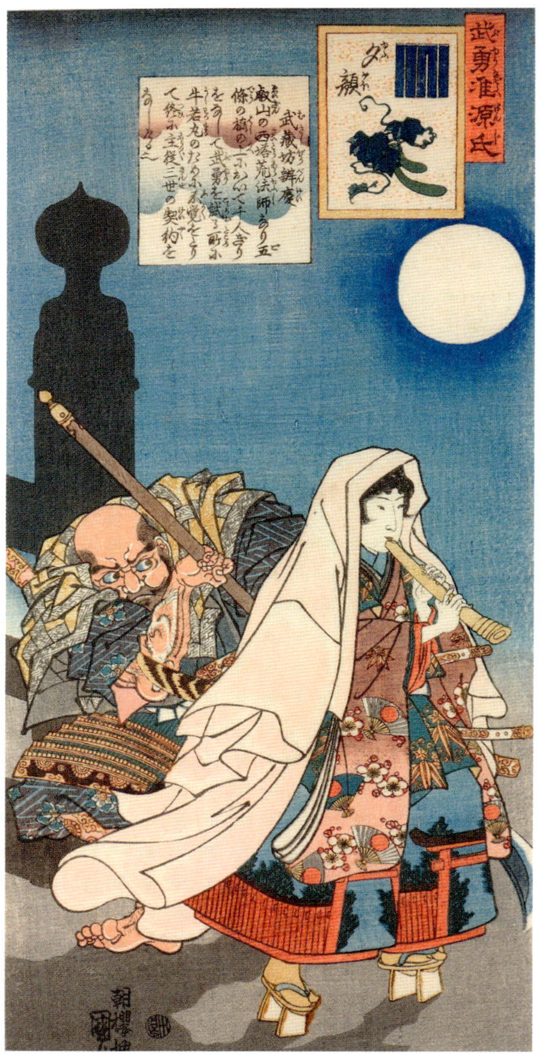

Yūgao (*Evening Faces*), from the series *Buyū nazorae Genji* (*Heroic Comparisons for the Chapters of Genji*). Utagawa Kuniyoshi (1797–1861), colour woodblock print, 1843. 36.1 x 16.8 cm. British Museum 2008,3037.05501. Loaned by the American Friends of the British Museum (Prof. Arthur R. Miller collection).

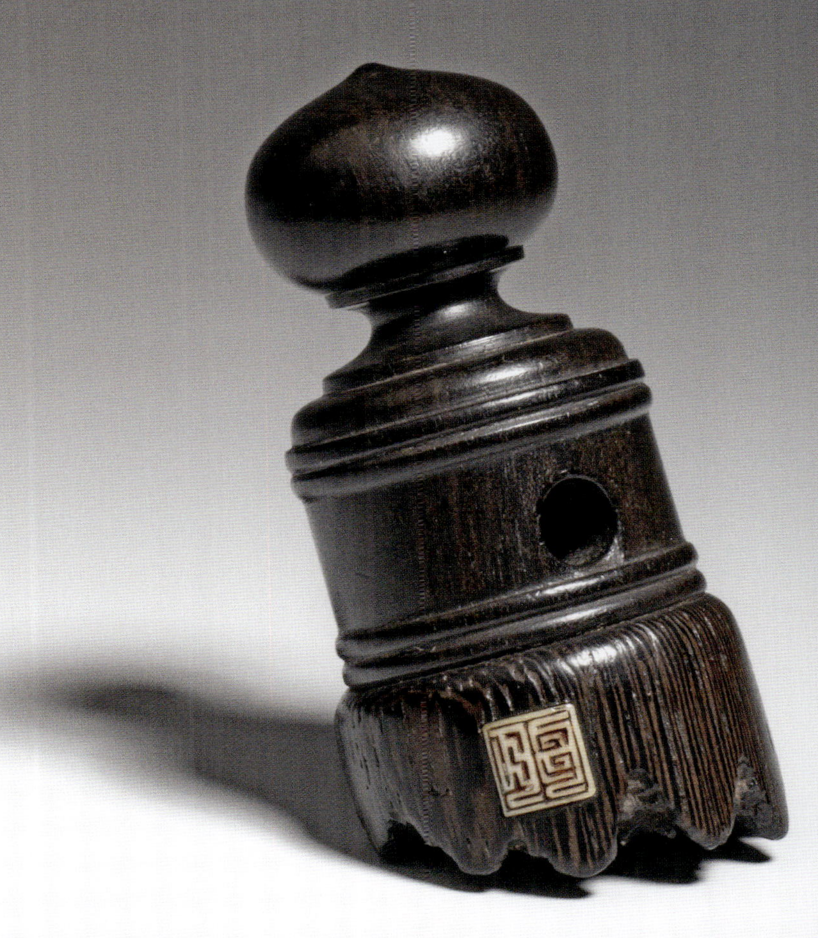

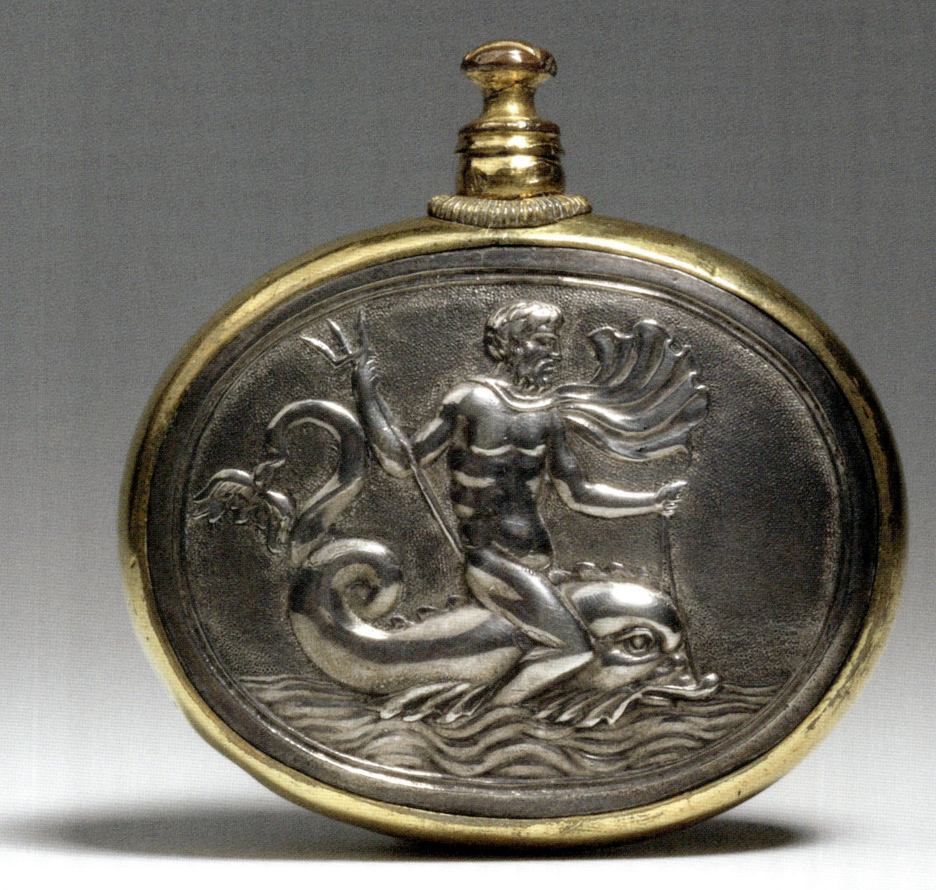

Pocket watch with Neptune

This unusual metal netsuke is probably an imitation of a
pocket watch of the type brought to Japan by Dutch traders.
During the Edo period (1615–1868), the Dutch were the
only Europeans permitted to trade with and live in Japan,
and they were confined in the port-city of Nagasaki.
The case of the watch netsuke has a simulated winder stem
at the top, and the silver cover is beautifully carved with a
European neoclassical design of Neptune riding on a
dolphin-like sea creature amid waves. Neptune is the god of
the sea, usually depicted as a bearded, powerfully-built man
holding a trident. As the god of seafarers, Neptune was a
popular talismanic motif in Europe, and objects with this
image, in various media, must have been carried while at
sea. On the back of the watch, a floral design surrounded
by a fret pattern (the running pattern around the edge) is
delicately carved into the gilt metal ground. A ring is
attached to facilitate use as a netsuke.

—

Unsigned
Silver and gilt metal, early 1800s
H. 4.6 cm; w. 4.3 cm
British Museum HG.238
Given by Professor John and Mrs Anne Hull Grundy

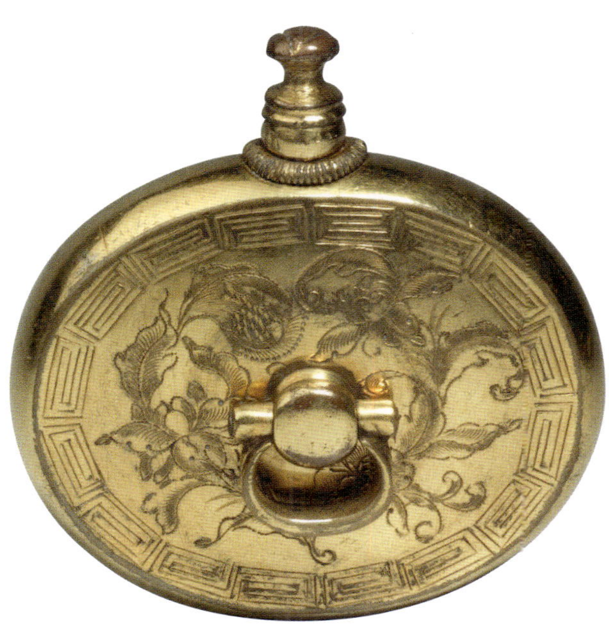

Flower basket

This delicate netsuke of a flower basket is carved from a
very rare material, hornbill ivory. The ivory comes from the
casque, a decorative growth on the upper mandible of the
bird's bill, and is characterized by its beautifully contrasting
golden yellow and bright orange-red colourations.
A precious material, it is difficult to secure a piece
sufficiently large for a carving in the round. In some fine
animal netsuke, the red part of this material was used for
inlaid eyes. In this netsuke, flowers of the four seasons –
cherry blossom, lotus, chrysanthemum and peony – are
arranged in a woven basket. The natural colouration of
the hornbill is most effectively exploited. An arrangement
of blossoms from all four seasons was an elegant and
idealized image that was much appreciated during the
later Edo period (1615–1868).

This netsuke was previously published in Harris 1987,
pp. 94–95, fig. 462.

—

By Ono Ryōmin
Hornbill ivory, late 1800s
H. 3.8 cm; w. 3.3 cm
British Museum HG.709
Given by Professor John and Mrs Anne Hull Grundy

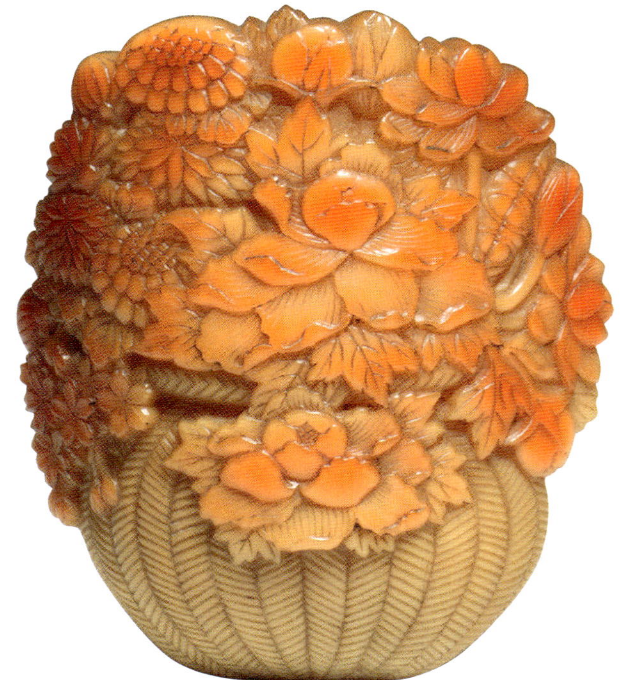

Sake **gourd in a net**

This double-gourd-shaped netsuke realistically simulates a *sake* container in a knotted-cord carrying net. Dried gourds have long been adapted to carry water or *sake* (Japanese rice wine), their inherent lightness and durability making them ideal for travelling. The netsuke is inlaid with various materials: the cord around the neck is rendered in red carved lacquer; the fastening cord of the net in green-stained ivory; the fastening *ojime* bead in dark wood; and the stopper in the mouth of the gourd in horn. The net covering the gourd, amazingly, is carved in wood with fine detailing.

The carver, Suzuki Tōkoku, lived and worked in Tokyo during the second half of the nineteenth century. Although it is recorded that he was self-taught, his works are especially distinguished by the masterful use of inlay in various coloured materials, a technique which he himself developed. These inlays are never overly-elaborate and as a result the appearance of the netsuke is refined and understated. A strong and pleasing contrast is created between the gourd's sleek polished skin and its net covering. The cord holes (*himotōshi*) are also ringed with green-stained ivory.

This netsuke was previously published in Barker and Smith 1976, p. 89, fig. 146.

—

By Suzuki Tōkoku (1846–1931)
Wood, with details in red lacquer, green-stained ivory and horn, Tokyo, about 1900s
w. 4.6 cm
British Museum 1945,1017.580
Bequeathed by Oscar Charles Raphael

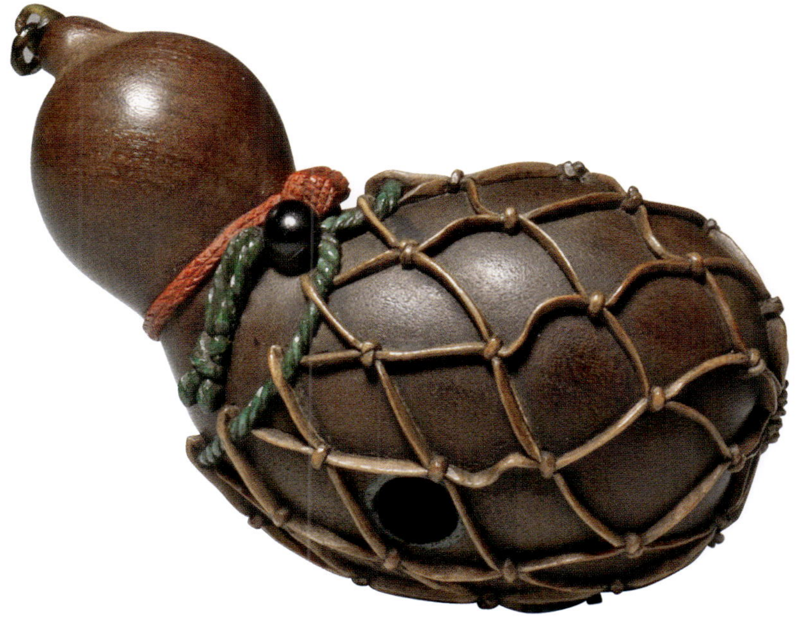

Aubergine with Mount Fuji and a hawk

This clever, playful netsuke when closed represents a round Japanese aubergine, but once opened into two halves it reveals Mount Fuji and a hawk. The subject is based on a Japanese proverb about the first dream of the New Year, 'One: Fuji, two: hawk, three: aubergine' (*ichi Fuji, ni taka, san nasubi*). Traditionally, it is believed that the contents of the first dream will foretell the luck of the dreamer during the coming year. It is considered particularly good fortune to dream of (in order) Mount Fuji, a hawk and then an aubergine. The saying is thought to list the three highest objects in Suruga province (present-day Shizuoka prefecture) where Tokugawa Ieyasu (1542–1616), the first shogun of the Tokugawa shogunate, spent many years after his retirement. Mount Fuji and Mount Ashitaka (the sound '*taka*' means hawk in Japanese) are the first and the second highest mountains in Suruga. Fabulous prices were paid for the earliest aubergines of the season grown there. Another theory suggests that they were all favourites of Ieyasu who loved Mount Fuji as a view, falconry as a hobby and aubergine as a food.

This netsuke was previously published in Harris 1987, p. 101, fig. 503.

—

Unsigned
Boxwood, partially lacquered, mid 1800s
H. 5.2 cm
British Museum HG.215
Given by Professor John and Mrs Anne Hull Grundy

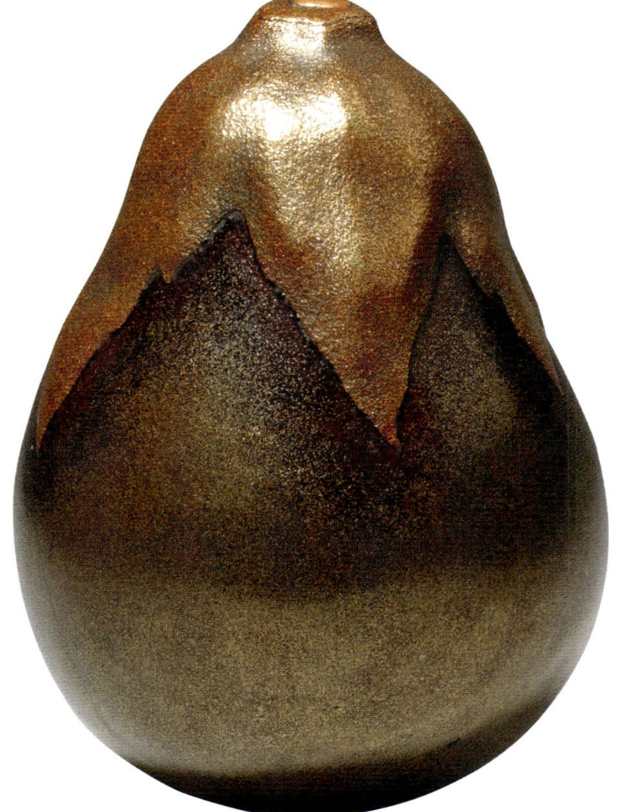

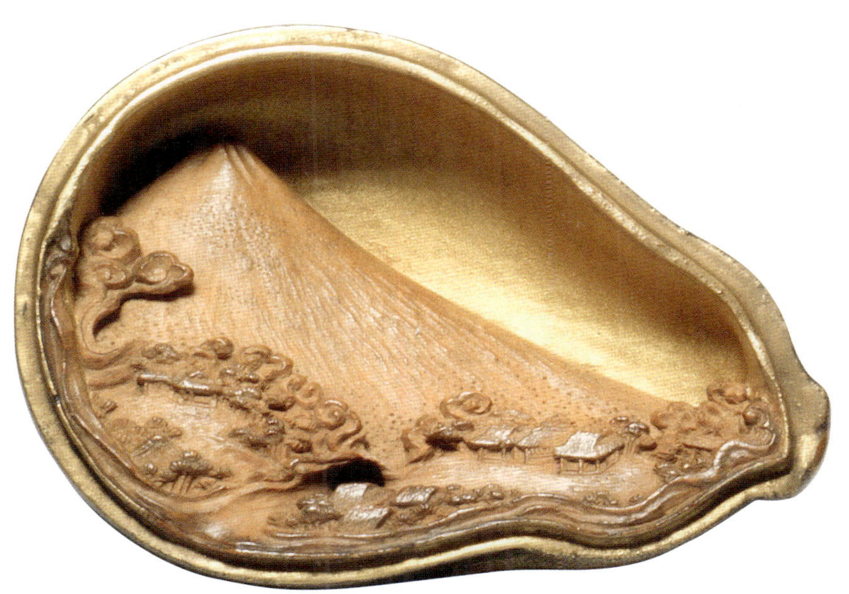

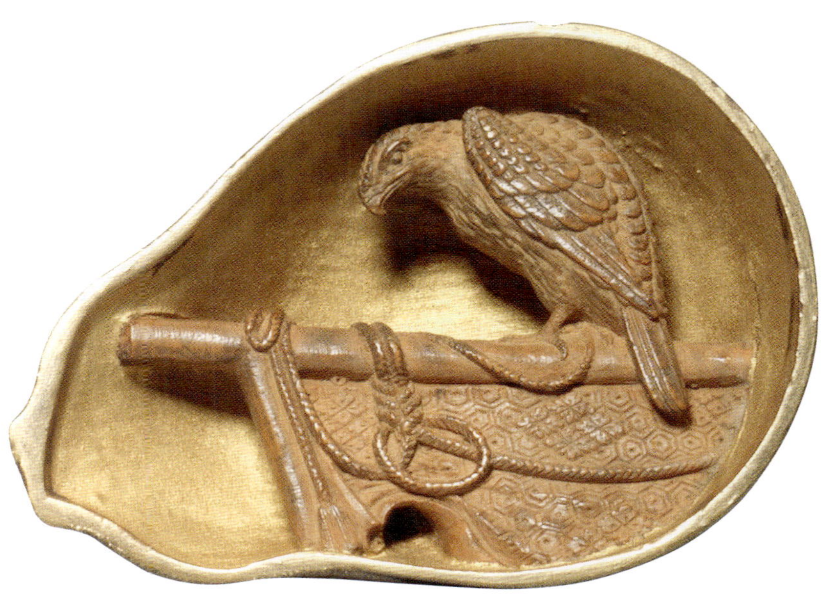

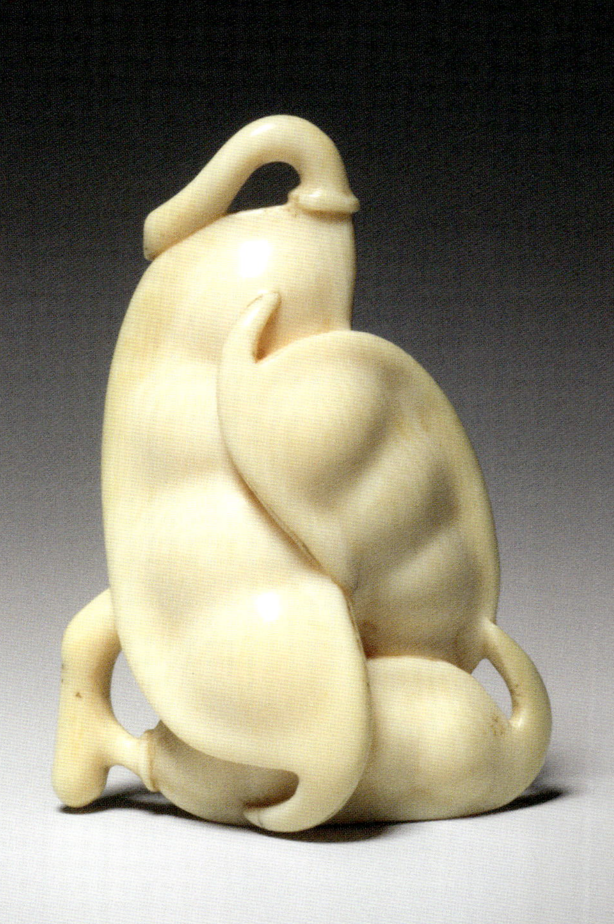

Three pea pods

This netsuke of three pea pods (*endō*) is naturalistically carved into a compact format. In Japan, *endō* is a common food that is eaten roasted or boiled, or used for making sweat bean paste. The carver, Kiyokatsu, who lived in Kyoto in the early nineteenth century, was renowned for his realistically carved netsuke in the shape of shells, nuts and vegetables. Here, he succeeds in capturing the delicacy and smoothness of the pea pod in a simple and fluid form. The gentle contours of the peas themselves can be seen inside their pods, and appear compellingly tactile.

This netsuke was previously published in Barker and Smith 1976, pp. 56–57, fig. 70.

—

By Kiyokatsu
Ivory, Kyoto, early 1800s
H. 5.3 cm
British Museum 1945,1017.591
Bequeathed by Oscar Charles Raphael

Signatures

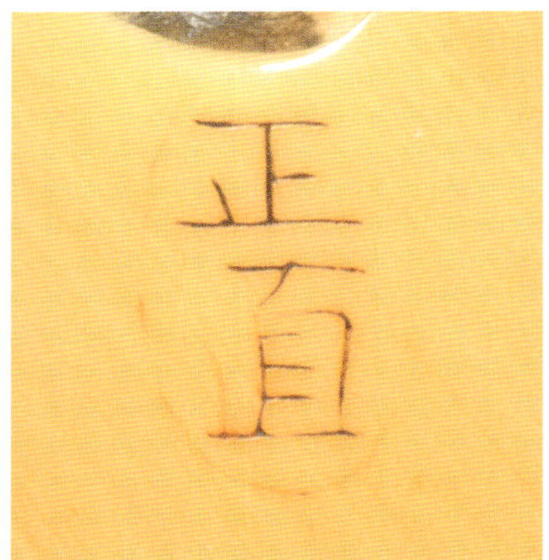

Page 31
Signed on the base Masanao of Kyoto.

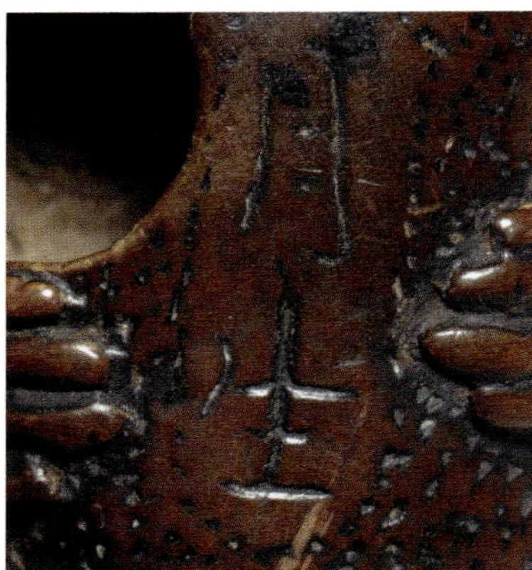

Pages 34–35
Signed on the base Gesshō.

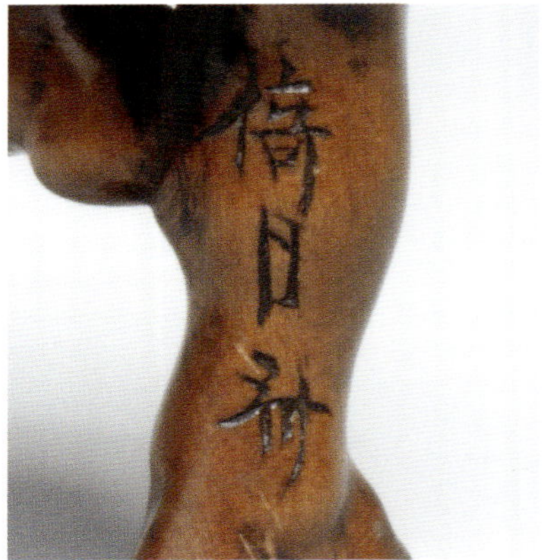

Pages 36–37
Signed on the calf of the right leg Kijitsusai.

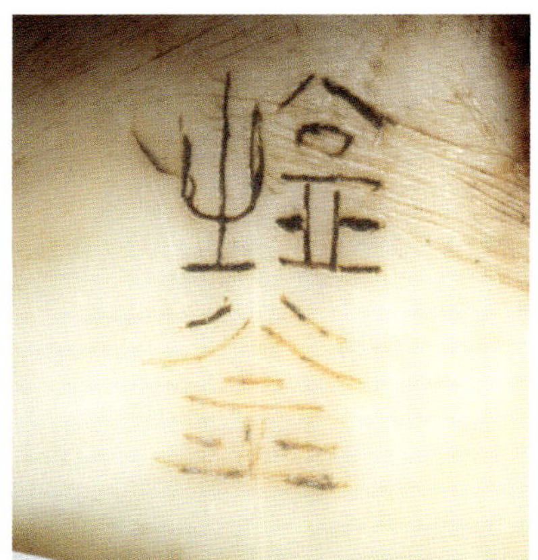

Pages 40–41
Signed Atokama in seal-script at the hem of the robe.

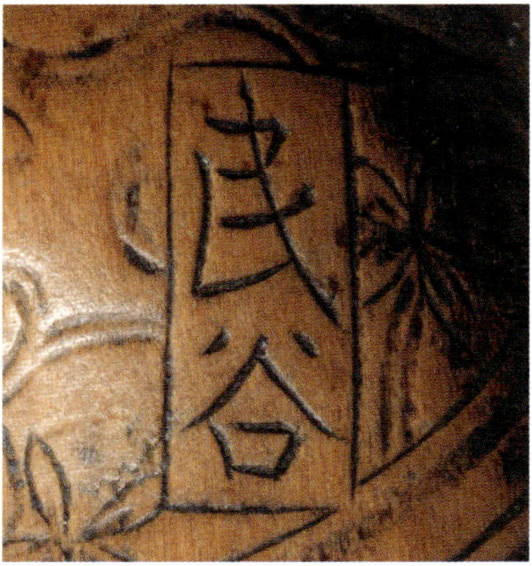

Page 42
Signed on the back Minkoku.

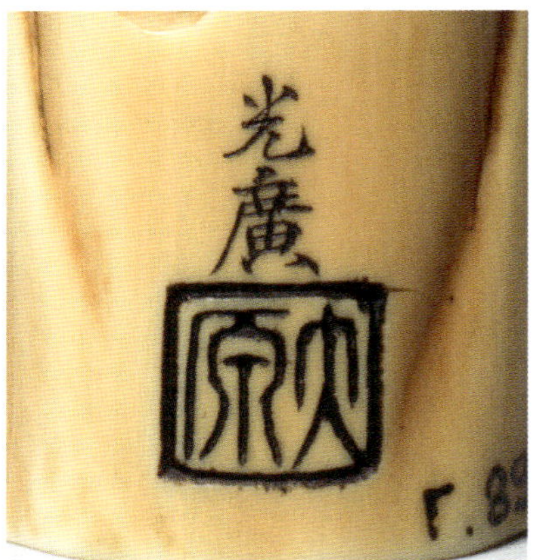

Pages 44–45
Signed on the back Mitsuhiro, with seal Ōhara.

Pages 46–47

Signed Kikugawa on the base.

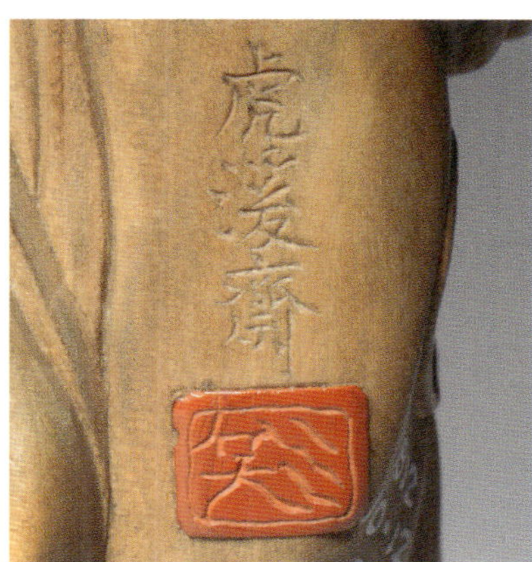

Page 48

Signed on the back Kokeisai, with seal Sanshō.

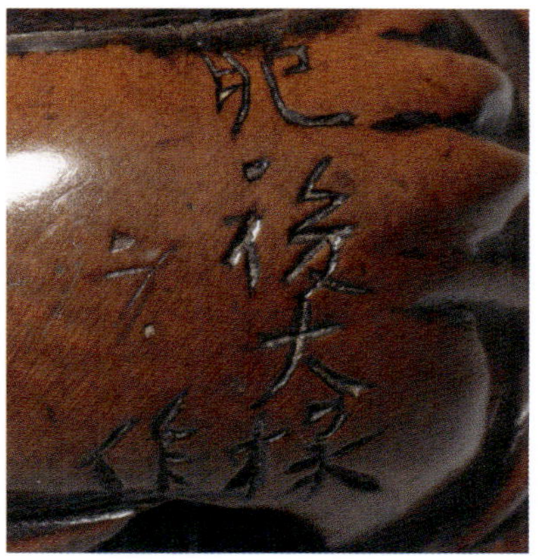

Pages 50–51

Signed Higo Daijō saku ('Made by Higo Daijō') on the posterior of one of the figures.

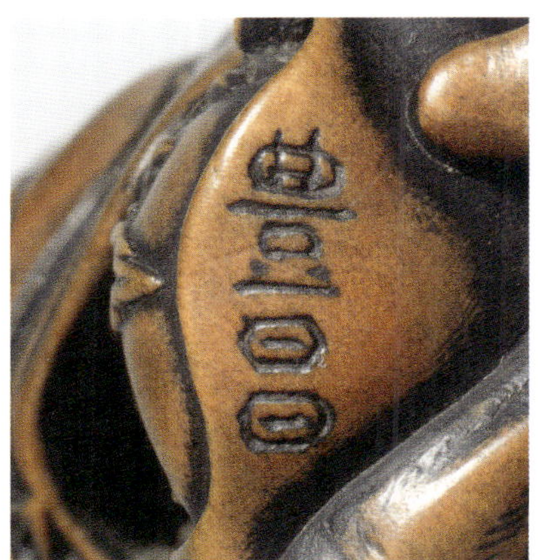

Pages 52–53

Signed on the base Toyomasa.

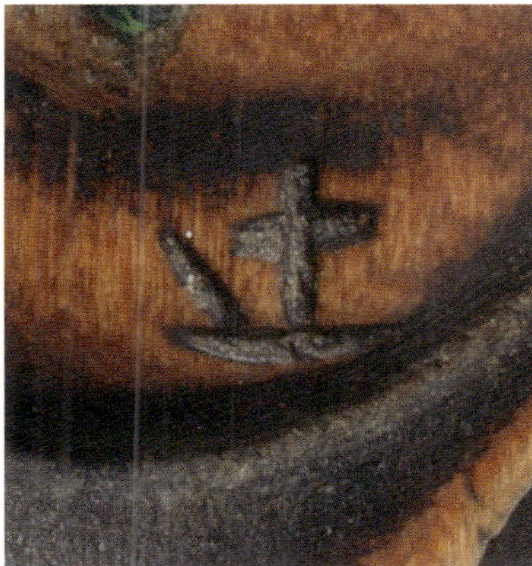

Pages 58–59

Signed with the small single character of Tsuji's name, here carved at the hem of the robe.

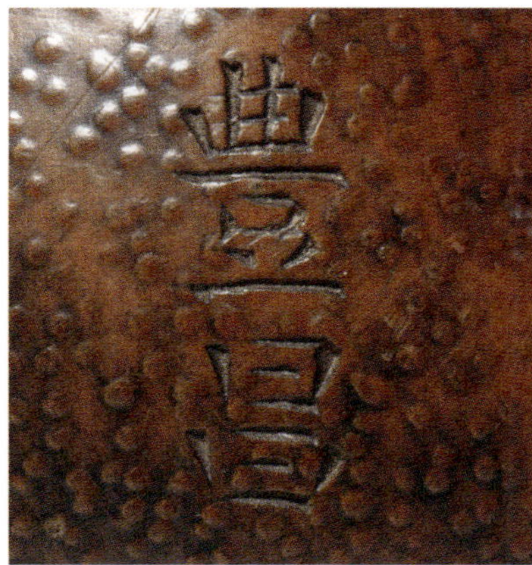

Pages 62–63

Signed on the base Toyomasa.

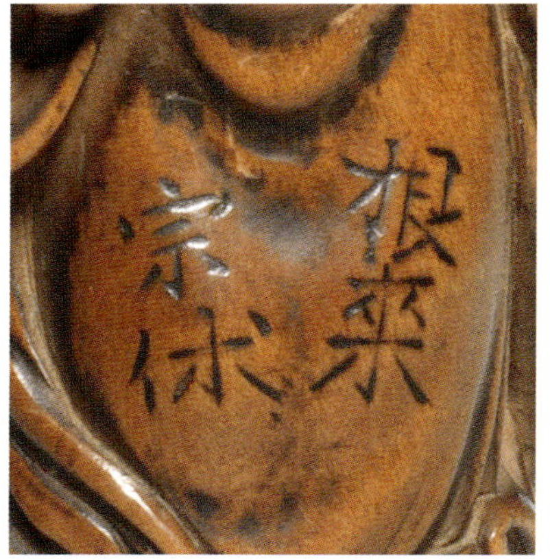

Pages 64–65
Signed on the back Negoro Sōkyū.

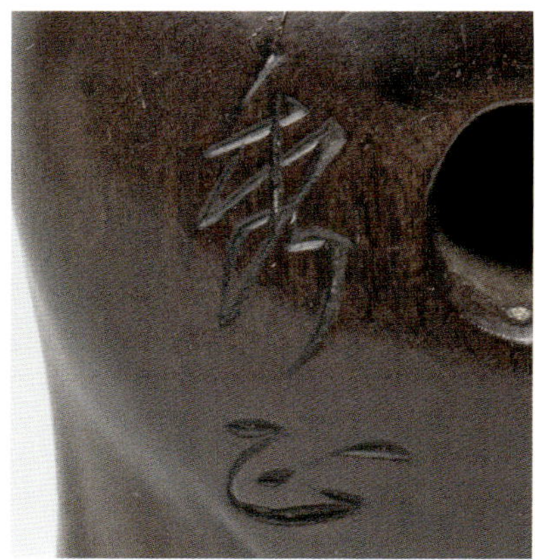

Pages 66–67
Signed on the posterior Hidemasa.

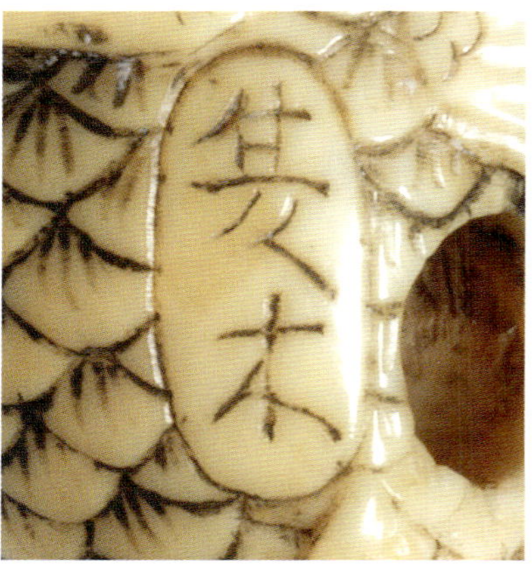

Pages 74–75
Signed on the underside Natsuki.

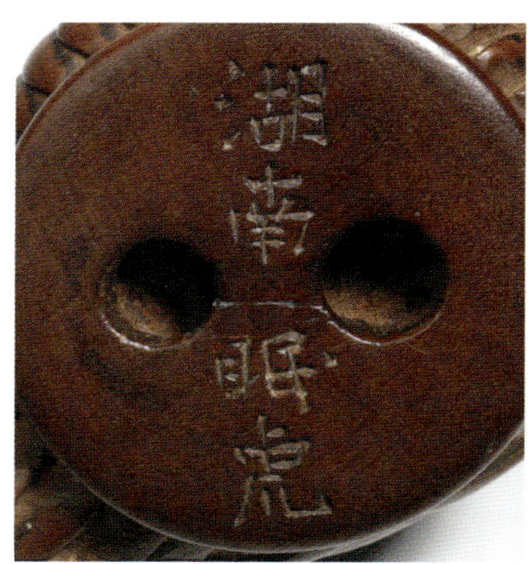

Pages 78–79
Signed on the base Konan Minko.

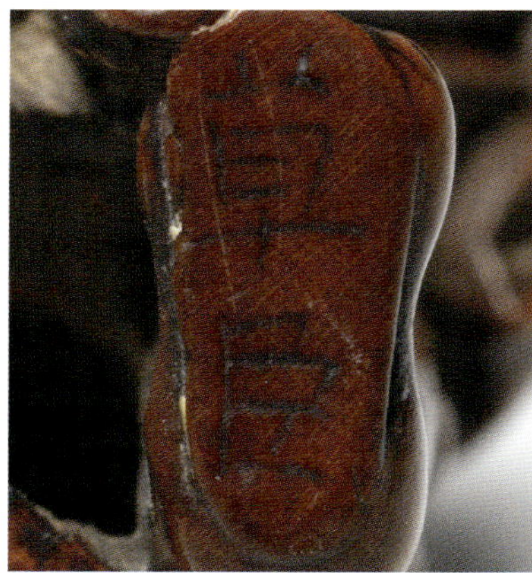

Pages 84–85
Signed Sōshin on the underside of the ghost's left foot.

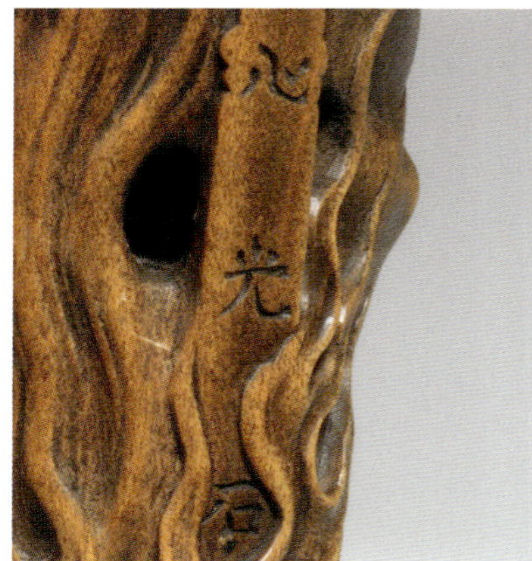

Pages 88–89
Shin Kōseki is incised on the narrow wooden grave marker that forms part of the netsuke.

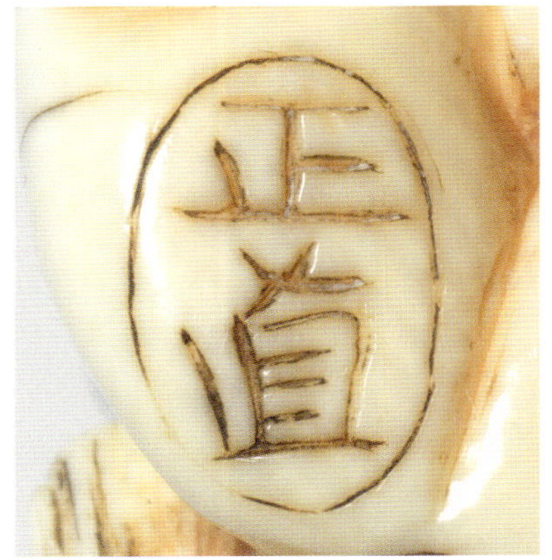

Pages 96–97
Signed on the base Masanao.

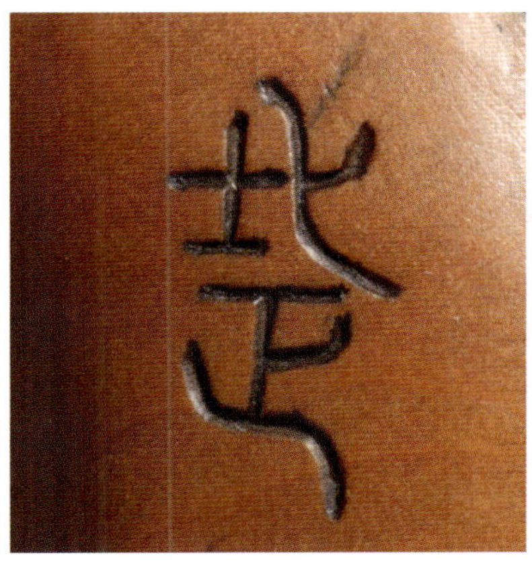

Pages 98–99
Signed on the back Hokushō or
Kitamasa.

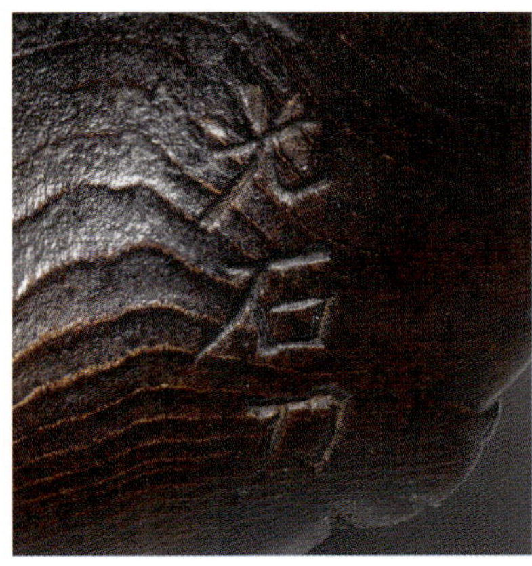

Page 101
Signed on the back Kōseki tō ('Carved
by Kōseki').

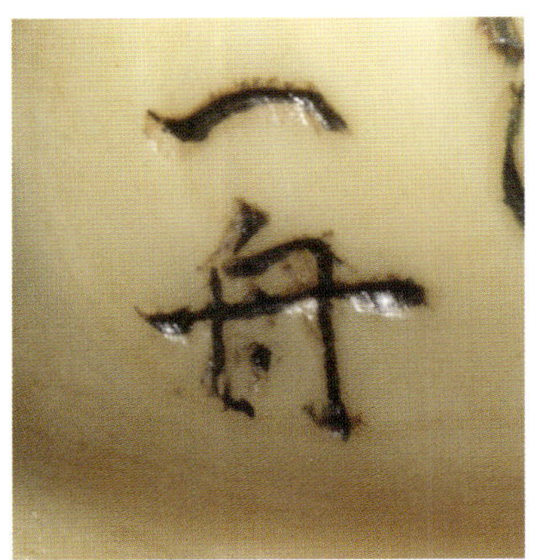

Pages 104–105
Signed on the side Isshū.

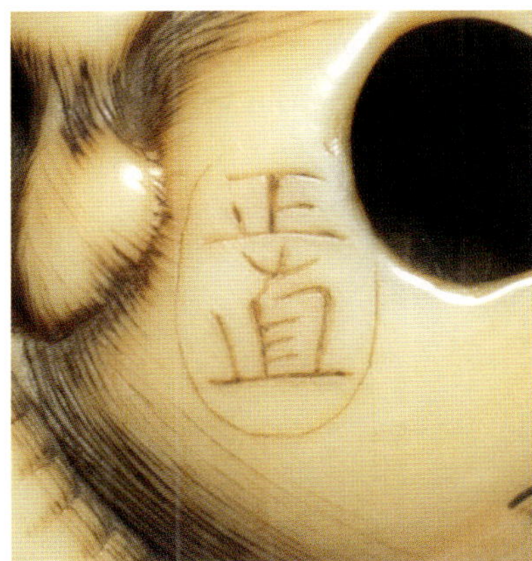

Pages 108–109
Signed on the base Masanao.

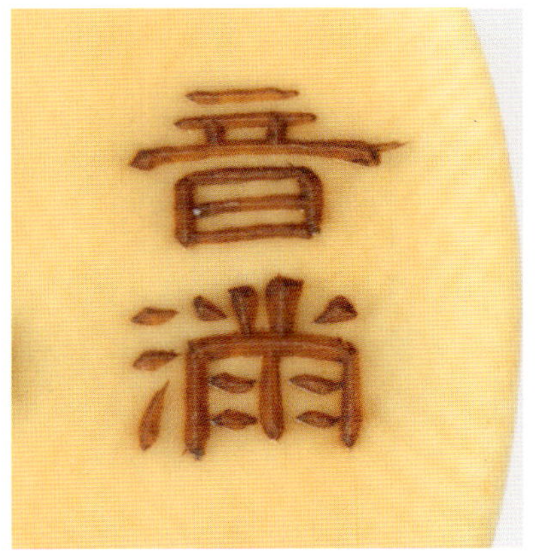

Pages 110–111
Signed on the base Otoman, with
red stain.

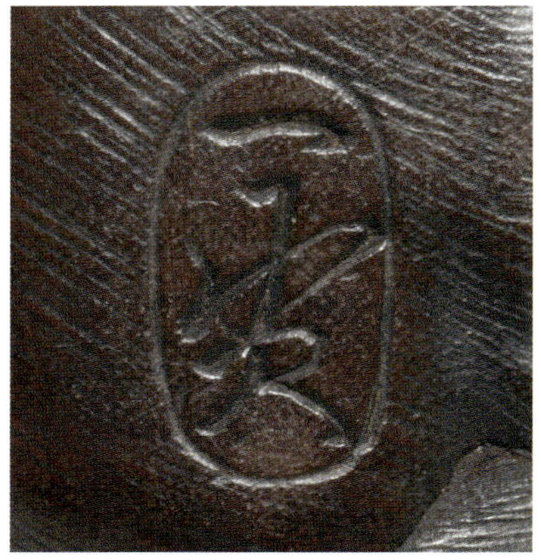

Pages 112–113
Signed on the base Ikkan in cursive script.

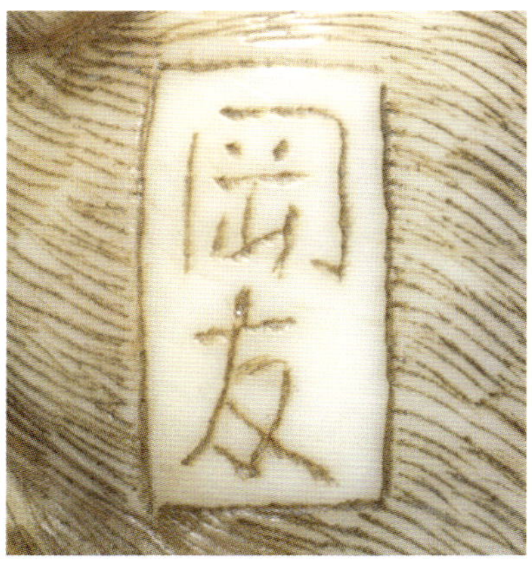

Pages 118–119
Signed on the left rump Okatomo.

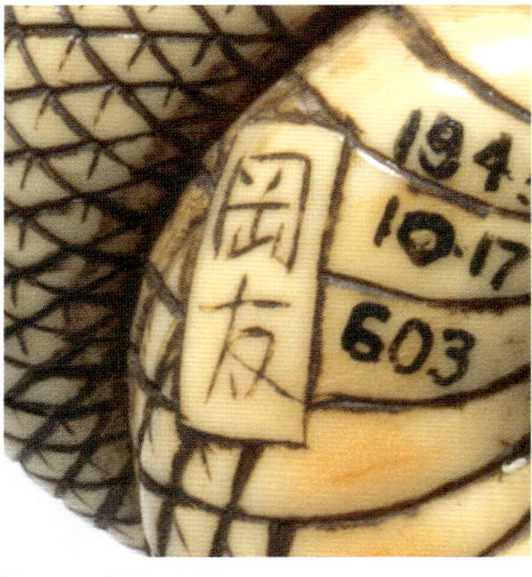

Pages 124–125
Signed on the underside Okatomo.

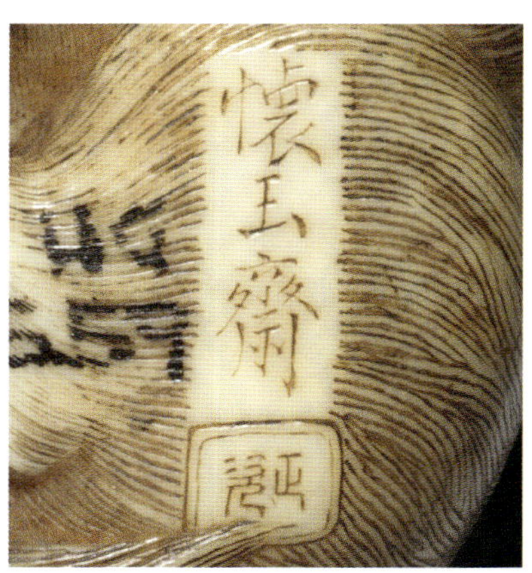

Pages 128–129
Signed on the base Kaigyokusai with seal Masatsugu.

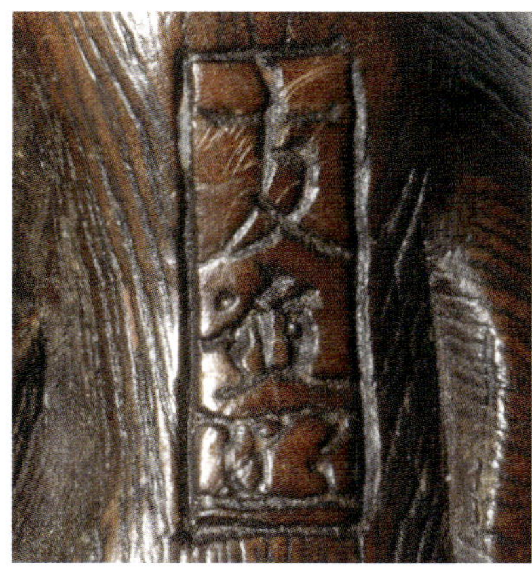

Pages 130–131
Signed on the base Tomochika, with cursive seal (*kaō*).

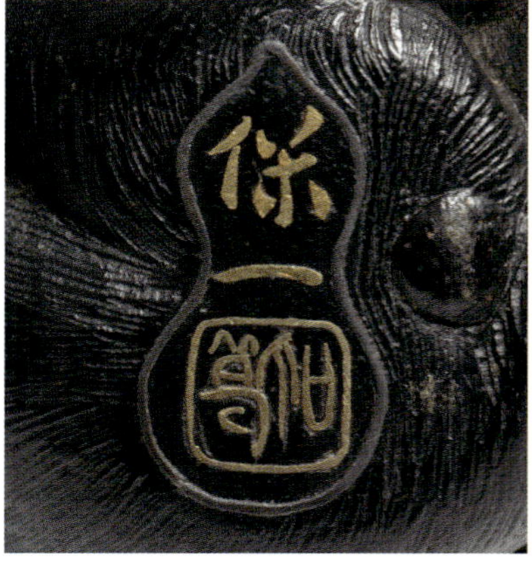

Pages 132–133
Signed on the underside Hoichi (or Yasukazu) with an unread seal, both in gold wire, inside a gourd-shaped cartouche.

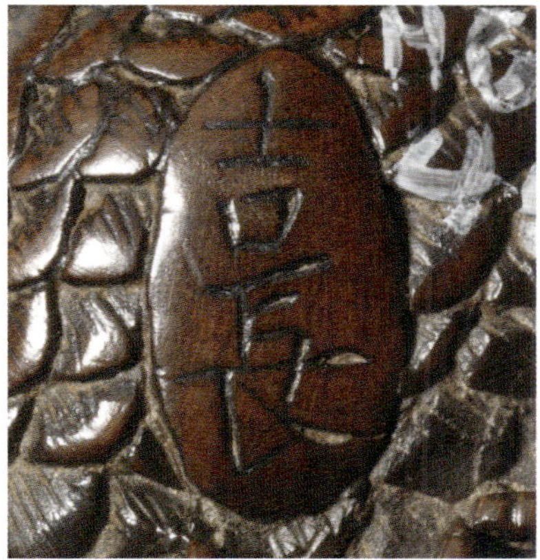

Pages 134–135
Signed on the base Yoshinaga.

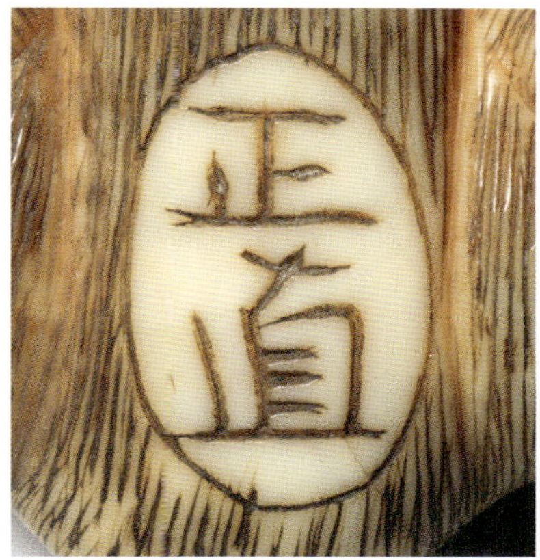

Pages 136–137
Signed on the base Masanao.

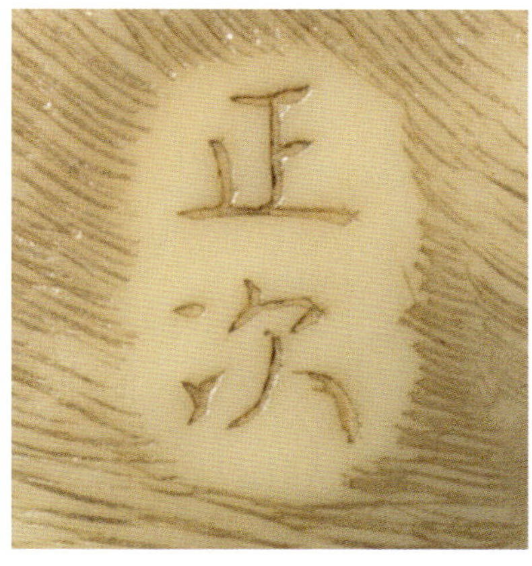

Pages 138–139
Signed on the base Masatsugu.

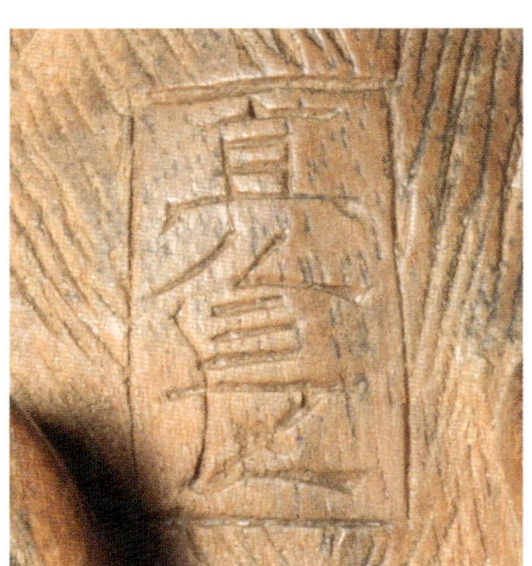

Pages 140–141
Signed on the base Sukenaga.

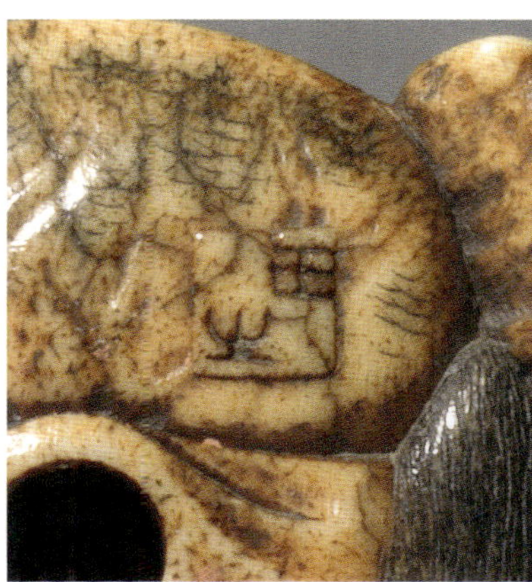

Pages 154–155
Signed on the base Masayuki in seal form.

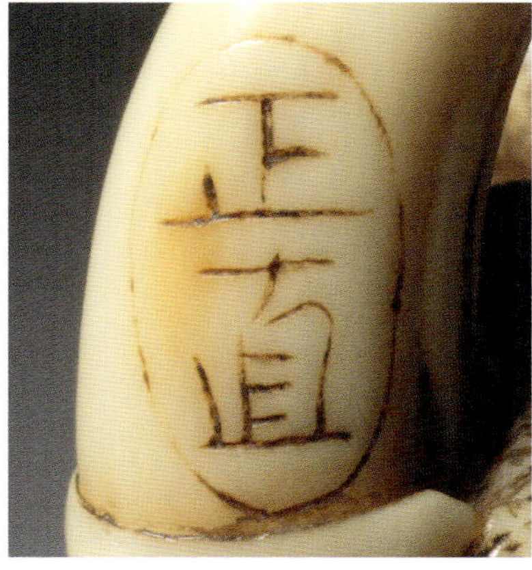

Pages 156–157
Signed Masanao at the side of the hallux (the first digit).

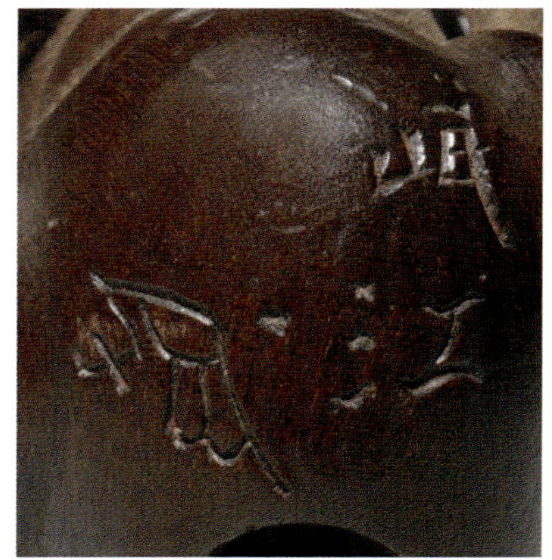

Page 159
Signed on the back Minkō, with cursive seal (*kaō*).

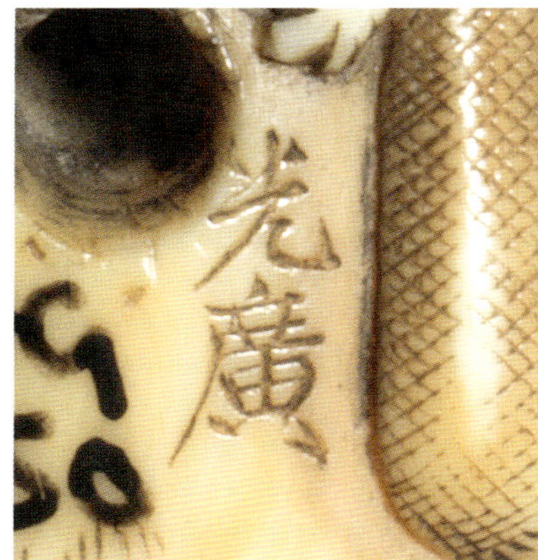

Pages 160–161
Signed on the base Mitsuhiro.

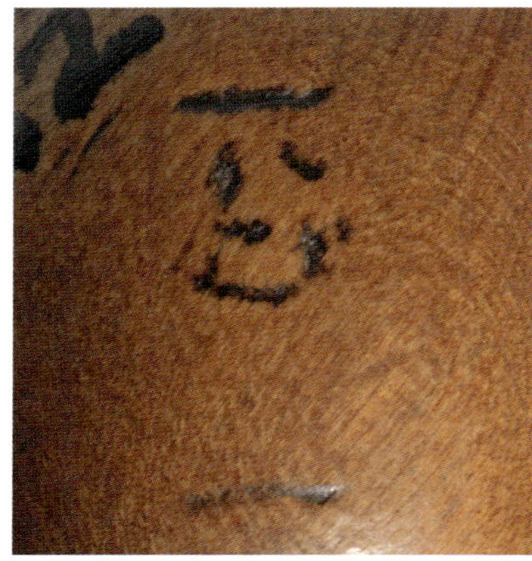

Pages 162–163
The signature on the base is almost illegible, but has been read, tentatively, as Masakazu (or Shōichi).

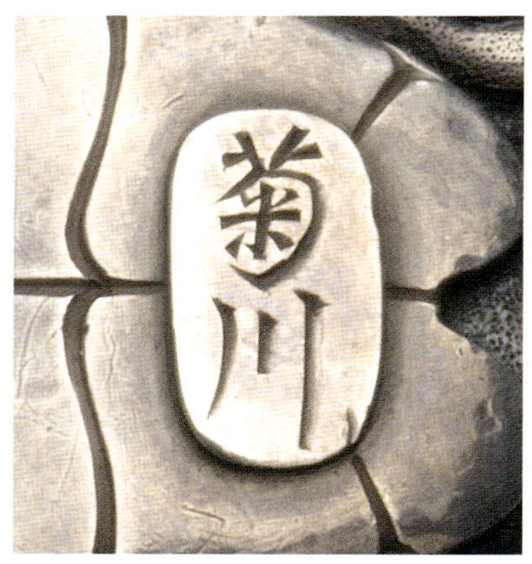

Pages 164–165
Signed on the underside Kikugawa, with separate cursive seal (*kaō*).

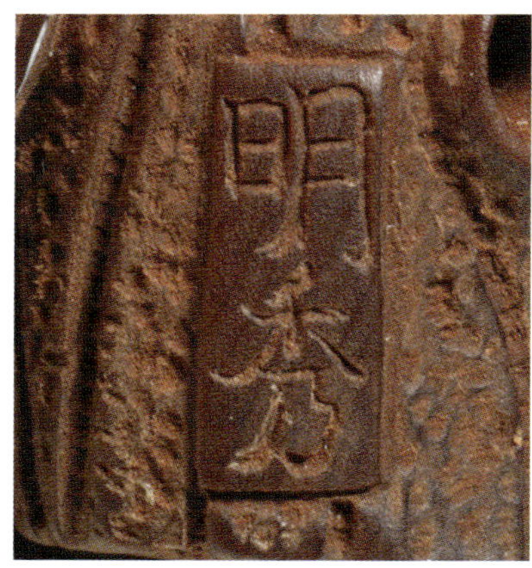

Pages 166–167
Signed Meishū on the base of the branch.

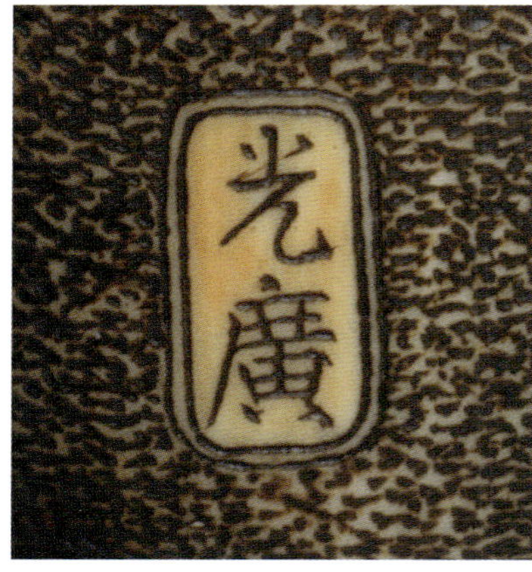

Pages 168–169
Signed on the side of the pot Mitsuhiro.

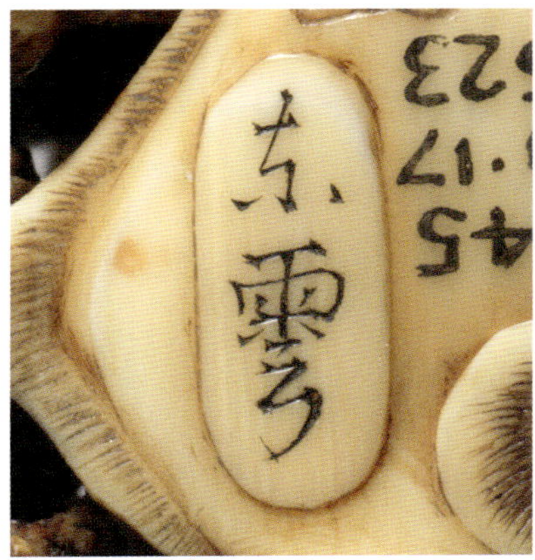

Pages 172–173
Signed on the reverse of the ray Tōun.

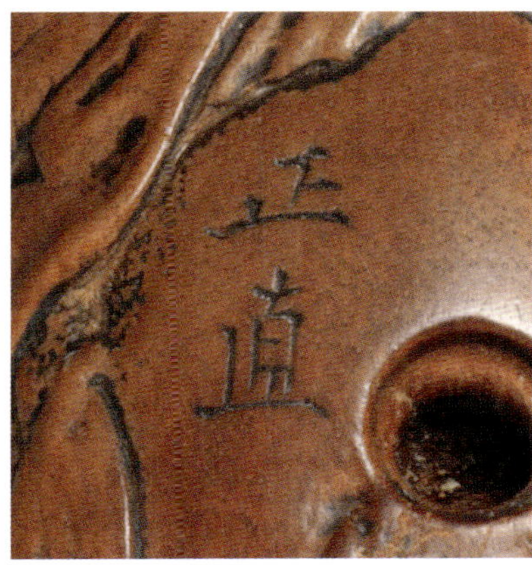

Pages 176–177
Signed on the base Masanao.

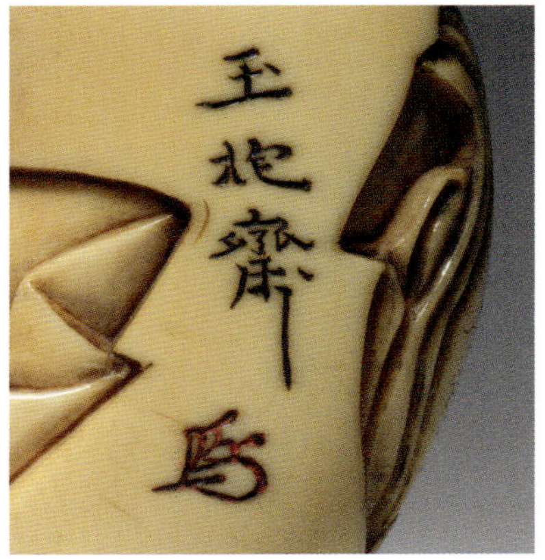

Pages 180–181
Signed on the reverse Gyokuhōsai
with cursive seal (*kaō*).

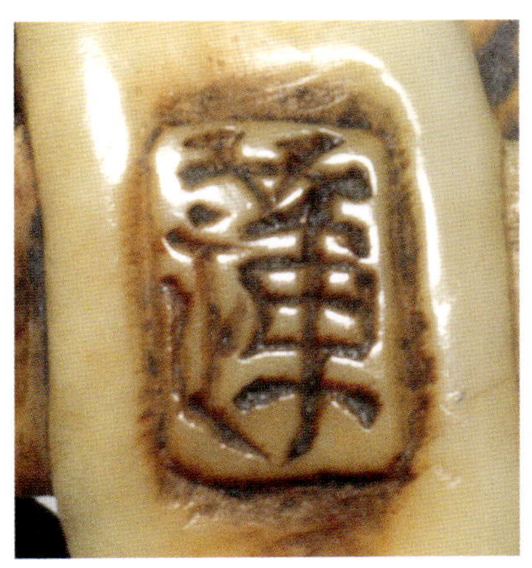

Pages 182–183
Rensai often signed or sealed himself
simply 'Ren', and this piece has a seal
that reads Ren on the side.

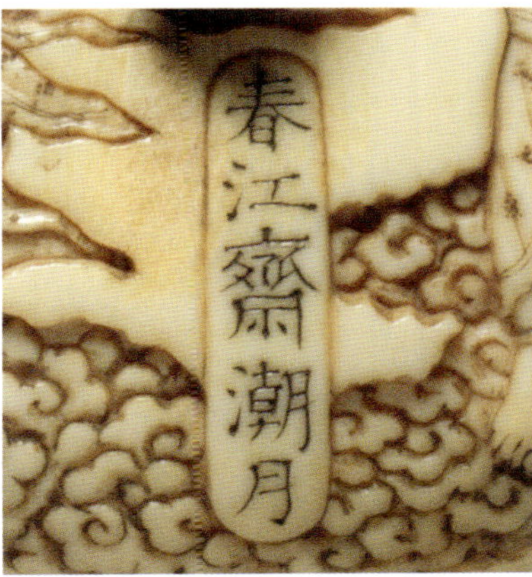

Pages 184–185
Signed on the reverse Shunkōsai
Chōgetsu.

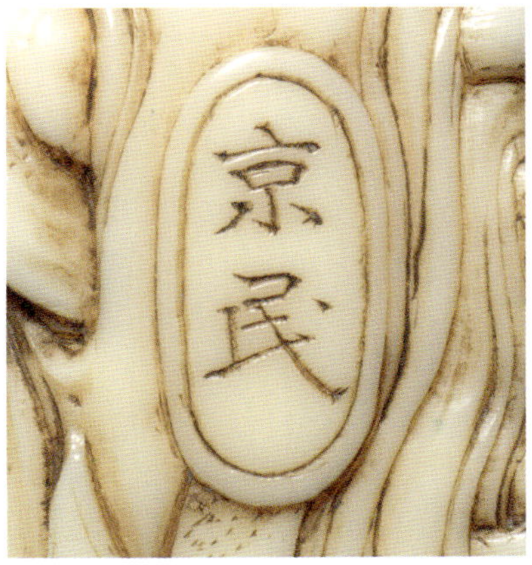

Pages 186–187
Signed on the side Kyōmin.

Signatures

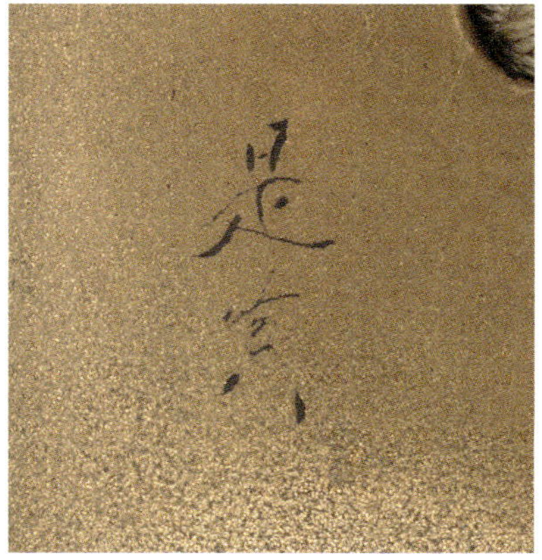

Pages 188–189
Both the base of the *inrō* and the back of the netsuke (shown here) are signed Zeshin in carved characters.

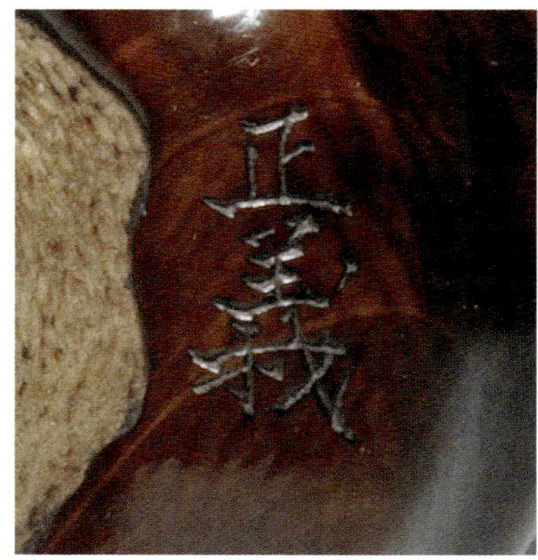

Pages 192–193
Signed Masayoshi at the edge of the base.

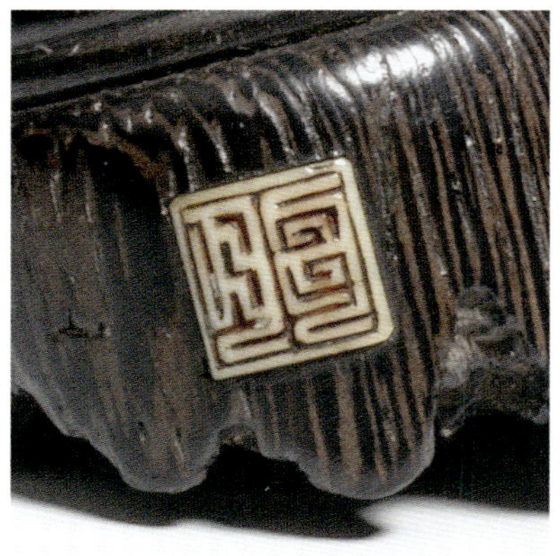

Pages 196–197
Signed Shūgetsu in seal-script (*tensho*) characters on an inlaid ivory tablet.

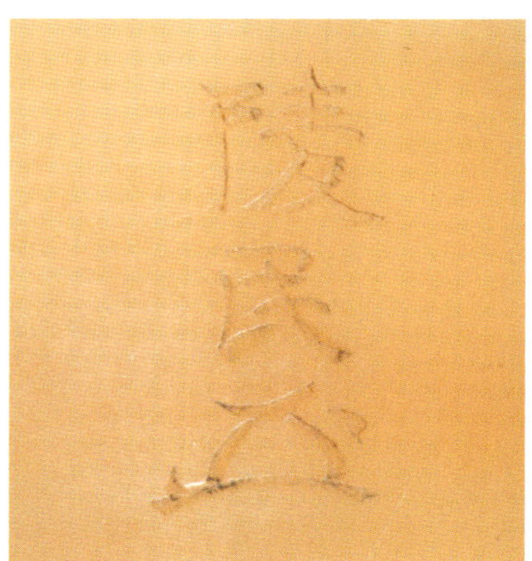

Page 200
Signed on the back Ryōmin with cursive seal (*kaō*).

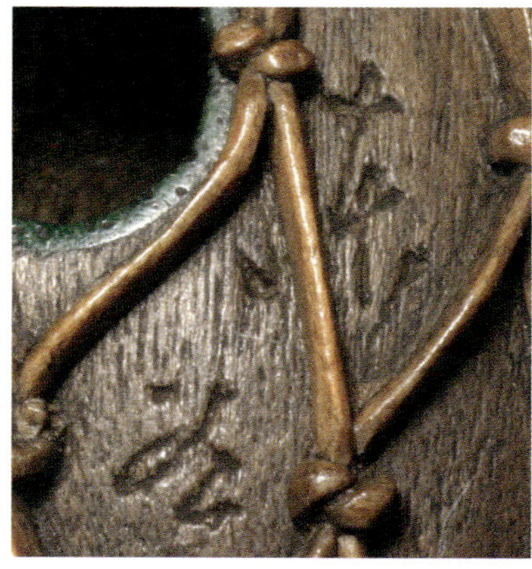

Page 201
Signed on the side Tōkoku, with gilt metal seal Bairyū.

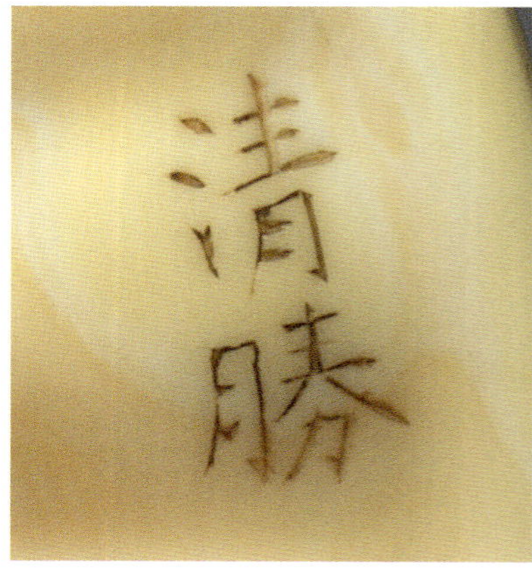

Pages 204–205
Signed on the reverse Kiyokatsu.

Acknowledgements

The publication by the British Museum of *Netsuke: 100 miniature masterpieces from Japan* is timely indeed. There has recently been increased appreciation of this intricate and imaginative Japanese art form. Collectors and scholars of netsuke convened in May 2013 in London for the biennial convention of the International Netsuke Society, the first in Europe for over 20 years. In conjunction, the Embassy of Japan in the UK, with the guest curatorship of Rosemary Bandini, staged an important loan exhibition of netsuke, with scholarly catalogue, humorously entitled *In a Nutshell*. The best-selling book *The Hare with the Amber Eyes*, published in 2010 by British ceramic artist Edmund de Waal, has brought the art form to a new and much wider audience. Recent rotations in the British Museum's Mitsubishi Corporation Japanese Galleries and an Asahi Shimbun 'Objects in Focus' display in Room Three have also given renewed attention to these diminutive carved 'toggles'. Netsuke have indeed come a long way from the sartorial accessory of the Edo period (1615–1868), to prized art form for connoisseurs and collectors today.

I am grateful to many people for their support, help and encouragement in writing this book. Firstly, I would like to thank Her Imperial Highness Princess Takamado, who kindly assisted with biographical information on contemporary netsuke carvers. Research for the book would not have been possible without the financial backing and support of Robert White and the Duke of Omnium Fund. Max Rutherston, Rosemary Bandini and Sem Djelal generously gave me their professional advice on the selection of the 100 pieces and helped me to better understand them. I am particularly indebted to Tim Clark, Nicole Coolidge Rousmaniere, Uchida Hiromi, Alfred Haft and Matsuba Ryōko of the Japanese Section and Jan Stuart, Keeper of the Department of Asia at the British Museum for their unfailing encouragement and their assistance in the editing of the book. The Conservation department at the British Museum provided valuable assistance and research on materials used in the netsuke. Morohashi Kazuko from the Sainsbury Institute for the Study of Japanese Arts and Cultures created the map. Anna Wilkinson of wilki.creative created the netsuke, *inrō* and sash drawing. I should also like to thank Ken Adlard of New Moon Photography who brilliantly captured the essence of these miniature works; also Rosemary Bradley, Emma Poulter and Kate Oliver at the British Museum Press who oversaw publication of the book. Finally I am grateful to Professor Kawai Masatomo for his academic nurturing and to my husband Aki and my family for their support.

Further reading

Arakawa Hirokazu (ed.), 'Inrō to netsuke', in *Nihon no bijutsu* no. 195, Tokyo, Shibundō, 1982.

Arakawa Hirokazu, *The Gō Collection of Netsuke, Tokyo National Museum*, Tokyo, New York and San Francisco, Kōdansha International, 1983.

Arakawa Hirokazu (ed.), *Netsuke: Takumi to Share*, Kyoto, Tankōsha, 1995.

Bandini, Rosemary, *Shishi and Other Netsuke: The Collection of Harriet Szechenyi*, London, Rosemary Bandini, 1999.

Bandini, Rosemary, *Tiny Titans: The Sumo Netsuke Collection of Karl-Ludwig Kley*, London, Rosemary Bandini, 2006.

Bandini, Rosemary, *Japanese Netsuke, Inro and Works of Art*, London, Rosemary Bandini, 2010.

Bandini, Rosemary, *In a Nutshell: A Loan Exhibition of Japanese Netsuke from European Collections*, exhibition catalogue, International Netsuke Society and The Embassy of Japan in the United Kingdom, 2013.

Bandini, Rosemary, *Japanese Netsuke, Inro and Lacquerware*, London, Rosemary Bandini Japanese Art, 2013.

Barker, Richard and Smith, Lawrence, *Netsuke: The Miniature Sculpture of Japan*, London, British Museum Publications, 1976.

Treasured Miniatures: Contemporary Netsuke, British Museum and Los Angeles County Museum of Art, exhibition catalogue, 1994.

Buckland, Rosina, *Shunga: Erotic Art in Japan*, London, British Museum Press, 2010.

Bushell, Raymond (ed.), *The Netsuke Handbook of Ueda Reikichi*, Rutland, Vermont and Tokyo, Charles E. Tuttle Company, 1961.

Bushell, Raymond, *Collectors' Netsuke*, New York and Tokyo, Weatherhill, 1971.

Bushell, Raymond, *Netsuke Familiar and Unfamiliar: New Principles for Collecting*, New York and Tokyo, Weatherhill, 1975.

Bushell, Raymond, *Netsuke Masks*, New York and Tokyo, Weatherhill, 1985.

Clark, Timothy, et al. (eds), *Shunga: Sex and Pleasure in Japanese Art*, London, British Museum Press, 2013.

Coullery, Marie-Thérèse and Newstead, Martin S., *The Baur Collection, Geneva: Netsuke (Selected Pieces)*, Geneva, The Baur Collections, 1977.

Davey, Neil K., *Netsuke: A Comprehensive Study Based on the M. T. Hindson Collection*, London, Faber & Faber Ltd in association with Sotheby Parke Bernet Publications, 1974.

Davies, Barry, Oriental Art: *An Exhibition of The Robert S. Huthart Collection of Non-Iwami Netsuke*, exhibition catalogue, 1998.

Ducros, Alain, *Netsuke & Sagemono 2*, Granges-les-Valence, 1987.

Earle, Joe, *An Introduction to Netsuke,* Victoria and Albert Museum, London, The Compton Press Ltd and Pitman House Ltd, 1980.

Earle, Joe, *Fantasy and Reality in Japanese Miniature Sculpture*, Boston, Museum of Fine Arts, 2001.

Eijer, Dieuwke, *Kagamibuta: Mirrors of Japanese Life and Legend*, Leiden and Geneva, Heinz Kaempfer Fund and The Baur Collections, 1994.

Eskenazi Ltd, *Japanese Netsuke from the Carré Collection*, London, Eskenazi, 1993.

Goodall, Hollis et al., *The Raymond and Frances Bushell Collection of Netsuke: A Legacy at the Los Angeles County Museum of Art*, Chicago and Los Angeles, 2003.

Harris, Victor, *Netsuke: The Hull Grundy Collection in the British Museum*, London, British Museum Publications, 1987.

Hutt, Julia, *Japanese Inrō*, London, V&A Publications, 1997.

Hutt, Julia, *Japanese Netsuke*, London V&A Publications, 2003.

Irvine, Gregory, *Masks, Myths & Monsters in Japanese Art*, London, Sun Tree Publishing Ltd, 1996.

Joly, Henri L., *W. L. Behrens Collection Part I: Netsuke*, London, 1912, reprinted by Paragon Book Reprint Corp., 1966.

Kinoshita Muneaki, *Netsuke Art of Kinoshita Collection*, Kyoto, Seishū Netsuke Art Museum, 2009.

Kinsey, Miriam, *Contemporary Netsuke*, Rutland, Vermont and Tokyo, Charles E. Tuttle Company, 1977.

Kinsey, Miriam, *Living Masters of Netsuke*, Tokyo and New York, Kōdansha International, 1984.

Lawrence, Louis, *Hirado: Prince of Porcelains*, Chicago, Art Media Resources, Ltd, 1997.

Lazarnick, George, *Netsuke & Inro Artists, and How to Read Their Signatures*, 2 vols, Honolulu, Reed Publishers, 1981.

Lazarnick, George (ed.), *The Meinertzhagen Card Index on Netsuke in the Archives of the British Museum*, New York, Alan R. Liss, Inc., 1986.

Masatoshi (by Masatoshi as told to Raymond Bushell), *The Art of Netsuke Carving*, Tokyo, New York and San Francisco, Kōdansha International Ltd, 1981.

Meinertzhagen, Frederick, *The Art of the Netsuke Carver*, London, Routledge and Kegan Paul, 1956.

Moss, Paul, *Eccentrics in Netsuke*, London, Sydney L. Moss Ltd, 1982.

Moss, Paul, *Zodiac Beasts and Distant Cousins: Japanese Netsuke for Connoisseurs*, London, Sydney L. Moss Ltd, 1993.

Moss, Paul, *Meeting with Remarkable Netsuke: 108 Masterpieces Selected from Private Collections*, London, Sydney L. Moss Ltd, 1996.

Moss, Paul, *Myth, Reality and Magical Transformation: Aesthetics and Connoisseurship in Japanese Netsuke*, Sydney L. Moss Ltd, 2000.

Okada, Barbara Teri, *Netsuke: Masterpieces from the Metropolitan Museum of Art*, New York, The Metropolitan Museum of Art, 1982.

Rutherston, Max and Bandini, Rosemary, *The Sheila M. Baker Collection of Japanese Netsuke and Inro*, London, Rutherston & Bandini, 2012.

Rutherston, Max and Bandini, Rosemary, *Japanese Netsuke, Inro and Works of Art: An Exhibition to Coincide with the International Netsuke Convention 2011*, London, Rutherston & Bandini, 2011.

Smith, Lawrence and Harris, Victor, *Japanese Decorative Arts: From the 17th to the 19th Centuries*, London, British Museum Publications, 1982.

Smith, Lawrence, Victor Harris and Timothy Clark, *Japanese Art: Masterpieces in the British Museum*, London, British Museum Publications, 1990.

Prince Takamado, Norihito, *Contemporary Netsuke: The H.I.H. Prince Takamado Collection*, Tokyo, Hakuchōsha, 2003.

Princess Takamado, Hisako, *The H.I.H. Prince Takamado Collection II*, Kyoto, Shibunkaku, 2006.

Princess Takamado, Hisako, *Netsuke: Have Netsuke, Will Travel – H.I.H. Princess Takamado Contemporary Netsuke Collection*, Tokyo, Kōdansha, 2008.

Tokyo National Museum (eds), *Netsuke: The Prince Takamado Collection*, Tokyo, Tokyo National Museum, 2011.

De Waal, Edmund, *The Hare with Amber Eyes: A Hidden Inheritance*, London, Chatto & Windus, 2010.

Yoshida Yukari, and Gabor, Wilhelm, *The Netsuke Dancers*, Tokyo, Yabane Co. Ltd, 2005.

Yoshida Yukari and Gabor, Wilhelm, *Netsuke Opus 20*, Tokyo, Yabane Co. Ltd, 2011.

Index